Teaching science

The Open University Postgraduate Certificate of Education

The readers in the PGCE series are:

Thinking Through Primary Practice
Teaching and Learning in the Primary School
Teaching and Learning in the Secondary School
Teaching English
Teaching Mathematics
Teaching Science
Teaching Technology
Teaching Modern Languages
Teaching History
Teaching Music

All of these readers are part of an integrated teaching system; the selection is therefore related to other material available to students and is designed to evoke critical understanding. Opinions expressed are not necessarily those of the course team or of the University.

If you would like to study this course and receive a PGCE prospectus and other information about programmes of professional development in education, please write to the Central Enquiry Service, PO Box 200, The Open University, Walton Hall, Milton Keynes, MK7 6YZ. A copy of *Studying with the Open University* is available from the same address.

Teaching science

Edited by Ralph Levinson
at The Open University

ROUTLEDGE

London and New York
in association with
The Open University

First published 1994
by Routledge
11 New Fetter Lane, London EC4P 4EE

Simultaneously published in the USA and Canada
by Routledge
29 West 35th Street, New York, NY 10001

Reprinted 1995

Typeset in Garamond by Florencetype Ltd, Stoodleigh, Devon
Printed and bound in Great Britain by
Biddles Ltd, Guildford and King's Lynn

British Library Cataloguing in Publication Data
A catalogue record for this book is available from the British Library

Library of Congress Cataloguing in Publication Data
A catalogue record for this book is available from the Library of Congress

ISBN 0-415-10253-7

Contents

Part IV Assessment: a way through

Part V Making science accessible to all

Part VI Science education: a debate

Foreword

The form of teacher education is one of the most debated educational issues of the day. How is the curriculum of teacher education, particularly initial, pre-service education to be defined? What is the appropriate balance between practical school experience and the academic study to support such practice? What skills and competence can be expected of a newly qualified teacher? How are these skills formulated and assessed and in what ways are they integrated into an ongoing programme of professional development?

These issues have been at the heart of the development and planning of the Open University's programme of initial teacher training and education – the Postgraduate Certificate of Education (PGCE). Each course within the programme uses a combination of technologies, some of which are well tried and tested, while others, on information technology for example, may represent new and innovatory approaches to teaching. All, however, contribute in an integrated way towards fulfilling the aims and purposes of the course and programme.

All of the PGCE courses have readers which bring together a range of articles, extracts from books, and reports that discuss key ideas and issues, including specially commissioned chapters. The readers also provide a resource that can be used to support a range of teaching and learning in other types and structures of course.

This series from Routledge, in supporting the Open University PGCE programme, provides a contemporary view of developments in primary and secondary education and across a range of specialist subject areas. Its primary aim is to provide insights and analysis for those participating in initial education and training. Much of its content, however, will also be relevant to ongoing programmes of personal and institutional professional development. Each book is designed to provide an integral part of that basis of knowledge that we would expect of both new and experienced teachers.

Bob Moon
Professor of Education, The Open University

Introduction

Ralph Levinson

I looked around and saw in a corner an ordinary dry battery. Here is something we could do: the electrolysis of water. . . .

I put some water in a beaker, dissolved a pinch of salt in it, turned two empty jam jars upside down in the beaker; then found two rubber-coated copper wires, attached them to the battery's poles, and fitted the wire ends into the jam jars. A minuscule procession of air bubbles rose from the wire ends: indeed, observing them closely you could see that from the cathode about twice as much gas was being liberated as from the anode. . . .

Enrico was in a bad mood and doubted everything. 'Who says that it's actually hydrogen and oxygen?' he said to me rudely. 'And what if there's chlorine? Didn't you put in salt?'

The objection struck me as insulting: How did Enrico dare to doubt my statement? . . .

'Now we shall see,' I said: I carefully lifted the cathode jar and, holding it with its open end down, lit a match and brought it close. There was an explosion, small but sharp and angry, the jar burst into splinters . . . and there remained in my hand, as a sarcastic symbol, the glass ring of the bottom. . . .

I experienced retrospective fear and at the same time a kind of foolish pride, at having confirmed a hypothesis and having unleashed a force of nature. It was indeed hydrogen, therefore: the same element that burns in the sun and stars, and from whose condensation the universes are formed in eternal silence.

(Primo Levi, *The Periodic Table*)

In this extract Primo Levi conveys the problems, principles, methods, techniques and, most importantly, the wonder of science – in short, the fundamental concerns of the science teacher. Teaching science can be immensely rewarding and frustrating. It is full of unsuspected traps and wonderful surprises and for the committed teacher science education raises many questions which become more challenging and fascinating with experience.

The aim of this book is to bring to light the experience and theory that inform the concerns of science teachers both at the beginning of their careers and in the years to come.

Part I deals with the changes in the science curriculum over the last 150 years. Joan Solomon explores the changes in the philosophy of science education over this time and concludes with questions raised about the role of the laboratory in learning science. Solomon describes *how* teaching methods evolved from a mix of external constraints and ideas generated from within the teaching profession. Hodson and Prophet address the question 'Why the science curriculum changes'. Their analysis is based on the concept of the socially constructed curriculum and they suggest that the selection of scientific knowledge for the curriculum is controlled by powerful interest groups.

Part II addresses the question of how children learn science. A considerable body of evidence now demonstrates that children have intuitive ideas about certain natural phenomena. Some of these ideas are common and part of the discourse of everyday life, for example young children conceiving of the Earth as flat, air as empty, plants getting their food from the soil and heavy objects falling faster than light ones. This evidence points to the view that children construct explanations from their own experiences.

Rosalind Driver discusses the implications of a constructivist theory of learning. She indicates those factors that are necessary for children to make the intellectual leap from their intuitive ideas to an understanding of the accepted or 'correct' scientific explanations. Michael Arnold and Robin Millar present a teaching programme consistent with the constructivist viewpoint.

Whilst Driver, Arnold and Millar focus on the construction of concepts in particular areas of science, Philip Adey describes the Cognitive Acceleration through Science Education (CASE) project which owes more to Piaget's general stage theory of development. Adey suggests that the attainment of formal operational skills, which include types of reasoning such as controlling variables and comprehending correlations between variables, can be accelerated through teaching. Whilst there are theoretical differences between these two approaches both have the aim of developing teaching strategies which promote effective learning in science.

Theories of learning have important consequences for teaching. But for any teaching to result in successful learning there has to be a channel of communication between teacher and pupil. This is particularly true in science where the introduction of new terminology, for example, can be a source of confusion.

It is language and, more generally, communication which forms a common theme amongst the articles in Part III. They deal with methods to advance learning and all give practical advice. Clive Sutton argues that the role of language should have greater prominence in the science curriculum.

Language does not merely label objects or events; everyone interprets language in their own way. Science is about ideas and values, specifically human ideas and human values. Thus, he proposes that the emphasis on practical work should shift to a balance between interpreting scientists' ideas through what they say and write, on the one hand, and practical work to test their validity, on the other.

The programmes of study in the National Curriculum in science are explicit about the role of communication and the nature of scientific ideas. Joan Solomon analyses discussion in the science classroom and suggests that group discussion is a particularly useful forum in the field of controversial social issues. Like Clive Sutton she emphasises the humanising aspect of science that this approach encourages.

Andrew Burns and Mike Hamlin describe a project for enhancing the quality of communication. This involved a cross-curricular link with the English department where the pupils explored issues arising from their chemistry course. It is worth noting that the success of the liaison was due to the appropriate organisational and planning structures that had to be set up.

Dorothy Dallas' piece about communication is eminently down to earth. It addresses the question: how do you carry out a class discussion in a fixed bench laboratory? Though Dorothy Dallas died in 1977 her tone will strike a note of familiarity, fun and good sense with any science teacher today, whether beginner or experienced.

Terry Hudson's article looks at the area of skill development in science. After defining and classifying skills he explores appropriate methods to improve cognitive, intellectual and motor skills.

Part III concludes with an attempt to bring in the perspective of teachers at the chalkface through their daily routines. At the end of the day the important interactions are between the teachers, the curriculum, the water taps, the children and the photocopier. Science teachers experience both despair and, in this case, elation, which illustrates that the learning curve for teachers has little in common with the regular certainty of Newtonian mechanics.

Assessment provides an important check on learning for pupils and teachers. John Skevington, in Part IV, provides an overview of assessment for science in the National Curriculum. He identifies some of the difficulties and suggests ways of overcoming them.

Part V looks at ways in which learning science can be made accessible to all including those who experience science as problematic. Patricia Murphy analyses some of the differences in achievement between girls and boys in a practical context. There is a great deal of evidence to show that girls and boys go about carrying out investigations and problem solving in very different ways which usually disadvantage girls when it comes to assessing achievement. However, she points out that change in the nature of the science curriculum can rectify this situation. The curriculum in Thailand is a striking case where a more 'feminine' image of science, amongst other factors, has resulted in girls achieving at least as well as boys.

Maggie Farrar deals with teaching chemistry to pupils who speak English as their second language, though her strategies are applicable to all areas of science. She gives practical advice on useful techniques. Language, as Clive Sutton has earlier indicated, is the medium through which children gain access to scientific ideas, and when sufficient attention is paid to presenting language this can facilitate learning for all children. The underlying message from both Murphy and Farrar is that effective science teaching addresses the needs of all pupils.

Teaching is a demanding vocation and a challenge. Reviewing and evaluating one's teaching methods is a difficult but rewarding task and is part and parcel of successful teaching. All the articles in Part VI are challenging in that they raise issues for debate within science education.

Derek Hodson suggests that computer-assisted learning (CAL) is a more effective teaching instrument than much laboratory bench work and under the right conditions enables children to become more active and creative learners. He does not dismiss bench work but argues that it should be used when essential, such as giving children first-hand experience in the use of a magnet, say, or using instruments such as telescopes and microscopes which extend our senses and acquaint us with parts of the world we could not experience any other way.

Robin Millar warns against any particular emphasis on teaching processes. He argues that instruction in processes such as observing, classifying, inferring and hypothesising are not linked by a set of procedures for doing science. Rather, they are activities which we all do anyway and there is no evidence to show that they are transferable. Millar proposes that the teaching of processes should not be an end in itself but that there are 'scientific processes' that we should be aiming to develop which depend on a basis of scientific knowledge. Ultimately, doing science is a craft which contains many tacit elements.

Richard Gott and Judith Mashiter argue for a task-based approach to curriculum design which would have the characteristics of motivating pupils and giving them a sense of ownership in the activities. A task-based curriculum would involve setting the learning in context and welding together procedural and conceptual understanding.

Finally, Bryan Chapman challenges the 'institutional truths' that support the dominant position of science in the National Curriculum. He questions many of the justifications for a compulsory science education and explores many contentious areas. His conclusions are disturbing and his contribution would jolt any feeling of complacency amongst science educators. It is important to engage with these arguments to give sense and purpose to teaching and learning science. All the articles in this reader have been chosen as a stimulus for effective teaching and as sources to reflect upon in the years to come.

Part I

The science curriculum
Where from, where to?

Chapter 1

The laboratory comes of age

Joan Solomon

Science teaching must take place in a laboratory; about that at least there is no controversy. Science simply belongs there as naturally as cooking belongs in a kitchen and gardening in a garden. Books of recipes or gardening manuals can be read anywhere, but the smells, taste, labour and atmosphere can only be evoked in those who already know the reality. It is the same with science, and so the teaching of it must involve real contact with those aspects of nature which are to be studied. This has one great advantage: for young children the first move out of the classroom with its familiar rows of desks into the exotic atmosphere of a laboratory is immensely stimulating. Excitement and expectation stir. What should we do with these invaluable commodities?

The children themselves have no doubt about the answer; they are all agog to 'do experiments', to touch and use the strange new instruments and perform exciting tricks with them. To put it at its lowest level, this is a wonderful opportunity for new play! Alone amid this throng the adult teacher has another, sterner ambition – that somehow out of this rough, untaught expectancy can be forged an understanding of the insights and the methods of science. Both teacher and pupil are united only in a belief that experiment is the right tool for their objective, and indeed it is a marvellously rich instrument, if well used, with a host of possibilities. The children bring to it their gifts of imagination, curiosity and argumentativeness; the teacher hopes to add scientific purpose, logical method and practical skill. From a marriage of these two sets of qualities may issue an understanding of scientific theory.

EARLY SCIENCE TEACHING

Now theory is not an alluring concept in the educational scene. It conjures up memories of rigidly formulated statements, dry as chalk dust, emphatically underlined on the blackboard, to be learnt and reproduced by rote. Of course it can well be argued that these theories, the end product of so many years of scientific endeavour, are the intellectual heritage of our children.

The atomic theory, the laws of motion, evolution, gravitation, electromagnetic theory, the concepts of energy and entropy, these were all hard-won laurels in the continued battle of science, giving to modern humans rich and subtle ways of visualising the world around them. In the days when scientific education was still in its infancy the objective was simply to present these theories, along with their proofs, to successive generations of pupils as efficiently as possible. Here, they said in effect, is the scientific achievement, learn this.

> It may be said that a boy takes more interest in the matter by seeing for himself, or by performing for himself . . . this we admit, while we continue to doubt the educational value of the transaction. The boy would also probably take much more interest in foot-ball than in Latin grammar; but the measure of his interest is not identical with the importance of the subjects. It may be said that the fact makes a stronger impression on the boy through the medium of his sight, that he believes it the more confidently. I say that this ought not to be the case. If he does not believe the statements of his tutor – probably a clergyman of mature knowledge, recognised ability, and blameless character – his suspicion is irrational, and manifests a want of the power of appreciating evidence.[1]

That extract, it must be admitted, has been included for sheer amusement. Colonel Blimp attitudes are always good for a laugh and no subject which can be as exuberant or as catastrophic as laboratory work should be viewed with exclusive sobriety! At this period science degree courses at the universities were still very new and school science was only just beginning. Some schools and technical colleges did offer a little student practical work even in those early days; at the City of London School, for example, pupils were asked to pay an extra seven shillings a term for such experimental tuition.[2]

Gradually school laboratories equipped for real experimental work became more common and yet, at heart, the method used to teach science differed very little from that used in history, geography or classical studies. Whatever the practical evidence that was offered to schoolchildren in the form of experiments, documents, maps, costumes, photographs or archaeological remains, it was always used to illustrate a concept or a theory which was also explicitly presented. In other words, it was evidence in support of taught theory and not designed as a child-orientated exercise in research. Until quite recently experiments performed in science lessons almost always fulfilled this supporting role; the theory was announced and then practical illustrations were paraded in its honour – some of them being notoriously obstinate in the yielding of obeisance! However, even if the experiments were not successful, it was a matter of no great importance, since all the details of procedure and the 'correct' results were to be found in the textbooks, which were required reading for all pupils. The discovery or establishment of a new theory was clearly far removed in spirit from any of the experiments that were taking place in the school laboratory.

ARMSTRONG AND THE DAWN OF DISCOVERY

The first attack on this approach to science teaching was made by H.E. Armstrong at the turn of the century. During this period, when Baden-Powell was trying to stimulate initiative and self-reliance in the young by his invention of Scouting for boys, Armstrong was attempting to instil the same spirit into the conduct of school experiments. It was an appeal for a new attitude towards education which sounds as fresh today as on the day it was written:

> Let it be realised that an experiment is something altogether different from a demonstration or verification, just as a trial is very different from an execution. . . . The one involves prolonged mental activity, the other mere mechanical obedience. In schools generally the work done is scarcely ever proper experimental work but merely work involving practical demonstrations or verifications – executions not trials. Much nonsense is talked by trainers of teachers and by not a few teachers who ought to know better about the impossibility of children doing 'original work'; it is forgotten that every conscious act done in ignorance of its consequences but with a distinct object of ascertaining what will happen is an act involving original enquiry.[3]

Suddenly it became possible to see a new dimension to education where experiment could be reinvested with all its original excitement and uncertainty. Not only would it be a real enquiry in itself, but it would also lead directly towards an understanding of theory. At one stroke this might both abolish the boredom of didactic instruction and also introduce the child to the new role of a scientific discovery: scientific practice elucidating scientific theory. Admittedly it was a very slow method of covering any syllabus, but for a while it did seem to be gathering support.

In the wider context Armstrong was no lone pioneering figure; it is possible to see him representing within science teaching an amalgam of many contemporary attitudes (those concerned with general child education) with the history and philosophy of science and even with the current psychology of learning. His outstanding importance, of course, lay in his application of these trends to the teaching of science.

THE NATURALIST MOVEMENT IN EDUCATION

Froebel, the originator of kindergarten education, and his mentor Pestalozzi had worked and written about their new liberal methods of teaching early in the nineteenth century, but it was only in Armstrong's time that their influence came to be widely felt. There were many strands of Froebel's system, but the one on which the 'naturalists' of the twentieth century laid most stress was the importance of allowing the latent powers of a child enough room to develop. It seemed to them that what children most needed was simply the freedom to cultivate their own individuality and exercise their own capacity for discovery. Some individuals, like Tolstoy, went so far along this path that it became hard to see much point in the continued existence of the teacher at all. Armstrong himself had been heard to complain that overdidactic teachers were one of his chief stumbling blocks but, as we shall see, he did have a definite task for instruction in his system. However, it is easy to understand how a liberal, discovery attitude towards education might well end by making the teacher seem an outmoded and redundant commodity. In more recent times also the doctrine of free discovery has often been linked with a movement to belittle or even to sweep away the interfering figure of the teacher.

THE PHILOSOPHY OF COMMON SENSE

By the first decade of the twentieth century the history of science seemed to present a gloriously uninterrupted march of progress. In particular, John Dalton's atomic theory and Charles Darwin's theory of evolution presented enthusiastic philosophers of science with a model of excellence for the discovery of truth in the natural world which they were anxious to transfer to every other field of study. The influence of optimistic scientism spread widely, from Bible criticism to social welfare, and a sadly mixed blessing it proved to be. Herbert Spencer, who wrote copiously about education, was also the author of an obnoxious brand of Darwinism in which he attempted to justify the absence of welfare for the urban poor by using the 'law' of the survival of the fittest.

The scientific method by which these prestigious laws had been discovered seemed to be no more than a simple mixture of observation, measurement and reasoning. T.H. Huxley, another colleague of Darwin, expounded a view of science which much influenced Armstrong's thinking. 'Science', he wrote, 'is nothing but trained and organised common sense.' The philosopher Karl Pearson had written in 1892, 'We must carefully guard ourselves against supposing that the scientific frame of mind is a peculiarity of the professional scientist.' If this were so, there was indeed no need for specialised teaching, only the encouragement of organisation and practical training as Armstrong had proposed.

It also followed that the scientific method was similar to the best methods to be used in history, politics or the law. Skills gained in one subject could be directly transferred to another. The net result of education, they argued, was a trained mind – 'education is what is left when all that has been learnt in school has been forgotten.' It is easy to see how welcome such attitudes would be to the traditional classics teachers in the public schools. Why then teach science at all? This was not a paradox that worried Armstrong himself, but many of his supporters struggled manfully with it on behalf of the new school study of science.

TRAINING THE FACULTIES

In the nineteenth century the infant science of psychology sought to divide the domain of the intellect into *faculties* which could be treated as separate and distinct elements. The task of education was to develop these faculties – the will, the imagination, the power of reasoning and the memory – by a carefully balanced programme of activities which was often compared to the training of an athlete's muscles.

Armstrong and other reforming educationalists of the time were expected to justify their new courses by reference to these faculties. In 1896 the Oxford and Cambridge Examination Board gave their approval to a school science syllabus which had very largely been designed by Armstrong. Two years later he published an account of his method under the title *Heuristic Method of Teaching or the Art of Making Children Discover Things for Themselves*. The use of the word 'making' is slightly forbidding; how it must have jarred upon the ears of contemporary followers of Froebel! Armstrong firmly believed that children could be *trained* to discover, and that the process involved the faculties of observation, reasoning and memory. His pupils were set a programme of practical exercises to perform and Armstrong argued enthusiastically for the value of experimental work as a training ground for the mind.

It was fundamental to Armstrong's whole position to believe that there was indeed a heuristic method in which pupils could be instructed. Few nowadays would be so sure that scientific discovery always chugs forward on such definite tramlines; in Armstrong's day this belief rested upon a confident and simple philosophy of science. The subtle and revolutionary changes of scientific theory in the present century were yet to make an impact and there seemed to be no mystery about scientific discovery. Urging children to form conclusions from the results of their experiments thus appeared to be both an ideal educational process and also a likeness to science itself.

Highly trained faculties were regarded as the pinnacle of the educational achievement, producing an intellectual elite who were ready and able to transfer these qualities of mind to any other understanding. So ran the credo of Victorian education – and the Foreign Office, the Indian Civil Service and the armed forces floundered or flourished in its wake. The send-up by W.S. Gilbert of the 'Modern Major General' speaks volumes for the depths of inappropriate learning such a system could produce!

CHANGING TIMES

This early period of educational reform is very instructive. We are now at a sufficient remove from it to observe the curious, inevitable way in which it included and complemented so many facets of current thinking. The moral speaks for itself. However isolated and intimate is the laboratory situation in which pupils and teachers meet during science lessons, they can never be completely insulated from outside influence. Teachers are notoriously impatient of the 'highbrow' theories of philosophy and psychology; this may even be a good and necessary defence of their own intuitive powers of reading their pupils' reactions. Nevertheless they too, as creatures of their age, are bound to be coloured in their thinking and their teaching by current attitudes towards both scientific knowledge and appropriate learning methods.

However, appreciating the power of this continuing interaction lends a sturdiness to the teacher's basis from which the teacher can innovate with greater confidence, and may add an extra dimension to the science which the pupils learn.

Then Armstrong's method began to fall from favour; by 1925 even he was ready to admit that it was out of fashion. There were probably a multitude of reasons for this and some of them are particularly interesting in the light of present arguments about the teaching of science.

In the first place there were complaints from the front line during the First World War that the almost total lack of elementary scientific knowledge was actually endangering the lives of soldiers. War had become more technological and in particular the advent of gas warfare threw up questions of diffusion and of the very nature of gases, about which the majority of soldiers, both officers and other ranks, seemed completely ignorant.

At the end of the war, Higher School Certificate, the forerunner of Advanced Level GCE, was expanded to include examination options in physics, chemistry, botany and zoology. These were intended to be relevant to university work in science and they had a considerable factual content. It soon became all too obvious that Armstrong's prolonged and free-ranging methods provided far too slow a method for covering such syllabuses.

There were also more remote influences from the realms of pure research and philosophy. The 1920s witnessed a shattering revolution in the basic concepts of physics; both quantum theory and relativity turned the older school-learnt theories on their heads and shortly afterwards chemistry and biology were also transmuted by their own quieter revolutions. Even if no immediate changes were made in the school science syllabus (school teaching and their textbooks have a large in-built inertia!) some dim echoes of the noise of revolution were bound to reverberate in the classrooms and laboratories. Science's triumphant march of progress began to look more like the two steps forward and one backwards or sideways of the contemporary tango. It was not the observations or experiments which were at fault, as they might be in the school laboratory, but the interpretations which were to be put upon them. If the findings of famous scientists could be thus reversed, what hope remained that children could make valuable discoveries by their own unaided experiments?

Inevitably this coloured the contemporary philosophy of science. The certain path of rugged common sense no longer yielded certain and unchanging theory, and the philosophy of science began to present a structure of much more subtle hue than the transferable training of Armstrong's hey-day. Nevertheless his initiative never quite lost its appeal, and when the educational system was ripe for another revolution it was ideas very similar to his that rose to the challenge.

AFTER THE WAR

By the 1950s a whole new battery of influences began to make changes in science education seem almost inevitable. The 1944 Education Act had set up a new system in which the existence of three different kinds of schools was supposed to match the range of potentialities within the secondary school population. The now notorious 11+ examination was relied upon to chop off the academic tip for the grammar schools; the rest were divided between the secondary modern and technical schools. At the same time the school-leaving age was raised to 15. To the optimistic it appeared that every child would now be given the opportunity to profit by the education best suited to their ability, always provided that this remained as forecast at age 11. However socially and academically divisive such a system may now seem, it can be argued that it demonstrated, at that time, a genuine wish to tailor the extended education to fit the children, rather than to force all pupils into the same academic mould. In this sense it reflected a general movement towards wooing the enthusiasm of children rather than coercing their attention.

This was also a period when early specialisation in education was being widely attacked. In public and grammar schools it was quite commonplace for pupils to be forced to opt for the 'science side', or against it, by the age of 13 or 14; the result was an apparently educated population in which many had never studied any science subject after this age. In a famous and influential lecture C.P. Snow attacked the 'Two Cultures' within society – science and the arts – which coexisted without respect for or understanding of each other's intellectual background. When, after a decade of appalling post-war shortages of teachers, equipment and laboratories, the Nuffield Foundation put generous funds at the disposal of school science in order to inaugurate new courses, the slogan adopted was 'Science for All'. Since these early courses were all designed for the grammar school, which catered for no more than the top 20 to 25 per cent of the school population, this battle-cry may seem more than a little misleading. It was to be understood only in the

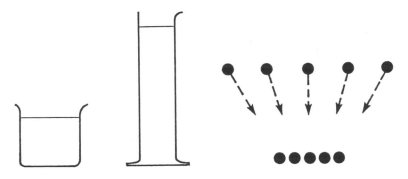

Figure 1.1 Which holds more water? Which line contains more beads? Think of *an action* which connects them

sense that all those able or lucky enough to be in such a school should have had the chance to savour the delights of school science!

It even proved possible to argue from the continuous upheaval within the world of science that another type of teaching should be adopted. By this time new philosophies of science, such as those due to Karl Popper and T.S. Kuhn, had developed. These systems both accepted as inevitable, even healthy, the confrontations between opposing scientific theories which occasionally led to the downfall of a long-accepted paradigm. Scientific revolutions and somersaults seemed almost more characteristic of science than the cherished Victorian picture of sedate forward progress. If pupils were to be trained for such an uncertain battlefield it could be more important that they were armed with a foretaste of discovery than with an armoury of well-learnt theories which might be superseded tomorrow.

It must be added that there were also those within the new educational movements, perhaps even a majority, who favoured the discovery method for almost opposite reasons. To them discovery was the irreversible method of science and 'to be a scientist for a day', another of the Nuffield catch-phrases, was to find for oneself the way forward by an impeccably reliable route.

In quite another sphere a whole new understanding of childhood learning and thinking about the natural world had been developing. This was the attractive, child-centred study made by Jean Piaget and his followers. By watching, questioning and testing groups of children of different ages he had managed to uncover a vital and unsuspected stage in their development which enabled the unstructured observation of a curious toddler to grow towards the sophisticated formal reasoning processes which are the aim of secondary science education.

In many of the problems and tests that Piaget posed to his sample of children, such as the constancy of a certain volume of water or the number of objects in two different arrays (Figure 1.1), there always seemed to be an operational stage of understanding when an actual course of action – pouring the water or grouping the objects – became a concrete mental process in its own right. In any explanation it was this action which was visualised and referred to. Purely abstract reasoning, concepts of the conservation of volume or number, arrived later. This seemed incontrovertible proof that the children were right in demanding to play on their own with the intriguing apparatus of the laboratory. In this way they would learn from experiment how to think about natural objects and phenomena before they were presented with the abstract theories of science which rightfully belonged to a later stage in their intellectual development.

THE NEW MOVEMENTS IN BRITAIN AND THE UNITED STATES

This build-up of pressure came to a head in the late 1950s with the planning of new courses. The next decade proved to be very fertile with a fine crop of new science syllabuses, the most famous of these being PSSC (Physical Science Study Curriculum) and the BSCS (Biological Science Curriculum Study) in the United States and the Nuffield Science Projects in England.

Parallel to this process and intermingled with it ran the other movement, involving a change in the approach to teaching which was to give discovery the pride of place. In the Nuffield scheme this idea was rooted in their much-used word *understanding*. They quoted in its support a supposedly Chinese proverb, 'I hear and I forget, I see and I remember, I do and I understand.' The progress of scientific research, psychological theories of intellectual growth, sympathy for the childhood experience and even the long-neglected teachings of Armstrong had all culminated in a repudiation of the old didactic routine in favour of child-orientated experiment.

A great deal of fundamental work and reorganisation was required. The old criticism of Armstrong's methods still held true: discovery exercises were bound to be slow and need extension over many teaching periods before any useful results could emerge; and these themselves might well prove to be of little weight in terms of knowledge acquired. Their true value would lie in the spirit of enquiry, enthusiasm and individually created understanding that was anticipated. In return for these priceless qualities the new method seemed to demand that the teachers should discard many items of the traditional syllabus; on the other hand, public examinations and the need to meet the requirements of university entrance challenged and menaced any curtailment of the learning process. Fortunately the Nuffield scheme had the resources both to design totally new syllabuses for their O- and A-level examinations and also the imagination to plan questions which would be in sympathy with the general approach that they were using. After a course which had emphasised understanding based on experimental work, it would have been a travesty of the whole method then to present the fresh, open minds of the pupils with the usual horror of slogging through answers thick with revised and memorised facts. Carefully, and with considerable success, the originators of the Nuffield courses steered their way round the many natural obstacles – and if the result was something of a compromise between free experiment and didactic teaching, at least it was workmanlike and planned to the last item of apparatus to be used and the weekly questions to be set for homework.

Another new feature of these courses was apparent from the first. The Nuffield Physics scheme, for example, was published in 1964 fully furnished with a complete set of Teacher's Guides and pupils' Question Books for each of the five years of the course – and yet there was not one regular textbook. This was deliberate policy. When the Nuffield Project listed the characteristics of the kind of science teaching they wished to promote, they concluded with the following three points:

– a well-grounded understanding of science (or a branch of science), not a knowledge of disconnected facts;
– encouragement of children to think freely and courageously about science in the way practising scientists do;
– experimental and practical enquiry for children as a means of awakening original thought.

This understanding of science was to be achieved in the first place not by reading about theories but by performing experiments and creating concepts at first hand in the laboratory. In this way the children would make their own discoveries and be sure.

In the United States at this time there was not so much an educational revolution as a public convulsion at the state of science teaching which had been sparked off by that colossal affront to national pride – the Soviet launching of Sputnik. School and college science teaching were quickly singled out to be the public scapegoats for this humiliation. Where the Nuffield Project was staffed largely by school science teachers seconded for the purpose from their usual work, in the United States their colleagues were castigated and then ignored by the new movement which was generated by college educationalists and working scientists. Both the newly created National Science Foundation and the National Academy of Science launched urgent projects for curriculum reform and in 1961 a most forceful and prophetic lecture by Joseph J. Schwab, Professor of Education at Chicago University, heralded a movement for 'Inquiry Methods' in science teaching. The stern admonishment of teachers in the name of national welfare is clear from the opening sentences:

Teachers and educators concerned with science face a new situation. They are being asked to fulfil an urgent national need, to act as executors of a public policy which is not of their making. They can no longer treat their duties as determined only by themselves.[4]

Schwab's analysis was based on a delineation between 'stable' and 'fluid' enquiry, similar to T.S. Kuhn's descriptions of 'normal' and 'revolutionary' science. When science is going through a normal or stable phase, the current paradigm of the subject, as developed in the contemporary textbooks, dominates all experiment and theory. More detail is added to the paradigm, but the whole activity is only to be reached through an intensive formal education in its operation. Fluid or revolutionary science, by contrast, only takes place at those moments in history when the previous paradigm is discredited and a new one is set up in its place. Examples include the Copernican revolution in astronomy or the wave mechanics revolution in electron theory. For such sparkling innovations it is not so much formal training in an established paradigm that is required as the creativity of new imagination – a far more difficult objective for any educational programme.

Schwab maintained that the rapid growth of science had so shortened the time span of stable enquiry that it was no longer viable itself as a guide for science teaching nor valuable as a source of technological innovation. Fluid enquiry, on the other hand, showed scientific knowledge as uncertain and hard to come by. Many of Schwab's examples were aimed at college students via the study of original papers. In practical work he aimed to give first-hand experience of the difficulties of specifying an actual problem and of collecting data. He too agreed that experiment should precede classroom instruction, and that practical manuals of instruction should be replaced by 'permissive and open materials which point to areas in which problems can be found'. He also discharged a volley of disapproval at the 'rhetoric of conclusions' contained in the usual student textbooks.

A comparison between this seminal lecture and one delivered on behalf of the Nuffield Teaching Project in England, say the well-known paper by Professor E.M. Rogers first read to an ASE (Association for Science Education) meeting in Birmingham in 1964, demonstrates vividly the effects of this divorce in the United States between the practice and theory of teaching. Schwab concludes his lecture:

> treatment of science as enquiry consists of a treatment of scientific knowledge in terms of its origins in the united activities of the human mind and hand which produce it; it is a means for clarifying and illuminating scientific knowledge.[5]

Compare that with the exuberant and child-centred conclusion to Rogers' paper:

> in teaching physics for understanding, we hope for great results in this generation of children but greater still in two generations, when these children can tell their children in turn 'Science is delightful, interesting,

powerful; science is great thinking and clever doing; science makes sense.'[6]

Despite this contrast the upshot of these two movements was similar. School textbooks were unanimously cast as the villains of the piece and were rejected as a respectable teaching implement. Experiment was promoted in their stead to pride of place in the teaching armoury either as enquiry into a problem posed by the teacher or, even more boldly, as an open-ended encounter between pupils and materials which was to generate problems, concepts and results. The role of the teacher was less clear. In England the teacher was given the task of radiating enthusiasm and encouragement, and was even allowed to adapt the course as he or she went along. In the United States he was to rally to the national call, to read widely in the philosophy and history of science, and to carry out the behests of the educationalists.

TIME FOR REVIEW

The lifetime of Armstrong's early initiative in education was about twenty years, and by now roughly the same span has elapsed since the 'golden years' of Nuffield. Once more, as time slips by there are subtle changes in our educational aspirations, our philosophy of science and our attitudes towards teaching which should enable us to take up a stance which is both critical and constructive.

We could begin by looking at those features of this attractive discovery method of teaching which have cried out for examination from Armstrong's day to the present. Admittedly it is an emotive area where thinly disguised terms of specialised abuse are apt to be hurled about in a blindly ideological way. 'Authoritarian', 'traditional', or 'radical', 'undisciplined', they cry! Just because the teaching of children is so important and so close to the heart, hardly to be attempted without care, sympathy and personal involvement, there is no reason why such awkward questions should not be asked and answered as far as is possible.

Are there any heuristics of discovery? Can one actually train children to discover? Are they to be guided to the brink or should they be left free to choose both the problems and the methods that they want? Are there different degrees of freedom within what we call discovery learning?

Where does the teacher fit into this? Would the children have greater space to exercise their valuable initiative without the teacher's presence? Is a worksheet of written clues better than an authoritative, talking teacher?

Should children be encouraged to work at their own individual pace? What place, if any, does the social interaction between children have in the discovery sequence? What can they teach each other?

Must the syllabuses be jettisoned? Is it possible to contrive that a sequence of discoveries will cover the appropriate topics? Can new concepts and theories also arise from practical experiments without exposition from a book or a teacher?

Does practical laboratory work itself need instruction like carpentry and metal work? Are there skills to be learnt by detailed instruction and demonstration, or will free experiment and practice prove to be its own tutor in such matters?

What about the hoary question of transferability? Is there any evidence that the initiative encouraged in one lesson transfers to another topic or another subject? Does an act of personal discovery make learning and remembering easier?

Any scheme of science teaching has two different sets of critics who stand poles apart and only too often make hardly any contact. At one extreme stand the professional lecturers on education; at the other stand the children, uniquely cast both as guinea-pigs and continual assessors of the courses. Between these are to be found the harassed, practising schoolteachers whose opinions are swayed now by one side and now by the other. In as much as they take an up-to-date, professional view of their task they will have imbibed some of the new philosophies of science education by spare-time reading and 'in-service' training, but their daily contact with pupils cannot fail to have seasoned their study with incidental surprises. Because teaching is not an intellectual pursuit, in the field either of education or of science, but rather a continual and intimate struggle to understand, stimulate and assuage the curiosity of the young, these teachers have the opportunity to interpret the interaction between children and science in the battlefield of the laboratory. Released from the dreary necessity for producing an atmosphere of chilling silence while notes and sample problems are taken down at dictation speed, the teacher can now permit, or even encourage, a chatty background to the group experimental work. At once a wealth of unselfconscious comment becomes audible. Mixed though it may be with local gossip and pop-culture crazes, this is immensely valuable source material. Argument, discussion and appeals to the teacher for arbitration show very clearly the efficiency of the methods being used and any difficulties that are arising. Boredom is unmistakable and both absorption and enthusiasm are contagious. If one sort of experimental approach succeeds more than another, then neither the teacher nor the pupils can be unaware of it. Children clamour characteristically for more of what they have enjoyed and criticise with uninhibited frankness what they have disliked or found incomprehensible.

With such ready critics to hand there is no need to stop at an examination of the discovery method. There are other areas of practical work that require investigation every bit as much – demonstration experiments by teachers, experience exercises and exhibitions of specimens and materials. Almost all the published courses include such activities, although not all the Teacher's Guides are as clear as they might be about the purposes behind these different kinds of experiment. Nor is it enough to consider the pedagogic purpose alone; the impact of such lessons in terms of class reaction and behaviour will be an essential, even devastating, aspect of any actual lesson.

In a wider sense the childhood experience of learning science will require some kind of programme to provide not only a steady crescendo of understanding which is effective and eloquent in its results, but also one which matches the teacher's own philosophy of science. This is inevitable; one can only sell a product effectively if one has a strong belief in its merit. For this purpose it will be illuminating to touch upon the experience of research at the front line of knowledge and upon the current theories of the philosophy of science. Once again, as these are applied within the classroom, the comments of our young critics-cum-guinea-pigs can be relied upon to give the thumbs up, or down, on any new method which is attempted.

The elusive but central motif of this discussion will be the power and training of the imagination. Few scientists would doubt the importance of this quality in understanding and interpreting the models of science all the way from animal transport systems to the kinetic theory of gases and black holes. Still less doubt exists about the vividness of children's own powers of imagination. These are demonstrated in everything they do from playground games to painting and story-telling. Yet, within science, this wayward faculty needs to be fined and sharpened to a purpose by way of concepts which need definition as well as the visualisation of mechanisms.

How then does the solid hardware of the laboratory, the prosaic bunsen burner, flask and ammeter, relate to a developing imagination? If we ignore this apparently ill-matched liaison between apparatus, measurement and imagination we shall reduce experiment to a level of importance on a par with cooking cakes to a given recipe.

NOTES

1 Isaac Todhunter, *Conflict of Studies and Other Essays* (Macmillan, London, 1873). Quoted in Robert L. Weber and E. Mendoza (eds), *A Random Walk in Science* (Institute of Physics, Bristol, 1973).
2 It is probably unnecessary to point out that such schools as did offer science were largely the well-established public schools. Indeed the forerunner of the present Association for Science Education was named 'The Association of Public School Science Masters', which had a predictably elitist view of its objectives. The first president of this association is on record for stating the aim of school science as 'the means of sifting out from the great mass of the people those golden grains of genius which are now too often lost among the sands of mediocrity'.
3 H.E. Armstrong, Address to the Portsmouth Secondary Educational League, 1908. Quoted in G. Van Praagh (ed.), *H.E. Armstrong and Science Education* (John Murray, London, 1973).
4 Joseph J. Schwab, *The Teaching of Science* (Harvard University Press, Cambridge, MA, 1962).

5 Ibid.
6 Professor E.M. Rogers. Paper given at an ASE Meeting, Birmingham, 1964. Quoted in *Nuffield Physics Teacher's Guides* (Longman/Penguin, Harlow/ Harmondsworth, 1966).

Chapter 2

Why the science curriculum changes
Evolution or social control?

D. Hodson and R.B. Prophet

Peter Uzzell[1] has traced the changing aims of science education from the early days of school science in the nineteenth century through to the Nuffield projects of the 1960s and the more recent Schools Council project in integrated science (SCISP). What is absent from this admirable article and from other works dealing with the history and development of the science curriculum (such as Jenkins,[2] Layton[3] and Turner[4]) is any convincing account of *why* the curriculum changed in the particular way that it did. In a later article exploring the changing status of science in the curriculum as reflected in official reports, Uzzell concludes:

> What is taught, the manner of teaching and the resources for teaching are of crucial importance, as are the needs of children and our country. *Who will decide and on what grounds?*[5] [our italics]

Our chapter speculates on these questions by taking a historical perspective, in the belief that some light may be shed on the question 'Who *will* decide curriculum issues?' by attempting to ascertain who decided them in the past – for example, in the period so carefully documented by Uzzell and others.

Underpinning the curricular arguments concerning the relative importance of 'content' or 'method', the role of practical work, the issue of separate versus combined (or integrated) science, which concerned the attention of teachers throughout this period, is the perception of 'science', and of 'school science' in particular, held by curriculum writers, teachers of science and scientists. Just as the science curriculum has changed, so too has the prevailing view of what is appropriate 'school science'. Layton[3] provides a most interesting and useful account of the process leading to the establishment of one particular conception of school science, that of *pure laboratory science*. It is this view which has provided the basic framework of school science in modern times. Layton argues that this particular view of science emerged in preference to alternative approaches because the alternatives had become 'casualties in a process of natural selection as the educational environment had become progressively more sharply defined'.[6] In our opinion, social

Darwinist explanations of this kind are inadequate and must be replaced by a more radical historiographic account. They are inadequate because they treat the social processes of decision making as though they are *natural* processes, and because they ignore the motives and interests of the decision makers.

In the mid-nineteenth century at least two alternative conceptions of school science were available to teachers: 'the Science of Common Things' and 'pure laboratory science'. That the latter became established as the *correct* view is not disputed in this chapter. However, Layton's explanation of *why* the latter view became established ('survival of the fittest') *is* challenged, and two important questions concerning the science curriculum are raised:

1 How does the selection of what is to count as worthwhile knowledge take place?
2 How is this *selected* knowledge presented to the learner?

Answers to these questions may lie in the dispute surrounding the nature of knowledge. Basically, there are two opposing views concerning the nature of knowledge. One view assumes a direct correspondence between reality and knowledge, and asserts that knowledge is *discovered*, the other claims that knowledge is *socially constructed* and may be understood only by reference to the social, cultural and historical context in which it arose.

THE FORMS OF KNOWLEDGE

There have been many attempts of late to derive a theory of knowledge to aid curriculum design.[7, 8] Perhaps the best known is that advanced by Paul Hirst,[9] who claims that all human knowledge may be differentiated into a number of 'logically distinct' *Forms* on the basis of four criteria.

1 The characteristic basic concepts.
2 The characteristic structures by which these concepts are related.
3 The characteristic ways by which knowledge statements are tested.
4 The characteristic techniques and skills for exploring experience.

Using these criteria, Hirst identifies *seven* Forms of Knowledge:

- Mathematics and formal logic
- The physical sciences
- The human sciences, including history
- Moral understanding
- The religious form of knowledge
- Philosophy
- Fine arts

For Hirst, the central aim of education is the development of mind, so that a curriculum organised on the basis of the Forms of Knowledge represents the most appropriate way of achieving that goal – because it introduces children to the *various ways of knowing*.

A number of distinguished educationists have argued that an effective teaching strategy requires that learning experiences should be designed in such a way that they reflect and illustrate the conceptual and methodological structure of the disciplines. Jerome Bruner may be taken as representative of this tradition of curriculum design.

> The curriculum of a subject should be determined by the most fundamental understanding that can be achieved of the underlying principles that give structure to that subject. Teaching specific topics or skills without making clear their context in the broader fundamental structure of a field of knowledge . . . makes it exceedingly difficult for the student to generalize from what he has learnt to what he will encounter later . . . has little reward in terms of intellectual excitement . . . [and produces knowledge] that is likely to be forgotten.[10]

SOCIALLY CONSTRUCTED KNOWLEDGE

Directly opposed to Hirst's theory is the view that knowledge is the product of the interaction of individual minds with experiences, resulting in a highly *personal* system of interpretations and rationalisations. On this theory, knowledge develops through social processes, as individuals categorise experience and infer meanings. Thus, the status of knowledge as an *objective* entity is severely questioned. Statements about curriculum content are then seen not as statements about objective entities, but as particular views of the world advanced by particular groups of individuals, or (as Blum puts it) as 'products of the informal understandings negotiated among members of an organized intellectual collectivity'.[11]

The sociology of knowledge has a long history. In *History and Class Consciousness*, published in 1923, Lukacs asserted that consciousness, and consequently knowledge of all kinds, is the product of interaction between men, reality and *interest*. This third variable is just as powerful as the other two in limiting and determining the kind of knowledge that different groups in society acquire. Lukacs believed that 'under ideal conditions' reality *is* accessible to man's rational appraisal, but that in practice *both* classes in society (the 'dominant' and the 'oppressed') will, because of their different *interests*, attain only a partial understanding of reality (a 'false consciousness', as he calls it). In *Ideology and Utopia* (1936), Mannheim reasserted this theory of the social construction of knowledge, but he exempted scientific knowledge, which he regarded as 'disinterested knowledge' unrelated to its context of production and capable of a direct relationship with reality. Writers in the modern tradition of the so-called 'new sociology' – especially Keddie,[12] Esland[13] and Young[14] – deny special status to scientific knowledge and reject the distinction between academic knowledge and common-sense knowledge drawn by philosophers such as Karl Popper.[15] They argue that *all* knowledge is socially constructed, that we do not know the world as it really is, but only as mediated through the conceptual framework we have. This framework is a human construction, which could have been different and is relative to the social system. Clearly, the way we see the world is partly influenced by the way we have been brought up ('socialised'), by our language and by our experiences, but these writers suggest that it is *totally* determined by these factors and that all knowledge and all kinds of truth are simply 'institutionalised conventions'. Thus, they lead us to a theory of 'cultural relativity' in which a particular view of reality is neither right nor wrong. In other words, 'truth is as you see it!' They refuse to allow limiting features in the nature of reality: the validity of arguments, the truth of statements, and the correct application of concepts to experience are to be explained *only* in terms of the socially dominant group. Hence, different groups could legitimate different standards of validity, truth and correctness. It is only a short step from suggesting that all knowledge is socially constructed, and therefore arbitrary, to suggesting that the *criteria* by which we decide on truth and falsehood are also socially constructed and could, therefore, be altered. Thus, rationality itself becomes merely a convention and the rules of logic and argument are shaped and selected in accordance with the purpose of the argument or the intentions of the arguer. C.W. Mills had argued in similar vein when he asserted that 'the rules of the game change with a shift of interest'. Zones of knowledge (as he called them), because they are human constructs, have 'careers' in which *the norms of truth change*.

> Criteria, or observational and verificatory models, are not transcendental. There have been, and are, diverse canons and criteria of validity and truth, and these criteria, upon which determination of the truthfulness of propositions at any time depend, are themselves, in their persistence and change, open to socio-historical relativization.[16]

At the other extreme is Phenix's view that the disciplines are perfected, *absolute* forms of knowledge, existing independently of man.

> The structure of things is revealed, not invented, and it is the business of enquiry to open that structure to general understanding through formation of appropriate concepts and theories. Truth is rich and varied, but it is not arbitrary. The nature of things is given, not chosen.[7]

Whilst not wishing to accept Phenix's proposition that 'the nature of things is *given*', we believe that there is a point at which it makes no sense to ask if things could be conceived otherwise. There *are* limiting features in the world. There *are* events in the world subject to cause and effect. There *is* some degree of stability and order. If there were not, we could not perceive it. The way we discriminate and explain must be *partly* due to stable features in our environment and *partly* due to cultural influences. Richard Pring sums this up quite succinctly when he says that choosing to distinguish between cats and dogs may be a consequence of our particular cultural environment, but *being able* to distinguish between them says something about cats and dogs.[17]

SOCIAL CONTROL

Whilst rejecting the extreme position advocated by the 'new sociologists', it is still possible to use the theoretical framework of socially constructed knowledge and the notion of *social control* as an explanation for *why* the science curriculum changes in a particular way.

Sociologists of knowledge assert that all groups in society attempt to legitimate and disseminate the knowledge which best suits their interests. As Karl Marx reminds us, the groups with the most power, the ruling groups, are in a better position to succeed in establishing their particular version of reality.

> The ideas of the ruling class are in every epoch the ruling ideas: i.e. the class which is the ruling material force of society, is at the same time its ruling intellectual force. The class which has the means of material production at its disposal, has control at the same time over the means of mental production . . . hence among other things [they] rule also as thinkers, as producers of ideas, and regulate the production and distribution of the ideas of their age; thus their ideas are the ruling ideas of the epoch.[18]

However, to suggest that the imposition of a particular view of the world by a ruling group implies both a huge conspiracy of manipulation on the one hand, and large-scale human subservience and passive acceptance on the other hand, is to oversimplify grossly the complex interactions in society. We are all born into a specific social and historical context, with its already existing ideas and interactions; we live within an 'ideological matrix' which influences and determines our whole consciousness, so that we acquire a set of beliefs, values and practices which we accept as 'common sense'. This view of society is then reinforced and stabilised through institutions such as schools, so that it appears to be the only way the world *can* be. Thus, the education system may be an important aspect of the social control mechanism.[19] It is inappropriate to enter into a discussion of the concept of social control here, but it is worth noting (as Donajgrodzki[20] points out) that the identification of social control processes at work does *not* imply that the control element is the major or the only factor, or that the 'controllers' and 'controlled' are aware of the process. A particular interest group may, of course, make a conscious and cynical use of education, or any other social structure or institution, but that group is just as likely to have a genuine passion for its cause and to assign itself motives for its actions, which only later appear to have been false. This would appear to be the state of affairs at the time of the great changes in the school science curriculum in the mid-nineteenth century. It may also be happening now!

THE SCIENCE OF COMMON THINGS

The earliest attempt to include science in the curriculum seems to have been Charles and Elizabeth Mayo's *Object Lessons*, designed for 'the cultivation of habits of accurate observation, correct description, and right judgement upon the things of nature and art'.[21] Following the publication of textbooks written by the Mayos (*Lessons on Objects*, 1831, and *Lessons on Shells*, 1832) and backing from the Home and Colonial Infant School society, Object Lessons quickly became established as the basis of science lessons in the early years of a child's elementary schooling. In the 1840s a small but influential group of clerics existed, who saw the teaching of science as essential for the moral and religious salvation of the labouring classes. Notable among them was the Rev. Richard Dawes, who became Rector of Kings Somborne in 1837 and, with the help of a government grant, opened a National Society school there in October 1842.[22] This village school soon achieved remarkable educational results, in large measure attributable to the use of secular reading books with a large scientific content and to the teaching of science as applied to 'the understanding of common things'. The first favourable reports from HM Inspectorate appeared in 1845[23] and, in 1848, the Minutes of the Committee of Council on Education contained a long account of the organisation and teaching of the Science of Common Things by the Rev. Henry Moseley.[24] From this time, Dawes found a staunch ally in Moseley, who applied himself to the diffusion of Dawes' curriculum scheme.

In the early 1850s more well-defined support for the teaching of science in elementary schools became apparent, possibly due to the Great Exhibition of 1851, when it was realised that British manufacturers compared unfavourably with those from overseas. Layton[3] describes how the supporters of the movement for science education recognised three priorities if science were to be firmly established in the curriculum: well-designed and inexpensive apparatus and books; suitably trained teachers; and a sound administrative framework. A government grant scheme for the purchase of school science apparatus and books, promoted by Moseley, went some way to meeting this first priority. Moseley's influence was also crucial in meeting the second priority, when he was instrumental in establishing the requirement that all students in training schools should study science. Additionally, grants were made available to supplement the salaries of lecturers who showed skill in adapting topics in science for elementary instruction. The third essential resource for the establishment of science in the curriculum was a sound administrative framework. Much of the basic groundwork had, of course, already been done by Moseley through his work for the Committee of Council. Further impetus was supplied in 1853 by the creation of the Department of Science and Art, with Dr Lyon Playfair as Head of Science. Playfair strongly endorsed the view that science should be introduced into elementary education, and early signs were that much fruitful work would be done in cooperation with the Committee of Council on Education.

By 1854, with the three essential resources necessary for the development of Dawes' scheme reasonably satisfied, the movement seemed poised for success. Journals such as *Educational Expositor* carried many articles discussing and suggesting further developments for the scheme.

Suddenly, in mid-decade, when all seemed set for a significant advance, several crucial changes occurred. Dawes was moved to the Deanery of Hereford where, even though he retained his interest in education, much of his time was taken up with his new duties. In 1855, a year after influencing grant regulations favourable to science and introducing a large amount of physical science into the examinations of training schools, Moseley was appointed resident Canon of Bristol Cathedral, being replaced as Inspector with special responsibility for the Church Training Colleges by the Rev. Frederick Temple, who within two years had revised the scheme of examinations for students, reducing the amount of mechanics and demoting physical science from its prime position to one of several *optional* subjects. By 1859 mechanics had disappeared as an examination subject and the number of teachers able to claim grant aid for scientific apparatus had been drastically reduced. The most vital resource of all for the continued success of the Science of Common Things movement, the supply of trained teachers, had been virtually halted. In the administrative sphere a significant change of priority was apparent. Playfair, a strong supporter of the Dawes scheme in the early years of the decade, shifted his ground significantly regarding the most appropriate kind of science for the elementary school curriculum. The aims and objectives of science education were moved firmly into the affective domain, with prime place being afforded to 'love of nature', for which natural history and the 'sciences of observation' were regarded as the most appropriate vehicles. In 1858 Playfair left the Department of Science and Art to resume his academic career as professor of chemistry in the University of Edinburgh. By 1859, with a new and very limited system of claiming grant aid for science teaching, the role of science in the curriculum had been severely curtailed. With the Revised Code of 1862, following the Report of the Newcastle Commission, all financial assistance towards science in elementary schools was withdrawn. It is worth noting that in assessing the state of popular education the Commissioners, rather surprisingly, did *not* seek the views of Dawes or Moseley. The result of these new regulations was that science disappeared from the elementary school curriculum, and did not reappear until 1882.

The question of particular interest in this chapter is *why* this change should have come about. The 'social Darwinist' explanation given by Layton – that better and more acceptable alternatives had become available – may appear reasonable from a common-sense viewpoint, but does not stand up well to close historical scrutiny. Rather than failing, the experiment with the Science of Common Things was showing signs of marked success: children were successfully learning science! Hence it would be more correct to say that it was *abandoned* rather than it failed, and that its abandonment represents an attempt at social control. It is reasonable to ask, therefore, *to whom* the new science curriculum alternative of *pure laboratory science was* 'more acceptable'? It is reasonable to ask *whose interests* were furthered by the introduction of this alternative and why this group's interest was being threatened by the success of the Science of Common Things?

THE EMERGENCE OF PURE SCIENCE

During the early 1850s the traditional orthodox conception of a classics-based liberal education, which set apart the aristocracy and gentry from the rest and restricted the entry of the emergent middle class to the ruling order, was beginning to come under attack. An important and forceful essay by Herbert Spencer[25] on the relative merits of various branches of knowledge directly questioned some of the basic assumptions of this classical education, and put forward a case for the inclusion of *science* in the curriculum. He suggested four main 'areas' in which scientific knowledge had a greater 'worth' than any other form of knowledge.

1 It cultivated a superior type of memory.
2 It was superior in cultivating judgement.
3 It was superior in instilling moral discipline, through its appeal to reason.
4 It was essential for developing a religious culture – science could not be separated from religion without harmful effects to both.

Spencer and Herschel[26] were adamant that the science promoted in schools should be 'practically useful' in various professions, manufactures and businesses, but such an emphasis was roundly condemned by Whewell, who considered that it would inhibit scientists in moving towards 'laws of a more exalted generality and higher speculative beauty'.[27] Such an attitude is representative of the increasingly prominent advocates of education in *pure abstract science*. Robert Hunt, Secretary to the Society of Arts, argued that whilst the practical aspect of science was of 'some importance', it is the study of *abstract science* that 'refined and elevated human feelings'. He claimed that any idea of measuring the value of science in terms of its utility was degrading it from its 'far higher and holier ends'. By training the young to 'estimate truth by its money value' and by seeking scientific knowledge for 'purely mercenary ends' we would ensure that scientific knowledge advanced no further. He suggested, instead, 'more noble' ends for science education:

> I would venture to impress upon all teachers of the young, not to attempt to teach science in all its details, but to excite curiosity, stimulate inquiry and quicken the powers of observation.[28]

His concluding words presented a view of science designed to advance it for serious consideration as a component of a liberal education:

> by allowing the young mind to expand itself over the fields of nature 'like a wild bird of the wilderness', to embrace within its flight the whole truth in its illustration of creation's great phenomena, by ascending from practical science to the high poetry of science, we shall produce a nobler being.[28]

The opposition to the teaching of the Science of Common Things and the promotion of Pure Abstract Science for inclusion in the curriculum for liberal education of the upper classes merged with the movement for the improved status of natural history. In this context the work of Henslow[29] and T.H. Huxley is particularly important. The views of many eminent scientists of the time were represented in a report presented to the British Association by its Parliamentary Committee.[30] Under the chairmanship of Lord Wrottesley, this committee undertook a survey of opinion among scientists on what they saw as the most effective measures to be adopted in improving the position of science. On the basis of the report (presented in 1857), Wrottesley drew up twelve resolutions to be submitted to Parliament. Implicit in the resolutions was the value of *pure science* – prestige for abstract science was deemed to be essential for the progress of science. Of the four resolutions directly concerned with education, none was concerned with science at the elementary school level. It may be assumed from this that Wrottesley and his committee either (i) considered science at the elementary level to be unimportant, or (ii) considered that developments at this level were already satisfactory and needed no further comment. It is *our* view that the report implicitly reflected a growing awareness of a serious problem: that developments in science at the elementary level were not only 'satisfactory' as far as science *learning* was concerned, but were highly *successful*, and that social hierarchy was being threatened because there was no corresponding development for the higher orders. Giving the labouring poor access to a particular form of knowledge, seen as a very important resource, and at the same time denying this resource to their superiors, was coming to be regarded as a very dangerous state of affairs. Wrottesley himself expressed his concern over elementary school science in a section of his book on the 'present condition of England'. He comments on the impressive grasp of scientific principles in schools for the labouring poor compared with the lack of any science in the curriculum of grammar and public schools, and describes in detail an incident in a pauper school where he asked a class for the explanation of the principle of a pump:

> a poor boy hobbled forth to give a reply; he was lame and humpbacked, and his wan emaciated face told only too clearly the tale of poverty and its consequences, unwholesome and scanty diet in early years; but he gave forthwith so lucid and intelligent a reply to the question put to him that there arose a feeling of admiration for the child's talents combined with a sense of shame that more information should be found in some of the lowest of our lower classes on matters of general interest than in those far above them in the world by station.[31]

Wrottesley's conclusion confirms the worst fears of the upper classes concerning the education of the lower orders:

> It would be an unwholesome and vicious state of society in which those who are comparatively unblessed with nature's gifts should be generally superior in intellectual attainments to those above them in station.[31]

Similar views, showing the depth of the disquiet, were expressed by many other influential individuals. In an article in the *Edinburgh Review*, A.C. Tait (who followed Arnold at Rugby and later became Archbishop of Canterbury) expressed concern that the education of the poor was making such good progress that the higher orders were being left behind. Consequently it was 'absolutely necessary for government to attend to education of the rich'. He predicted a complete overturn of the social order if 'the son of a labourer possesses better knowledge than the son of the squire'. It is interesting to note that he also makes direct reference to Dawes at Kings Somborne and to the undesirability of the children of labourers being educated with the sons of the higher orders.

The principal goal of the Science of Common Things was intellectual development of children, the acquisition of scientific knowledge and the provision of experiences for the exercise of reason, speculation and imagination. Improvements in the moral and religious condition of the children of the poor were assumed to follow as a matter of course once self-confidence and integrity of thought had been achieved. By giving a prominent place in the curriculum to applied sciences such as mechanics and agricultural chemistry, education could be related to a culture which was familiar to the labouring classes. Furthermore, the restricted linguistic experiences of so many elementary school children need no longer be an insuperable obstacle to the growth of rationality. As Layton remarks:

> Here was no crumb of upper-class education charitably dispensed to the children of the labouring poor. Instruction was related to a culture which

was familiar to them and provided opportunities for the use of reason and speculation by drawing upon observations which pertained to everyday life. *Understanding and the exercise of thought were not the prerogative of the upper and middle classes.*[3] [our italics]

As a consequence, the upper classes felt threatened. Influential scientists of the day, men such as Owen, Hooker, Lyell and Faraday, advanced the view that the ruling class was in danger of losing its position through lack of scientific knowledge. These views are evident in the *Report of the Public School Commission* set up in 1861.

> In a political point of view, it is not only an unhealthy but also a dangerous state of things in some respects, that the material world should be very much better known by the middle classes of society than by the upper classes.[32]

If it was considered such a 'dangerous state of things' that the new middle class had access to a form of knowledge denied to the upper class, how much more serious must have seemed the 'state of things' when the *lower* orders were seen to be becoming superior in scientific 'intellectual attainments to those above them in station'. By the middle and late 1850s a campaign backed by *The Times* newspaper had been mounted on two levels. On the one hand it advocated the merits of *pure science* as a component of the liberal education of the higher orders, on the other it advocated a *halt* in the scientific education of the lower orders, whom it saw as being 'overeducated'. The higher orders had realised that those below them in the social hierarchy were gaining access to scientific knowledge which might be used as a resource in future socially undesirable activity. Since, however, the continuing insistence of the higher orders on a classics-based liberal education excluded science to a large degree, it was in their interests to exclude science from the education of the poor. It is suggested that this, and *not* the appearance of 'better alternatives', was the reason behind the abandonment of the Science of Common Things. From this perspective it is possible to speculate that the Revised Code of 1862, which finally removed science from the elementary school curriculum, was the institutionalisation of these beliefs legitimated on administrative and financial grounds. The curriculum proposed for the elementary schools was a watered-down classics curriculum, containing *no science*. Clearly, a curriculum based on 'general training' offered the possibility of more direct control. Prominent amongst the advocates of this 'new' curriculum was Joshua Fitch, appointed Principal of the British and Foreign School Society Training College in 1854, and promoted to the Inspectorate in 1863. His Elementary School curriculum comprised reading and writing, arithmetic, English grammar (the 'classics of the poor'), a little geography and history. A knowledge of common things was not to be obtained by the direct study of science, but through 'country walks, star gazing and domestic experiences'.

> If children go into the world ignorant of common things, it is not for the want of technical instruction about them; but either because their daily life has been confined to a narrow and unlovely world, their homes are wretched, and God's fairest works kept far out of their sight (circumstances over which we have but small control), or else because their powers of observation and of thoughtfulness have been insufficiently developed; and this is a defect which I believe would be more truly corrected by the good and sound teaching of arithmetic, geography, grammar, history and the Holy Scriptures, than by all the catechisms and manuals of miscellaneous information ever written.[33]

When science eventually reappeared in the curriculum of the elementary schools, some twenty years later, it was in a very different form from that advocated by the liberal reformers. Objectives were now firmly in the affective domain: the principal goal was 'love of nature', which was considered necessary for ensuring success in later stages of a scientific education. Pure science had become accepted as the *correct* view. This marks the start of the conception of science education as it is known today. The 'new' view was described in some detail by Professor Roscoe in an address to commemorate the opening of new buildings at Owens College, Manchester. He argued for 'the educational value of original research', which he saw as 'personal communication with nature for its own sake'. Through this type of scientific enquiry, which was value free and disinterested, 'habits of independent thought and ideas of free enquiry are thus at once inculcated'. In claiming that the purpose of science education is to select and supply future scientists of talent to the universities, he described the teaching of science in schools as 'the means of sifting out of the great mass of the people those golden grains of genius which are now too often lost amongst the sands of mediocrity'.[34] This new view of science was designed to develop an elite who conformed to the image of the 'pure scientist' rationalised by the higher orders. Science had been allowed into the curriculum once more, but only on terms which effectively excluded the mass of the population from any meaningful scientific education. In this way it was ensured that the resource, available to all in theory but only accessible to the higher orders in practice, no longer posed a threat to the social hierarchy. As far as the elementary schools were concerned, the science component was to be natural history. As long ago as 1854, T.H. Huxley had defined scientific method as 'extended and applied common sense'.

> Science is nothing but trained and organized common sense, differing from the latter only as a veteran may differ from a raw recruit.[35]

For Huxley, biology was the experimental science which best exemplified scientific method and was ideally suited to the disciplining of the mind. Moreover, biology was ideally suited to the promotion of 'a love of nature'.

THE CURRENT SITUATION

The major thesis of this chapter is that the way in which school science is perceived today is *not* the end result of 'inevitable progress' in the disinterested search for truth. Rather, it is *socially constructed*, being the product of particular sets of choices made by particular groups of people at particular times. Its final form represents the triumph of a particular interest group. In providing a way of understanding nature that by definition *excludes* knowledge of the natural world as it is experienced by the mass of the population, the conception of school science that we have today was not designed to achieve the full potential of the majority. Hence it is unsuited, in its present form, to a common curriculum in comprehensive schools.

Michael Young has argued that science teachers continue to see the main purpose of science education as the supply of future scientists, with the result that two very different kinds of school science courses have arisen: academic science and non-academic science – 'the former claiming credibility from the professional scientific community, and the latter through notions of "relevance" and immediate interest for pupils'. Thus, 'relevance' and 'intellectual credibility' have come to be regarded as incompatible, and even mutually exclusive. The inevitable consequence of this dual policy towards science education is the emergence of two classes of citizen: the scientifically literate and the scientifically illiterate. According to Young, curriculum decision makers have social control motives in wishing to create a large scientifically illiterate workforce, 'who see themselves as dependent on experts in more and more aspects of their life'. He argues that those in power see it as desirable that 'except in the specific context of their work, and possibly in leisure pursuits such as car maintenance, our increasingly technologically dominated world remains for the majority as much a mystery as the theological mysteries of feudal times'.[36]

Jenkins[37] has attempted to discern some social control element in the nature study movement of the early twentieth century and Millar[38] claims to have detected similar concerns in the proposals of the Newsom Report and the influential Scottish Education Department's curriculum paper *Science for General Education*. Millar claims that these documents betray a concern with social control both *within* the classroom and outside (for example, in industrial relations), which determines both the content and the teaching methods employed.

As soon as a course module is refined to the point where its use in the class keeps the pupils occupied, enables a satisfactory staff-pupil atmosphere to develop, and therefore permits the teacher to feel unthreatened by an incipient loss of control, it is endorsed as 'satisfactory'. . . .

The hope here is clearly that a 'scientific' attitude to information, characterized by a desire to consider all sides of a question, to keep an open mind, to hold a point-of-view subject to experimental verification, will be transferred to areas which are far removed from the school science area.[38]

It is tempting to look for social control mechanisms operating during other periods of significant change in the science curriculum. What motives lay behind the other important curriculum changes described by Uzzell,[1] Layton[3] and Jenkins?[2] Were there social control factors at work during the great changes brought about by the Nuffield courses in the 1960s? What lay behind the General Science movement in the mid-twentieth century and the more recent attempts to promote integrated science? Which interest groups are promoting the current drive to increase the number of girls taking up careers in science, and why? As we enter a new phase of curriculum development in science we need to ask two questions:

1 *Whose* view of school science is being adopted in the curriculum?
2 *Whose* interests are being promoted by the particular view of school science that is adopted?

All proposals present a *particular* view of science. For example, the Association for Science Education's *Alternatives for Science Education* includes the following statements:

a good science education should seek to develop a range of intellectual skills and cognitive patterns which would help youngsters to handle the problems of growing up in, and integrating with, a society that is heavily dependent on scientific and technological knowledge and its utilization . . . provide opportunities for explaining, and therefore understanding, the nature of advanced technological societies, the complex interaction between science and society, and the contribution science makes to our cultural heritage.[39]

The document goes on to urge teachers to 'provide opportunities whereby youngsters can gain a sense of social meaning and identity' and sets out six 'personal and social aims of science education for all'. Typical of these is the aim identified by the ASE as *science in the world of work*: 'The development of an understanding of the way in which scientific and technological ideas are used to maintain an economic surplus.' Similarly, one is tempted to look for social control intent in the ASE policy statement *Education through*

Science when it sets out the aims of science education for *all* in the following terms:

> the development of an appreciation and understanding of the ways in which science and technology contribute to the worlds of *work, citizenship, leisure* and *survival*. We would include under this heading an understanding of the way scientific and technological ideas are used to create and maintain an economic surplus, facilitate participation in democratic decision-making in a technological society, enrich and sustain a wide range of leisure activities and pursuits, and enable the individual to utilize scientific ideas and technological processes in the context of increasing self-sufficiency, the conservation of resources and the utilization of alternative technologies.[40]

At least three of the six aims of science education listed in *Education through Science* could be regarded as having a social control intent:

1 'The attainment of a perspective or way of looking at the world. . . .'
2 'The attainment of a basic understanding of the nature of advanced technological societies, the interaction between science and society, and the contribution science makes to our cultural heritage.'
3 'The realization that scientific knowledge and experience is of some value in the process of establishing a sense of personal and social identity.'[40]

In view of the foregoing discussion one is tempted to ask:

1 *Whose* 'way of looking at the world' is being advanced?
2 *Whose interest* is being promoted by the curriculum?
3 *Whose* view of society is to be projected?

NOTES

1 Uzzell, P.S. 'The changing aims of science education', *S.S.R.*, 1978, 210, **60**, 7–20.
2 Jenkins, E.W., *From Armstrong to Nuffield* (John Murray, 1979).
3 Layton, D., *Science for the People* (Allen & Unwin, 1973).
4 Turner, D.M., *The History of Science Teaching in England* (Chapman and Hall, 1927).
5 Uzzell, P.S., 'The curriculum: whence, why and whither', *S.S.R.*, 1981, 223, **63**, 343–8.
6 Layton, D., 'The educational work of the parliamentary committee of the British Association for the Advancement of Science', *History of Education*, 1976, **5**, 25–39.
7 Phenix, P.H., *Realms of Meaning* (McGraw-Hill, 1964).
8 King, A.R. and J.A. Brownell, *The Curriculum and the Disciplines of Knowledge* (Wiley, 1966). Schwab, J.J., 'The structure of science', in Ford, G.W. and L. Pugno, *The Structure of Knowledge and the Curriculum* (Rand McNally, 1965). Broudy, H., *Building a Philosophy of Education* (Prentice Hall, 1961).
9 Hirst, P.H., 'Liberal education and the nature of knowledge', in Archambault, R.D. (ed.), *Philosophical Analysis and Education* (Routledge & Kegan Paul, 1965).

10 Bruner, J.S., *The Process of Education* (University of Chicago Press, 1960).
11 Blum, A.F., 'The corpus of knowledge as a normative order', in Young, M.F.D. (ed.), *Knowledge and Control* (Collier-Macmillan, 1973).
12 Keddie, N., 'Education as a social construct', in Jenks, C. (ed.), *Rationality, Education and the Social Organization of Knowledge* (Routledge & Kegan Paul, 1977).
13 Esland, G.M., 'Teaching and learning as the organization of knowledge', in Young, M.F.D. (ed.), *Knowledge and Control* (Collier-Macmillan, 1973).
14 Young, M.F.D. (ed.), *Knowledge and Control: New Directions for the Sociology of Education* (Collier-Macmillan, 1973).
15 Popper, K.R., *Objective Knowledge* (Oxford University Press, 1972).
16 Mills, C.W., 'Language, logic and culture', *American Sociological Review*, 1939, **4**, 670–80.
17 Pring, R., *Knowledge and Schooling* (Open Books, 1976).
18 Marx, K. and F. Engels, *The German Ideology*, 1845, quoted in McLellan, D., *The Thought of Karl Marx: An Introduction* (Macmillan, 1971).
19 Barnes, S.B., *Interests and the Growth of Knowledge* (Routledge & Kegan Paul, 1977). Berger, P. and T. Luckmann, *The Social Construction of Reality* (Penguin, 1967). Johnson, R., 'Educational policy and social control in early Victorian England', *Past and Present*, 1970, **49**, 96–119. Mulkay, M., 'Knowledge and utility: implications for the sociology of knowledge', *Social Studies in Science*, 1979, **9**, 63–80.
20 Donajgrodzki, A.P. (ed.), *Social Control in Nineteenth Century Britain* (Croom Helm, 1977).
21 Mayo, C. and E. Mayo, *Practical Remarks on Infant Education* (Home and Colonial School Society, 1849).
22 Ball, N., 'Richard Dawes and the teaching of common things', *Educational Review*, 1964, **17**, 59–68.
23 Committee of Council on Education, *Minutes 1844–5*, Report by Rev. J. Allen.
24 Committee of Council on Education, *Minutes 1847–8*, 7–27.
25 Spencer, H., 'What knowledge is of most worth?', *Westminster Review*, 1859, XVI, 1–41.
26 Herschel, J.F.W., *Preliminary Discourse on the Study of Natural Philosophy* (The Cabinet Cyclopaedia, 1830).
27 Quoted in Layton, D., *op. cit.*, p. 46.
28 Hunt, R., 'On familiar methods of instruction in science', *Lectures in Connection with the Educational Exhibition* (Society of Arts, Manufactures and Commerce, 1854).
29 Chapter 3 of Layton, D. (1973) is devoted to J.S. Henslow.
30 Layton, D., 'Lord Wrottesley FRS, pioneer statesman of science', *Notes and Records of the Royal Society of London*, 1968, **23**, 230–47.
31 Lord Wrottesley, *Thoughts on Government and Legislation* (John Murray, 1860).
32 Report of Her Majesty's Commissioners appointed to Inquire into the Revenues and Management of Certain Colleges and Schools, and the Studies pursued and Instruction given therein (HMSO, 1864), Vol. 4, Part 2.
33 Fitch, J.G., *The Relative Importance of Subjects Taught in Elementary Schools* (Bell and Daldy, 1854).
34 Roscoe, H.E., 'Original research as a means of education', in *Essays and Addresses, Owens College, Manchester* (1874), 21–57.
35 Huxley, T.H., 'On the educational value of the natural history sciences', lecture 1854, republished in Huxley, T.H., *Man's Place in Nature and other Essays* (J.M. Dent, 1906).

36 Young, M.F.D., 'The schooling of science', in Whitty, G. and M.F.D. Young (eds), *Explorations in the Politics of School Knowledge* (Nafferton Books, 1976).
37 Jenkins, E.W., 'Science, sentimentalism or social control? The nature study movement in England and Wales, 1899–1914', *History of Education*, 1981, **10**, 33–43.
38 Millar, R.H., 'Curriculum rhetoric and social control: a perspective on recent science curriculum development', *European Journal of Science Education*, 1981, **3**, 271–84.
39 *Alternatives for Science Education* (ASE, 1979).
40 *Education through Science* (ASE, 1981).

Part II

A picture of reality

Chapter 3

The fallacy of induction in science teaching

Rosalind Driver

Science is not just a collection of laws, a catalogue of facts, it is a creation of the human mind with its freely invented ideas and concepts. Physical theories try to form a picture of reality and to establish its connections with the wide world of sense impressions.

A. Einstein and L. Infield
The Evolution of Physics (1938)

In our everyday life as adults we operate with a very complex set of beliefs and expectations about events. An egg rolls across the counter top in the kitchen and we know where to make a grasp for it before it falls over the edge and smashes to the floor. The fact that so many of us can drive around on our roads without more accidents occurring is possible because of the sets of expectations we have developed enabling us to predict the speed and movement of other vehicles on the road and the probable behaviour of pedestrians. Such sets of expectations mean we can live our daily lives without being constantly in a state of disorientation and shock. Similarly, children construct sets of expectations or beliefs about a range of natural phenomena in their efforts to make sense of everyday experiences.

A 10-year-old switched off the radio, noticed with surprise that it took over a second for the sound to fade away and commented: 'What a long length of electric wire there must be in that radio when you think how fast electricity travels.' Without any formal instruction, this child had already developed certain ideas about electricity, notably that it travels down wires, and that it travels very fast.

From the very earliest days in its life, a child develops beliefs about the things that happen in its surroundings. The baby lets go of a rattle and it falls to the ground; it does it again and the pattern repeats itself. It pushes a ball and it goes on rolling across the floor. In this way, sets of expectations are established which enable the child to begin to make predictions. Initially, these are isolated and independent of one another. However, as the child grows older, all its experiences of pushing, pulling, lifting, throwing, feeling and seeing things stimulate the development of more generalised sets of expectations and the ability to make predictions about a progressively wider range of experiences. By the time the child receives formal teaching in science it has already constructed a set of beliefs about a range of natural phenomena. In some cases, these beliefs or intuitions are strongly held and may differ from the accepted theories which science teaching aims to communicate.

One of the features of the science teaching schemes which have been developed over the last twenty or thirty years is a rejection of science as a catalogue of facts. Instead, teaching schemes have been produced which present science as a coherent system of ideas. Focus is on the integrating concepts or big ideas such as atomic theory in chemistry or kinetic theory in physics. Apart from doing justice to the nature of scientific theory itself, one of the important arguments for such an approach suggested by Bruner[1] is that it helps pupils to apply ideas to new situations if the connections between those ideas are made explicit in teaching. Put in psychologists' jargon, it encourages 'transfer'.

One of the problems with this argument is that the connections that are apparent to a scientist may be far from obvious to a pupil. It is, after all, the coherence as perceived by the pupil that matters in learning. In developing science teaching material little attention has yet been paid to the ideas which children themselves bring to the learning task, yet these may have a significant influence on what children can and do learn from their science lessons. Over a decade ago, the psychologist David Ausubel commented on the importance of considering what he called children's preconceptions, suggesting that they are 'amazingly tenacious and resistant to extinction . . .' and that 'unlearning of preconceptions might well prove to be the most determinative single factor in the acquisition and retention of subject matter knowledge'.[2]

This perspective on learning suggests that it is as important in teaching and curriculum development to consider and understand children's own ideas as it is to give a clear presentation of the conventional scientific theories. After all, if a visitor phones you up explaining he has got lost on the way to your home, your first reaction would probably be to ask 'Where are you now?' You cannot start to give sensible directions without knowing where your visitor is starting from. Similarly, in teaching science it is important in designing teaching programmes to take into account both children's own ideas and those of the scientific community.

By the time children are taught science in school, their expectations or beliefs about natural phenomena may be well developed. In some cases these intuitions are in keeping with the ideas pupils will meet in their science lessons. They may be poorly articulated but they provide a base on which formal learning can build. However, in other cases the accepted theory may be counter-intuitive with pupils' own beliefs and expectations differing in significant ways from those to be taught. Such beliefs I shall refer to as 'alternative frameworks'.

Another characteristic of the science curriculum development of the last few decades has been an emphasis on the heuristic method. This was prompted by the admirable concern to allow children to experience something of the excitement of science – 'to be a scientist for a day'.[3] We are now recognising the pitfalls of putting this approach into practice in classrooms and laboratories. Secondary school pupils are quick to recognise the rules of the game when they ask 'Is this what was supposed to happen?' or 'Have I got the right answer?'[4,5] The intellectual dishonesty of the approach derives from expecting two outcomes from pupils' laboratory activities which are possibly incompatible. On the one hand pupils are expected to explore a phenomenon for themselves, collect data and make inferences based on it; on the other hand this process is intended to lead to the currently accepted scientific law or principle.

Some insight into this problem can be gained by considering different views of the nature of science. The most simplistic view of the scientific enterprise is, perhaps, the empiricist's view, which holds that all knowledge is based on observation. Scientific laws are reached by a process of induction from the 'facts' of sense data. Taking this view of science, observations are objective and facts immutable. Also, such a position asserts that science will produce a steady growth in knowledge: like some international game of 'pass the parcel', the truth about the natural world will be unwrapped and gradually more will be revealed.

This inductivist position was criticised when it was first suggested by Bacon nearly 400 years ago, yet it has reasserted itself early in this century in the heuristic movement and later in some of the more naive interpretations of the discovery method adopted by the Nuffield science schemes.

For a long time philosophers of science and scientists themselves have recognised the limitations of the inductivist position and have acknowledged the important role that imagination plays in the construction of scientific theories. In this alternative constructivist or hypothetico-deductive view, theories are not related by induction to sense data, but are constructions of the human mind whose link with the world of experience comes through the processes by which they are tested and evaluated.

Currently there are different views about the criteria for acceptance or rejection of scientific theories.[6] The philosopher Popper asserts that, in addition to the individual's mental world, there exists a world of objective knowledge[7] which has properties which can be assessed by logical principles without regard to the person or group of people who generated that knowledge. Others subscribe to a more subjective position. Polanyi,[8] for example, in his writings, indicates the importance of the commitment of an individual to a theory, a commitment which may be influenced by factors other than logic, with aesthetic criteria playing an important part. Science as a cooperative exercise as opposed to an individual venture is emphasised in the writings of Kuhn[9] and Lakatos.[10] Viewed from a sociological perspective, such writers suggest that the criterion for acceptance of a scientific theory is that it is scrutinised and approved by the community of scientists.

Although there are these differences of view on the objectivity of scientific knowledge and the criteria for assessing theories, there is general agreement on two matters of importance to school science. The first is the recognition of pluralism in scientific theories. Following from this is acceptance of the revolutionary nature of science; that progress in scientific knowledge comes about through major changes in scientists' theories (or paradigms). This gives science educators the task of 'teaching consensus without turning it into an orthodoxy'.[11] The second point of agreement is about the nature of observations: these are no longer seen as objective but influenced by the theoretical perspective of the observer.[12] As Popper said, 'we are prisoners caught in the framework of our theories'.[13] This, too, has implications for school science, for children, too, can be imprisoned in this way by their preconceptions, observing the world through their own particular 'conceptual spectacles'.

I will illustrate some main points with a couple of classroom examples. The first example illustrates the hypothetico-deductive nature of science enquiries. It shows an investigation taking place, not from observation to generalisation, but being initiated by a hypothesis which in this case derives from a pupil's alternative framework.

Two 11-year-old boys, Tim and Ricky, are doing simple experiments on the extension of springs when loaded. They have made their own spring by winding wire round a length of dowel. One end of the spring is supported in a clamp and a polystyrene cup is hanging from the other end (Figure 3.1). Following instructions, they investigate the extension of the spring as they add ball bearings to the polystyrene cup. Ricky is adding the ball bearings one at a time and measuring the new length of the spring after each addition. Tim is watching him, then interrupts:

> How far is that off the ground? Pull it up and see if the spring does not move any.

He unclamps the spring, raises it higher up the stand, and again measures its length. Apparently satisfied that the length is the same, he continues with the experiment. Later, when he was asked the reason for doing this, he explained that he thought the weight of the cup of ball bearings would increase if it were raised. To explain his reasoning, he picked up two marbles and held one up higher than the other:

> This is farther up and gravity is pulling it down harder – I mean the gravity is still the same but it turns out it is pulling harder the farther away. The higher it gets the more effect gravity will have on it because,

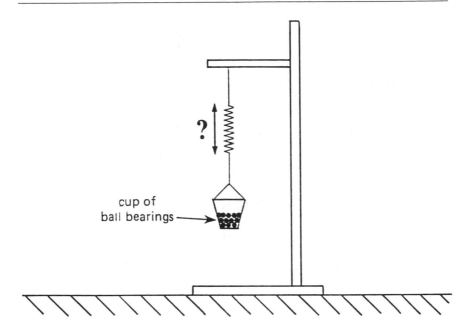

cup of
ball bearings ——→

Figure 3.1

like if you just stood over there and someone dropped a pebble on him, it would just sting him, it wouldn't hurt him. But like if I dropped it from an aeroplane it would be accelerating faster and faster and when it hit someone on the head it would kill him.

It appears that Tim's idea of weight encompasses the notion of potential energy and leads him to predict a greater extension of the spring when it is further from the ground. He uses the same framework when considering the force required to hold a trolley at different positions on an inclined board, predicting that it will be harder to hold when it is higher up than when it is lower down the slope.

Not only does this example indicate how pupils' alternative frameworks can intrude into their activities in science lessons, it illustrates how, in some cases, alternative frameworks are more than an idiosyncratic response to a particular task, they may be general notions applied to a range of situations.

There is evidence from a number of investigations that pupils have common alternative frameworks in a range of areas including physical phenomena such as the propagation of light, simple electrical circuits, ideas about force and motion and chemical change, also biological ideas concerned with growth and adaptation.

It follows from a constructivist philosophy of science that theory is not related in a deductive, and hence unique, way to observations; there can be

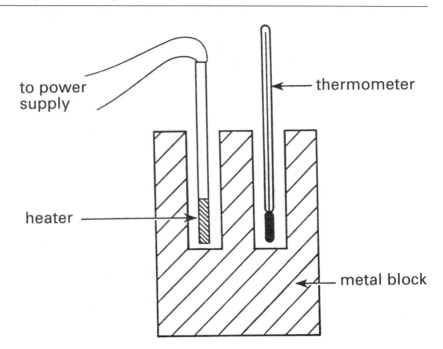

Figure 3.2

multiple explanations of events which each account for the data. In the example of Tim's idea of weight we see how he had developed an idea based on common experiences with falling objects, yet he had explained them to himself in a way that differed from the accepted physicist's view. The possibility of multiple interpretations of an event is also illustrated in the following example of work done in a science class of 12-year-old pupils. A pair of girls were doing an experiment in which an immersion heater was placed in blocks of different metals, each of the same weight (Figure 3.2). The pupils had been instructed on a worksheet to draw a temperature–time graph for each block as it was heated, the purpose of the experiment being to illustrate variation in specific heat capacities of different metals. The girls had chosen blocks of iron and aluminium, and towards the end of the lesson they were instructed to look at their graphs, compare them and suggest explanations for any differences. Here are their comments:

P1: We've got to do a graph for the aluminium.
P2: Good. Aluminium isn't so – um – it –
P1: Don't forget it has to go through, doesn't it? Through the thickness to reach there – the thermometer.
P2: That was only thin to get to that.
P1: Come on, we've got to put it away now.

The teacher enters the discussion.

T: What has your experiment shown you?

P2: That different – um – that different materials and that see how heat could travel through them.

T: What did you find out?

P1: Well – er – that heat went through the – the iron more easier than it did through the – er –

P2: Aluminium.

Here pupils had performed the experiment and had collected their data, yet it appears from their comments that they interpreted the difference between the graphs for the two metal blocks not in terms of the amount of heat required to raise the temperature of each by a certain amount, but in terms of the comparative conductivity of metals.

The more simplistic interpretations of the discovery approach in science suggest that we only need to give pupils the opportunity to explore events and phenomena at first hand and they will be able to induce the generalisations and principles themselves. The position suggested here is that children do make generalisations from their first-hand experiences, but these may not be the ones the teacher has in mind. Explanations do not spring clearly or uniquely from data.

Through the eyes of those initiated in the currently accepted theories of science, common school demonstrations, such as trolleys and ticker tapes, experiments with batteries and bulbs, or work with ray boxes, mirrors and prisms, appear to offer self-sufficient support for the underlying principles they are designed to demonstrate, whether it is Newton's laws of motion or the laws of reflection of light. If children fail to abstract and understand these principles from their experiments, it may be seen as the children's error for either not observing accurately or not thinking logically about the pattern in the results.

The constructivist view of science, on the other hand, indicates the fallacy here. If we wish children to develop an understanding of the conventional concepts and principles of science, more is required than simply providing practical experiences. The theoretical models and scientific conventions will not be 'discovered' by children through their practical work. They need to be presented. Guidance is then needed to help children assimilate their practical experiences into what is possibly a new way of thinking about them.

The slogan 'I do and I understand' is commonly used in support of practical work in science teaching. We have classrooms where activity plays a central part. Pupils can spend a major portion of their time pushing trolleys up runways, gathering, cutting and sticking tangling metres of ticker tape; marbles are rattled around in trays simulating solids, liquids and gases, batteries and bulbs are clicked in and out of specially designed circuit boards. To what end? In many classrooms, I suspect, 'I do and I am even more confused'.

This process of 'making sense' takes on even greater significance when considering children's alternative frameworks. Not only do children have to comprehend the new model or principle being presented to them, but they have to make the intellectual leap of possibly abandoning an alternative framework which until that time had worked well for them.

To use the language of philosophy of science, children sometimes need to undergo paradigm shifts in their thinking. Max Planck suggested that new theories do not convert people, it is just that old men die. If scientists have this difficulty in reformulating their conceptions of the world, is it a wonder that children sometimes have a struggle to do so?

NOTES

1 J.S. Bruner, *The Process of Education*, Random House (1963).
2 D.P. Ausubel, *Educational Psychology: A Cognitive View*, Holt, Reinhart (1968).
3 *Nuffield Physics Teachers' Guide*, No. 1, Longman/Penguin (1966).
4 R. Driver, The name of the game, *Sch. Sci. Rev.*, **56**, 800–5 (1975).
5 J.J. Wellington, 'What's supposed to happen, sir?': some problems with discovery learning, *Sch. Sci. Rev.*, **63**, 163–73 (1981).
6 An account of current aspects of the philosophy and sociology of science is given in *What is Science?*, ASE Study series, No. 15 (1979).
7 K.R. Popper, *Objective Knowledge*, OUP (1972).
8 M. Polanyi, *Personal Knowledge*, Routledge (1958).
9 T. Kuhn, *The Structure of Scientific Revolutions*, University of Chicago Press (1963).
10 I. Lakatos and A. Musgrave (eds), *Criticism and the Growth of Knowledge*, CUP (1974).
11 J. Ziman, *Public Knowledge*, CUP (1968).
12 N.R. Hanson, *Patterns of Discovery*, CUP (1958).
13 K. Popper, Normal science and its dangers, I. Lakatos and A. Musgrave (eds), in *Criticism and the Growth of Knowledge*, CUP (1974).

Chapter 4

Teaching about electric circuits
A constructivist approach

Michael Arnold and Robin Millar

DIFFICULTIES WITH ELECTRICITY

There is little need to tell most science teachers that electricity is a difficult subject to teach effectively. The APU Short Report on *Electricity*[1] confirms that pupils have problems in understanding and using even basic electrical ideas.

A growing body of research has shown that children come to science lessons with prior conceptions about many, if not all, science topics and that many of these may conflict with the view promoted by formal teaching.[2,3] This can produce confusion, or rejection of the scientific perspective. Even 'successful' science students may have learnt an 'official' set of ideas for use in tests and examinations, overlaying *alternative* beliefs which are resorted to in 'everyday' contexts or in novel or difficult situations.[4,5] The everyday language of electricity (which includes terms like current and voltage) and informal observations about the use of electrical equipment at home contribute to the formation of pupils' prior conceptions about electricity. A further source of difficulty where electric circuits are concerned lies in the fact that the concepts involved (current, voltage, resistance) are not directly observable but are theoretical ideas used to explain a range of observations. Additional problems may arise from the fact that the simplified circuits commonly used in an introductory course of study are remote from the child's experience of everyday electrical applications, and may fail to serve as adequate models of them – preventing any effective linkage between 'school' and 'everyday' knowledge.

A CONSTRUCTIVIST APPROACH

Eliciting

In an attempt to develop an improved approach to the teaching of simple circuits, we have investigated the possibility – in a real classroom situation – of designing a short teaching sequence which begins by eliciting children's ideas and then builds on these existing beliefs in attempting to produce accommodation towards the accepted scientific view. Since this work was originally carried out as a research project,[6] the lesson sequence was preceded by a lengthy series of individual interviews to establish the group's initial ideas about electricity. This is time consuming and it is important to state at the outset that we do not feel that it is necessary for other teachers wishing to follow the approach outlined here to repeat this exercise each time. The likely alternative conceptions of a group of 12-year-olds can be anticipated with reasonable confidence from the research literature, where a fairly consistent pattern emerges from work with this age group.[7,8]

None the less some information about these initial interviews may be of interest. They began by asking each child to light a single torch bulb using a dry cell. The first attempts of many children showed that they did not realise that bulbs and cells have *two* connection points. Given a bulb, a cell and some pieces of wire, a majority could not get the bulb to light and persisted with 'one-pole' attempts to wire the components. When, after some further exploration and hints, a working circuit had been established, many children explained what they thought was happening in the circuit using a 'clashing currents' model, in which opposing currents flow from each end of the cell and 'clash' in the bulb to produce light. This model *has* predictive power, of course, since the removal of one of the two wires prevents the 'clash' occurring, even though the 'other' current is still present. Further, with two bulbs in series, the clashing currents model provides a plausible explanation of why the bulbs are half as bright as before – each bulb is now supplied through one end only! Though in this second case it is difficult to see how the 'clash' occurs, such inconsistency in explanation does not appear to trouble many pupils, who may use 'local reasoning' or 'instant invention' to 'solve' a conceptual problem. The fact that a non-scientific framework can nevertheless provide a workable explanation of an experimental result indicates that the teacher should carefully consider whether his/her experiments *are* demonstrating to the pupils the superiority of the accepted scientific model!

Discussion with individual pupils showed that the term 'electricity' is used as an umbrella term by most children, incorporating the separate ideas of 'current', 'power' and 'energy'. In particular, the inability of many children to discriminate between 'current' and 'energy' appeared to lie at the heart of their failure to conserve current. They considered that current was consumed by electrical components and decreased 'further around' the circuit (a 'sequence' model). This confusion has far-reaching consequences for more advanced learning. Ohm's law, for example, can mean little to a child who does not conserve current!

Planning

The great advantage of coming to think of children's learning of electrical ideas in these terms is that it helps in planning the instructional sequence. Rather than define learning in terms of content or experiments to be performed, the concepts which it was hoped the children would acquire were used as the basis of lesson planning. In order, these were:

1 Bipolarity (most devices have two terminals).
2 The rule of circuit closure (a working circuit has to have a loop of conducting material, including a cell).
3 A circulation model of current (something is flowing round the circuit – a current).
4 Some differentiation of electrical energy and electric current.
5 Conservation of current (current is the same at all points around a loop).
6 The relationship of current and resistance (very simply: as resistance increases current decreases, if everything else stays the same).

In deciding which concepts to teach, importance was attached to the logical sequence most appropriate for learning, rather than the logic of the subject matter as seen by scientists. Thus two topics 'traditionally' included, voltage and parallel circuits, were omitted. Research findings' indicate that 'voltage' is a particularly troublesome concept, best introduced after current is grasped, using a few simple operating rules. It was not explicitly mentioned in the present scheme for this reason, and was regarded simply as a number needed to match components (e.g. cells to bulbs). Similarly, no attempt to introduce branching (parallel) circuits was made in this introductory teaching (see Note 1)

Classroom activities

Experience showed that even this modest list of concepts may be too ambitious for a first course, and that current conservation presents a major stumbling block to understanding which deserves extended and careful consideration before progression to any more advanced study is attempted. The full teaching sequence involved six 70 minute lessons of practical work in groups of two or three, using circuit board equipment. Children were encouraged to formulate theories based on their existing conceptions, and where these differed from the accepted scientific ideas they were experimentally challenged to produce some degree of conceptual conflict. The scientific view was introduced only when its greater explanatory power might be seen to provide a solution to the child's conceptual difficulties. Speculation, argument and discussion (in small groups and with the whole class) formed an important part of the lessons.

Evaluation

One week after the end of the teaching sequence, children were reinterviewed to assess the extent to which their conceptions had been modified. The interviews involved practical demonstrations, puzzles and prediction exercises in which unfamiliar situations were used to investigate each pupil's reasoning and conceptual models. Most children now had an understanding of bipolarity and the rule of circuit closure. The circulation model of current was also adopted by the majority of the children. Over half demonstrated conservation of current and some conception of the relationship between current and resistance. The disappointing performance of those children who had moved least towards the scientific view could be traced in substantial measure to their lack of differentiation of the terms 'electrical energy' and 'electric current' and their consequent failure to conserve current.

Follow-up interviews one year later indicated that those children who had made progress towards the scientific view had substantially retained their new learning.

MANAGING THE LEARNING PROCESS

Identifying each child's existing beliefs and following his/her conceptual development throughout these practical sessions may appear to many teachers an impossibly complex task. Fortunately research findings indicate a reasonably consistent pattern and sequence of alternative conceptions, and teachers now may need only to identify a child's starting point within this sequence. It proved possible, even in a busy classroom, to gauge each child's progress from discussion and observation during the lesson, as the need to monitor the detailed content covered by the child is replaced by an assessment of the child's grasp of a small number of broad concepts. Regarding the topic area as a network of interrelated concepts, not only for planning purposes but as a basis for decision making during each lesson, retains the flexibility and freedom to pursue whichever line of enquiry is most appropriate for that child or group of children at that time.

The approach outlined above is within the *constructive* or *generative* model of teaching and learning.[9,10] It produced lessons of purposeful and intense activity enjoyed by children and teacher alike. We would suggest that a relatively restricted but secure conceptual framework on which to hang subsequent detailed content may be a more appropriate aim for an introductory course on electric circuits than a more extensive list of content-related objectives. Time spent at this early stage of learning may provide a basis for the more rapid development of further electrical ideas at a later stage.

NOTES

1 APU, *Electricity at Age 15*, Science Report for Teachers: 7 (DES, 1984).
2 Driver, R., E. Guesne and A. Tiberghien, (eds), *Children's Ideas in Science* (Open University Press, 1985).
3 Osborne, R.J. and P. Freyberg, (eds), *Learning in Science* (Heinemann, 1985).
4 Osborne, R.J., 'A method for investigating concept understanding in science', *Eur. J. Sci. Educ.*, 1985, **2** (3), 311–21.
5 Solomon, J. 'Learning about energy – how pupils think in two domains', *Eur. J. Sci. Educ.*, 1985, **5** (1), 49–59.
6 Arnold, M.S., *Changes in Middle School Pupils' Conceptions about Electric Circuits Resulting from a Short Teaching Sequence Designed to Produce Accommodation towards the Scientific View*. Unpublished MA thesis (University of York, 1985).
7 Tiberghien, A., 'Critical review on the research aimed at elucidating the sense that the notions of electric circuits have for students aged 8 to 20 years', in *Research on Physics Education: Proceedings of the First International Workshop*, La Londe les Maures (Paris: Editions du CNRS, 1983).
8 Shipstone, D., 'Electricity in simple circuits', in Driver, R., E. Guesne and A. Tiberghien, (eds), *Children's Ideas in Science*, op. cit.
9 Driver, R. and V. Oldham, 'A constructivist approach to curriculum development', *Stud. Sci. Educ.*, 1986, **13**, 105–22.
10 Osborne, R.J. and M.C. Wittrock, 'The generative learning model and its implications for science education', *Stud. Sci. Educ.*, 1985, **12**, 59–87.

Chapter 5

Pause for thought

Philip Adey

How good at thinking do you have to be to do science? Does learning science help you to think? The answers of teachers who have been working with a project looking at 'Cognitive Acceleration' are, respectively, 'Pretty good', and 'Yes, it can'.

'*Think*, child.' As pupils we heard this many times and as teachers we have probably at least felt like saying it. Surely, it is obvious that if you want to find out whether a pendulum with a heavy weight swings at the same rate as a pendulum with a light weight, you have to try two pendulums with different weights but of the same length. But it is not the daily experience of science teachers that such a solution is 'obvious', even to most 16-year-olds.

Why it should be difficult is a matter of some controversy. At the simplest level, one might say that the children have just not been taught enough. A few hours' hard work by the teacher and a bit of effort by the pupil are all that is required. Such is the educational wisdom of many whose first-hand experience of education is limited to their own school days, clouded or rose-tinted by lengthening memory.

A little less simplistically, one might say that the child who cannot solve such problems 'lacks intelligence'. This is the IQ explanation but is not, in fact, an explanation at all. It is a way of using a number obtained blindly from a test developed empirically to predict academic success within a particular system. No one knows what the number represents.

Up to a point, progress can be made without much theoretical under-standing. Victorian engineers, innocent of metallic crystal theory, were enormously successful at building bridges and ships (give or take a few Tay Bridge disasters). But the advent of weight-conscious aeroengineering out-lawed overdesigning, and strong, light, and reliable materials and structures could be developed only by using theoretical models of the behaviour of particles in solids.

Likewise, empirical curriculum development (write it, try it with a few enthusiastic teachers, revise it, and send it off to the publishers) has served us reasonably well in the last twenty years. But we are now at the point where more effective learning demanded by society can only be delivered on the back of a better theoretical understanding of the learning process.

We have been working with a psychological model to explain children's difficulties in learning, and applying it to the science curriculum. The origin of the model is Piagetian, and a central idea is that the development of thinking is more than the accumulation of knowledge. Thinking develops qualitatively as well as quantitatively, and the drivers of this development are genetics, maturation and stimulus. (I am not so foolhardy as to try to ascribe weightings to those three.)

Precise descriptions can be given of the different stages of thinking in many contexts. Thus the pendulum problem can be seen to require *formal operational* thinking because a dependent variable (rate of swing) has to be seen in relation to at least two independent variables (weight, length, etc.). That is a lot of variables to juggle with mentally at one time. A student who cannot yet use formal operations will not be able to solve the problem completely. 'Think' as he/she might, the solution will not come naturally.

This model was used to imply that curriculum objectives consistently demanded higher levels of thinking than were found in the student population at which they were aimed. Although many of the newer curricula have recognised and acted on this message, analysis of the national curriculum in science[1] shows that level 6 attainment targets, supposed to be achievable by average students aged 16, generally require formal operational thinking. Such thinking is currently only exhibited by some 30 per cent of that age group.

Of course, not everyone in the science education business accepts the validity of our model or the analysis based on it, although criticism usually comes from a sociological rather than a psychological perspective. We have, for instance, been accused of 'labelling children' and being deterministic about what they could and could not do. But labelling a banana as 'unripe' means neither that it never will become ripe, nor even that its rate of ripening cannot be retarded or accelerated.

Methods of retarding normal cognitive development are easily imagined: lack of stimulation, demotivating teaching, poor nutrition, or abuse. Methods of accelerating cognitive development are less easy to imagine. The term 'cognitive acceleration' begs the question: 'acceleration with respect to what'? To answer 'with respect to the current norm' *may* only mean removal of the present retardants.

The Cognitive Acceleration through Science Education (CASE) project took a more positive view of acceleration, as an extra spur that teachers and pupils together can apply with the specific intention of promoting higher levels of thinking. In a sense, CASE was trying to realise the claim often made for science in the curriculum that it provides a good opportunity for 'developing logical thinking'.

A set of thirty activities, called 'Thinking Science'[2] ('ThiSci') was developed. Each concentrates on one aspect of formal thinking such as control of variables, proportionality, or probability. Essential vocabulary needed to 'get inside' such reasoning is introduced and practised, initially in contexts which demand no more than concrete operations. Once the vocabulary and context of the problem is established, pupils are faced with problems which they find that they cannot solve with concrete operations alone. They are put in position where they need to reorganise their type of thinking, to accommodate reality. This strategy depends on the child being surprised at an observation, which explains the requirement to set up the problem parameters in the child's mind initially.

Other important features of the ThiSci method are that pupils are encouraged to be conscious of their own thinking processes, and the ideas from the ThiSci course are 'bridged' to the regular science curriculum. The reasoning patterns being developed are seen in many different contexts to assist their generalisation (see Figure 5.1).

In September 1985 we tested over 500 boys and girls aged 11 and 12, in schools all over England, for their level of thinking. Over the next two years half of these pupils used ThiSci activities instead of regular science lessons, at the rate of about one every two weeks. They were then tested again, and at this point there was some evidence for enhanced thinking among the ThiSci users, albeit with much variation between the different ages, genders and schools.

To which the sceptic might say '(a) your Piagetian tests only test what the ThiSci lessons were teaching, so of course users do better than controls, and (b), how long lasting is any effect?' Now we have looked at all of the pupils again, one year after the end of the project, and we have looked at their achievement in science, on the tests which they have been given in their schools, over which we had no influence.

What emerges clearly is that three out of four groups who had previously used Thinking Science achieved significantly higher scores in science than their control groups who spent the same time on regular science lessons. Of course, not every child has been equally affected. It seems that certain pupils have made particularly good use of the experience, while others have not been affected at all. We would like to find out more about the characteristics of the pupils who did particularly well – is there something in their learning style which responds to the sort of cognitive problem solving typical of ThiSci? We do know that these 'responders' came equally from low and from high pre-test scores, so it is not a matter either of starting from a low base, nor of being clever enough to benefit from the challenge. We also need to investigate more effective ways of introducing teachers to the methods of ThiSci.

Even without answers to these questions we have evidence which is encouraging to those who would like to believe that general intelligence can

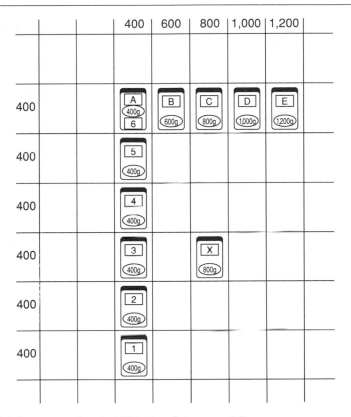

		400	600	800	1,000	1,200
400		A 400g 6	B 600g	C 800g	D 1,000g	E 1,200g
400		5 400g				
400		4 400g				
400		3 400g		X 800g		
400		2 400g				
400		1 400g				

Figure 5.1 Summary of part of *Thinking Science* activity

Floating and sinking jars: Five jars (A–E) are the same size, but increase in mass from 400 g to 1,200 g. Six jars (1–6) are the same mass but increase in size. (Jar A and jar 6 are the same jar.) For each jar, pupils note the mass and size, and then put it in water. They have a chart on which they mark whether the jar FLOATS or SINKS.

From this experience, they establish two concrete, two-variable, models: 'small things sink, big things float' (from 1–6); and 'heavy things sink, light things float' (from A–E). Each of these is adequate by itself.

Now jar X is produced. It has the same mass as jar C (which floats), and the same size as jar 3 (which floats). Pupils are asked to *predict* whether it will float or sink. Predictions made on the basis of the concrete models already established are that it will float. It is put in the water, and *sinks*.

To accommodate this, a new model involving three variables – mass, size, and buoyancy – must be constructed.

be raised in ordinary school settings. This could be a real meaning of that usually vacuous phrase 'raising standards of education'.

NOTES

1 Science in the National Curriculum. *Department of Education and Science 1989.*
2 Thinking Science, *by Philip Adey, Michael Shayer and Carolyn Yates, Macmillan Education 1989.*

Part III

The art of teaching in the science curriculum
(And some practical ideas)

Chapter 6

Well, Mary, what are they saying here?

Clive Sutton

The prospect of *adding* anything to an already crowded agenda for science is something I would want to resist, so in seeking to outline the day-to-day implications of my position I am also considering how the modern goals of school science might be achieved more effectively, more efficiently, and with greater satisfaction to pupils and teachers. I therefore want to explore the balance amongst the various activities that can go on in science lessons. How much telling? How much 'doing'? How much puzzling and problem solving? As I see it, good telling and good puzzling can both gain greater prominence, while 'doing' should be derived from these and made more purposeful by that connection, and less time consuming.

I am sure that if learners are to get a feel for language as an interpretive system, they must have experience of using it that way themselves. They should also regularly meet scientific ideas which are presented as expressions of thought rather than definite information, so that there is some point in puzzling over them. Most important, a reasonable proportion of the lesson time should be devoted to comparing different people's understanding. The phrasing in the title of this chapter is meant to point in that direction. There is an explanation of some scientific idea, probably on paper. The teacher signals that there is room for doubt about it, provides space for the pupil to make an interpretation, and tries to maintain a relationship which can carry discussion. Many teachers work this way intuitively in their informal interactions with pupils, but my contention is that the established routines of science lessons do not make adequate provision for it in the formal business of the lesson.

Puzzling and telling are complementary. A clear exposition by the teacher, or in the pages of a book, is one component, but the pupils' learning is in making sense of what is said or written. Lessons organised with this in mind should therefore include time for puzzling, and for pupils to restate what they understand to be the key ideas. Although this sometimes occurs informally in discussion, it will normally require some structure, and some formal means of public report about what they have made of the topic.

In practice, tasks of that kind are not given substantial periods of time, however much their use has been urged. There is something in the traditions of science teaching which marginalises them, and can even make them unsuccessful when first tried. It is partly the pupils' own expectations of language – i.e. of *not* using it to explore and interpret ideas, or at least not doing so in science. It is also an overconfidence in practical work. Teachers and pupils together have started to believe that handling things at the bench is the main source of understanding, that science lessons are a direct study of nature. My case in this chapter is that the principal object of study should be not nature itself but *sets of ideas*, as represented in the written or spoken words of *people*. Telling about these ideas, and puzzling over them, should be the core of lessons. Apart from improving the quality of learning, I believe this would immediately reinstate the human dimension, and overcome the criticism that science seems dehumanised. It would of course retain the importance of practical work, but place it in a very different light.

PRACTICAL WORK REVISITED

It has often seemed that the ideal science lesson is one in which pupils are actively engaged in bench work for a lot of their time. We expect to see them busily wiring a circuit with different numbers of bulbs, washing inks across absorbent paper, timing the fall of little parachutes, or soaking wrinkled raisins to see them swell. As teachers we have taken a pride in organising such events, because the pupils handle real materials and we believe that they 'learn by doing' rather than just by being told. We have seen ourselves as 'managers of learning' rather than as didactic dispensers of information. It seems quite odd therefore to question the system, particularly as I do not wish to imply that hands-on experience is not important. Nevertheless, there is a problem.

Practical work seems to offer many opportunities for interpretive activity, as we can say: 'What is going on here? What do you think is happening? Write down what happened.' Unfortunately, that kind of invitation places the pupil not in the reasonable role of interpreting what someone is trying to say, but in the *more difficult* role of interpreting nature. It is a tall order, when thoughtful minds have struggled for decades over the same phenomena! No wonder the experience sometimes fails to boost the self-esteem of the learners, and their confidence in the value of their own ideas!

The solution is to stop thinking of science lessons as the study of nature. Science itself may be a study of nature, but science lessons should be the study of what people have said and thought about nature. The main object of interpretive activity should be not the circuit itself, but *what someone has said about the circuit*, not the events in the test tube alone but *someone's way of talking about them*, not the raisin, but *a written account* of the dewrinkling, with its words about 'concentrations', 'membranes' and 'permeability', and behind the words an *author*, clearly envisaged as a *human being*. This person who told the 'story' we are considering: what was he or she trying to say? Science lessons should be the study of systems of meaning which human beings have built up. Practical work is necessary in order to get a feel for those systems, and to give an understanding of what the evidence is which supports the scientific view, but it should not be thought of as the source that ideas come from.

'WORD WORK' FOR THE EXTRACTION OF IDEAS

Let me try to represent this recommendation diagrammatically, with two kinds of activity – Task A and Task B. If the main object of study is *someone's words*, then the lesson will be planned around those words and not around the circuit board or the test tube. Equipment will be needed, but it will not dominate the time available for study, and there will be time for a proper interplay of tangible experience on the one hand, and interpretive talk and writing on the other. We will have something like the arrangement in Figure 6.1.

Within such a pattern the total time devoted to Word Work (within and between lessons) should exceed that spent on Bench Work. Well-chosen resource materials appropriate for it are required, and lots of good ideas for organising the work with them. In the past, most of the creativity of science teachers was channelled into organising Task B. The need now is for a corresponding inventiveness in relation to Task A.

SCIENCE LESSONS AS APPRECIATION OF IDEAS

It is important that what I have called a '**Story**' or **Statement** in Figure 6.1 is not seen as an account of fact, but as an expression of thought by some *person* who can be identified or at least envisaged. It offers a point of view, a kind of explanation, a way of talking about the topic. It forms the principal material of the lesson. It does not have to be written, though having something on paper can make it easier to argue about. To cater for a wide range of abilities, it will need to take many different forms on different occasions, for example:

- something the teacher says, briefly, or writes on the board
- a snippet from a textbook
- a newspaper cutting
- two slightly different explanations written by pupils in last year's class
- a snatch of videotape
- a food package label

Sometimes the words of actual scientists may be used. The art of selecting suitable items is one of considerable subtlety, as they must be capable of leading in to the key talk-system of the topic, and also of

AUTHOR
(teacher, scientist, writer,
sometimes another pupil)

PUPILS, working on what the
author is trying to say, conscious of
the author as a real person and of
the *story* as an expression
of that person's ideas

Task A: Word work
around a table or at a
desk, handling ideas

A 'STORY' or STATEMENT
–a point of view about the
topic (a set of ideas,
spoken or written)

Task B: Bench work
or other practical work
outside and at home

PRACTICAL EXPERIENCES. They
give reality to the ideas, but are not
in themselves the main source of
these ideas. Nor are they definitively
a test of their validity, though they
contribute to their credibility

Figure 6.1

engaging the pupils. Usually they must be short, so that there is opportunity to go over the material several times, to comment, interpret, query,
and go back to it, as well as to experience the relevant phenomena
practically.

The type of science lesson I am describing bears some resemblance to a
literature lesson in which the object of appreciation – be it a poem or a prose
paragraph – is presented quite quickly, leaving time and scope for reflection,
for talk, and for each participant to move towards a considered restatement
of their own. Certainly an academic proposition in science, such as $P_1 V_1 = P_2 V_2$ requires at least as much time and effort to make sense of it, as might be
given to a literary one like 'All the world's a stage'. What did the writer
mean, and how do we re-create that meaning for ourselves? We could call
this 'appreciation of scientific ideas' or even 'meaning extraction'.

Actually there are many classes in which it would not be the best strategy
to start with anything like such an academic message as $P_1 V_1$ and all that, but
the topic of Boyle's law has been so long established in science syllabuses

that I will stay with it for the moment in a form suitable for an academic group, and use it to illustrate how practical experiences can be short and purposeful, leaving more time for the meaning-extraction activities. Here then are some components for a couple of lessons on the squashability of gases:

1 A very short **experience** of 'the spring of the air', for everyone individually, squeezing a sealed syringe full of air or another gas.
2 A passage such as **Statement 1**, to be read and puzzled over in pairs and trios, leading to some agreed restatement of what they think the writer was trying to say.
3 A short **presentation by the teacher**, with demonstration apparatus, but not using large sections of lesson time to collect experimental results.
4 **Practical desk work** – plotting a graph using second-hand data (included in Statement 1), and then a restatement of what the graph says – made by pupils, with support as necessary.
5 For an extension, or homework with a high-ability group, one could add a further passage such as that in **Statement 2**, in which we can hear Boyle himself speculating about how to account for the spring of the air.[1]

STATEMENT 1
L'étude quantitative de la compressibilité des gaz

This is what it says in a French school book, in the section about compressing gases (see Figure 6.2) What are the main points that the writer of the book is trying to make?

Pour une masse donnée, à température constante, le produit $P \times V$, de la pression et du volume d'un gaz, est constant. C'est la loi de Boyle–Marriotte (*).

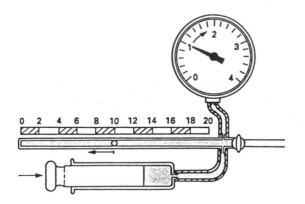

Figure 6.2

* Boyle (1627–91): physicien et chimiste irlandais. Découvrit la loi qui porte son nom en 1661–62, sans l'énoncer clairement.

* Marriotte (1620–84): physicien français. Verifia et précisa la loi de Boyle en 1676, il en donna l'énoncé correct.

Pression (en bar)	0.5	1.0	1.5	1.75	2.0
Volume (en cm^3)	20	10	6.7	5.7	5.0

STATEMENT 2
Boyle's speculations about the reasons for the spring of the air

Robert Boyle published his most famous account of the air in 1660, and called it *New Experiments Physico-Mechanical, Touching the Spring of the Air and its Effects; Made, for the most Part, in a New Pneumatical Engine.* Some years later he wrote more speculatively about what might account for its springiness:

Of the structure of the elastical particles of the air, divers conceptions may be framed, according to the several contrivances men may devise to answer the phaenomena: for one may think them to be like the springs of watches, coiled up, and still endeavouring to fly abroad. One may also fancy a portion of air to be like a lock or parcel of curled hairs of wool; which being compressed . . . may have a continual endeavour to stretch themselves out, and thrust away the neighbouring particles . . .

I remember too, that I have, among other comparisons of this kind, represented the springy particles of the air like the very thin shavings of wood, that carpenters and joiners are wont to take off with their planers. . . . And perhaps you may the rather prefer this comparison, because . . . these shavings are producible out of bodies, that did not appear, nor were suspected, to be elastical in their bulk, as beams and blocks, almost any of which may afford springy shavings . . . which may perhaps illustrate what I tried, that divers solid . . . bodies, not suspected of elasticity, being put into corrosive menstruums, . . . there will, upon the . . . reaction that passes between them in the dissolution, . . . emerge a pretty quantity of permanently elastical air.

But possibly you will think, that these are but extravagant conjectures; and therefore . . . I shall . . . willingly grant, that one may fancy several other shapes . . . for these springy corpuscles, about whose structure I shall not now particularly discourse. . . . Only I shall here intimate, that though the elastical air seem to continue such, rather upon the score of its structure, than any external agitation; yet heat, that is a kind of motion, may make the agitated particles strive to recede further and further . . . and to beat off those, that would hinder the freedom of their gyrations, and so very much add to the endeavour of such air to expand itself.

And I will allow you to suspect, that there may be sometimes mingled with the particles, that are springy, . . . some others, that owe their elasticity, not so much to their structure, as their motion, which variously brandishing them and whirling them about, may make them beat off the neighbouring particles, and thereby promote an expansive endeavour in the air, whereof they are parts.

How many distinctly different ideas does Boyle try out? What impression do you get about which if any of them he prefers, and what is your evidence?

The teacher must be confident of winning the involvement of the pupils in both kinds of task, and there are situations in which it would be easy to take the pessimistic view that only active benchwork will hold the attention of those pupils whose minds seem not so readily drawn to collective thought. That is not an adequate justification for practical work, and anyway such an estimate of pupils' abilities is too pessimistic; it indicates the need for a different task and a changed social relationship, not for abandoning the strategy. In this case I draw some confidence myself from the human interest of Boyle's identification of what he so interestingly called 'the spring of the air'.

For English-speaking pupils, a passage for Statement 1 would more usually be in English, and when I use the word 'interpret' I am not thinking primarily of that special subsection of interpretive activity which we associate with foreign languages. However, in this case a school book from France does give an added human dimension. What are they saying about this in Paris? Why do they say that? . . . and so on. The technical meaning of the passage hardly differs at all from that in a British book, but its historical and social significance to the French author was different, and there is an opening here for some discussion of the nature of scientific ideas. Data in a foreign language may seem daunting for pupils (and teachers) at first, more so than later experience justifies. Nevertheless, the teacher must judge the match of such a task to the age, experience and confidence of the pupils, and decide whether the task can be 'sold' to them as a worthwhile one, and how much support they may need in order to gain a feeling of success from it.

Statement 2 contains some very difficult language, but I think it is not appropriate to simplify it and replace it by teachers' words on paper. The result would too easily seem like something to be learnt rather than something to be puzzled over. I would feel the same if the data page were part of a modern technical manual on car engine compression ratios. The place for simplification is in the *speech* of both pupils and teachers, where difficult expressions can be taken alongside their more everyday equivalents.[2]

Many lessons on Boyle's law have no doubt been intended to have a structure of the kind I have described, dwelling on the appreciation of the idea. I think, however, that unless interpretation of meaning of the written word is advertised and proclaimed as the main purpose of the lesson, too much of the available time can be used in collecting figures from experimental equipment The impact of the lesson then is not of engaging the learners' minds with great scientific thoughts, but just of passing on authoritative knowledge.

Returning to the comparison of a science lesson and a literature lesson, probably there should be no fundamental difference, because in each case some person's meaning has to be sorted out and re-created in the minds of the learners. In a science lesson it is an advantage that we have access to tangible experience, but this cannot replace the interpretive work that must be done. Bench work should be primarily an aid to extracting the meaning from the words, and checking one's own interpretation of them. Pupils may seem to be checking Boyle's law, but what they should be checking is their own idea of what Boyle meant, and how he came to that view.

TYPES OF INTERPRETIVE ACTIVITY

In British schools, over-reliance on bench work may have passed its peak in the 1970s, when published schemes were characterised by long sequences of practical worksheet after practical worksheet. Moves to diversify learning activities are found in the more recent curriculum projects, and there is much talk of 'flexible learning and a *range* of teaching and learning strategies'. One guide for writers of new material for publication gives a list, of which the following is an abbreviated version.

Ways of learning: a checklist of (overlapping) approaches[3]

- by watching and listening
- by doing bench or field work, to a plan which someone else made for you
- by practical investigations which *you* plan, or help to plan
- by interpreting and evaluating data from charts, tables, graphs, etc.
- by tackling a technological problem, where you *try to design a solution*
- by *discussing ideas in a small group*
- by *writing – putting ideas together for an audience other than the teacher*
- by close reflective reading
- by teaching: *presenting a short talk or a poster to explain ideas to other students*
- by *devising maps, diagrams and charts* to express and communicate ideas
- by *taking part in role-plays*, simulations and games
- by manipulating ideas and information with a computer
- by searching through audiotapes, slides and video resource materials
- by careful analysis of 'case studies' of events outside school

In adult education or other sectors of the secondary school, such a list would not look at all strange, but for science teachers these activities are not so obviously right and necessary. 'Discussing ideas in small groups' surely lends itself to waffle, and 'writing for an audience other than the teacher' sounds a bit peripheral, and not what pupils expect to do in science. As for drama and role-play, that might be nice for a change, but is it really learning science? And if someone suggests that pupils should prepare speeches for a debate, it definitely seems like an extra rather than a crucial part of the learning. Debates are associated with opinions rather than with the consolidation of factual knowledge – more suitable for current affairs than for a science lesson.

The non-bench activities therefore have a somewhat uncertain status, not quite accepted by pupils or teachers as part of the real learning of science, and for that reason they may not be exploited to the full. Sometimes they are recommended on the common sense view that variety is a good thing, and the best way to avoid the boredom of repetitive routines. Although we do need variety, it would be a pity if these activities were seen only in that way. Part of my purpose in this chapter has been to express a rationale within which they can be seen to be more central to the learning. If pupils and their parents, as well as teachers, understand the need for interpretive effort, then the writing or the role-play will be used more positively for that purpose. To design a carefully thought-out flowchart on a poster, or to get ready to speak about it to the class, or to work out on paper how to explain to a younger child what (say) 'pasteurisation' is – these are exactly the tasks which make an appropriately high level of demand on the pupils, and require interpretive effort of them. With care, they also enable teachers to provide a supportive environment in which to encourage that effort. Diversified activities are not luxuries and extras, but necessary to the process of getting pupils to grapple with the ideas of science. Without them, I suggest that the bench work will continue to alienate as many pupils as it excites, and to leave others quite untouched by these ideas.

There is, however, the question of professional skills. A science teacher who can get an oscilloscope to work does not necessarily feel confident in organising a role-play, or in motivating pupils to set out their written reports for a non-scientific audience. Such skills were formerly outside the province of the science teacher, and although they are now being learnt, it is not in any systematic way. They are self-taught by enthusiasts and passed on slowly to others.[4] There are many helpful techniques which either will have to be assimilated to the repertoire of science teachers' skills, or else we shall need more differentiation of teachers' roles, with some members of the team specialising more in preparing pupils to work over ideas while others provide the backup of well-organised practical experience.

Table 6.1

Title of SATIS unit	Activities
The limestone enquiry	Analysing technical data, identifying by discussion the relevant facts and issues for consideration at a Planning Enquiry about a quarry extension, discussion of briefing papers for groups making representations at the enquiry, presenting ideas in a role-play of it
X-rays and patients	Analysing technical documents; selecting and presenting information in a form suitable for patients in a waiting room
The label at the back	A survey at home of fabrics and their uses; collating the information and presenting a summary, with explanation
The retrial of Galileo	Studying role-description cards, identifying ideas important to original participants; discussing each role, then playing them in a dramatised re-enactment of the trial.

KINDS OF RESOURCE MATERIAL

In Britain, the most extensive collection of resources to stimulate alternative activities is found in the SATIS units – *Science and Technology in Society*.[5] They offer a great diversity of activity and place in the hands of pupils data which is both more problematic than commonly found in a science text-book, and of much greater human interest. Using them generally involves much more talking, discussing and interpreting, relative to the standard bench work. Does such material automatically switch teachers and learners into a different style of language use, or does the rationale have to be made explicit? Many SATIS activities can be justified on several different grounds, not the least of which is that they are fun, but often the gains might be greater if parents and pupils were quite clear that (say) a technological problem is being set in order for the pupils to clarify their understanding of the relevant scientific concepts in their own words. A few examples of activities are listed in Table 6.1.

Most of these units provide material which requires the readers to get at the writer's intention, and to re-express it for themselves. They are a direct stimulus to word work as I have described it, and they make it legitimate for the learner to have a point of view based on a clear understanding of relevant science, in a way which textbooks and instruction sheets do not. This is one of the reasons why a technological problem is sometimes a better starting point for learning some science than is direct study of the science itself. Technological problems are not closed ended, and it is usually clear that more than one solution is acceptable, so it is easier for a learner to put forward an idea which draws on scientific knowledge, without fear of looking foolish. It is also easier for the teacher to be open to varied suggestions, whereas when discussion of a scientific problem directly is attempted it is hard for a teacher to avoid the trap of searching the class for the 'expected' answer, and greeting others with such faint praise that genuine discussion dies out.

SATIS-type activities will not automatically lead into the clarification of the full vocabulary and network of concepts in the related scientific topics, unless pupils and teacher approach them with that intention in mind. They are, however, a way of engaging the minds of the learners, placing them in positions of initiative in relation to ideas, and giving them a different concept of the part played by their own use of language in their learning.

MAINTAINING THE LEARNER'S FREEDOM

Freedom of interpretation is a key feature of good resource materials. There should be enough doubt in them to set the pupil's mind moving, and keep it moving, and also it should be legitimate for the doubt to lead to more than one acceptable conclusion, so that anyone may make reasoned estimates of the meaning without fear of being totally wrong. Under those circumstances language will naturally be used to explore what is meant, what was intended, and what we now understand. Teaching and learning will involve a degree of negotiation of the meaning: 'This is what I think is meant; how do you and other people understand it?' Some activities designed to support inexperienced readers work by artificially increasing the amount of uncertainty about what is being said.[6] In this connection, the power of narrative material about science seems to have been neglected. We know that a story can hold average readers much more easily than other kinds of writing, and Bruner[7] points out that narrative prose exerts its effect by recruiting the reader's imagination and triggering presupposition about what may be coming next, or what underlies what has already been said. The reader's mind is working on what is *not* present on the page, as well as what is there. The lack of explicit spelling out of every aspect is the feature which makes it possible for the reader to enter into and engage with the story. It offers freedom to do that, whereas explicitness would reduce the freedom, and hence the degree of involvement with the text. Perhaps one reason why a factual account of a scientific topic in a textbook often fails to hold attention is that it does not leave enough doubt, or lead the reader to fill it out from his or her own thought. There are not enough cues to uncertain possibilities to keep the average reader thinking ahead. Of course scientific books make a virtue of spelling things out, and leaving no doubt. Here is one of several places where features appropriate to science itself are not so appropriate for education.

For the future we may need two types of reading material – one to encourage the exploration of scientific ideas, the other to form a reliable quick guide to their structure. The traditional textbook is the latter only. There is also a case for making a clear division between two different kinds of lesson – one called 'Exploring scientific ideas' and the other 'Learning the systematics of science'. In the first of these, the freedom of the learner could be preserved absolutely, with a rule that there are no assumptions about 'right answers'; we are just exploring what people have thought and said about scientific matters. The teacher's role could be unambiguously one of encouraging and supporting speech and writing by the pupils, and the resources for these lessons would be of the types already discussed. In the second kind of lesson it would then be more legitimate to present the currently accepted structures of thought through clear exposition, without encroaching on the freedom of the learner to think. A relatively old-fashioned style of textbook, as a grammar of the subject, would also have its rightful place in that second kind of lesson, so avoiding the confusions of recent years when so-called 'textbooks' have attempted to do too many things at once.

SUPPORT FOR THE INTERPRETIVE WRITER

What happens to pupils' writing is of crucial importance if the habit of using language interpretively is to be established. The individual learner's idea of what writing is for can be extensively shaped by the attitudes of the teacher, and what the teacher explicitly or implicitly encourages. Teachers therefore need to be aware of the power of their taken-for-granted routines. For pupils to make full use of writing for the purpose of sorting out meaning probably requires the system of intermittent dialogue between teacher and pupil about what they write, a system which has been fully described elsewhere.[8]

Factors which matter include:

1 What the teacher does with pupils' writing when it has been completed.
2 The amount of time spent beforehand on discussing the purpose of the writing, its possible form and content, expectations in terms of style, and reasons for these.
3 The writer's sense of audience while attempting to set down ideas.
4 The extent to which the teacher allows and encourages a variety of styles.

All these are all deeply affected by the teacher's beliefs about what the writing is for. An extended account of these beliefs has recently been published by Douglas Barnes.[8]

SOCIAL AND EMOTIONAL CLIMATE

None of what I have described in this chapter can occur unless appropriate social relationships are established between teacher and pupils and amongst the pupils themselves. Much of this chapter has been about the cognitive functions of language, and I had better acknowledge therefore that in the classroom it is the emotional functions which have priority. What, for example, is happening in the following exchanges?

TEACHER: Gather round here please . . . . One at a time now . . . Listen to Vijay . . . I think you can make a good job of the graph, can't you?

PUPILS: Do we have to do it now? . . . I'm no good at graphs . . . [and later] Hey, Miss, it really works!

It would be silly to seek the importance of what is said here just in terms of the instruction or information that seems to pass. Questions of feeling, of a learner's self-concept, and of organisation and social control, are threaded through the words; they remind us that language has many functions in addition to the interpretation of ideas.[9] At the simplest level, there is often a direct clash in the classroom between using language to encourage thought, and using it for social control. For example, when teachers are helping pupils to elaborate their first thoughts, and to gain confidence in reasoning out an idea, they use long attentive pauses,[10] yet a common and successful technique for the management of large groups involves a kind of dominance strategy with very short pauses in the teacher's delivery!

To adopt an interpretive view of language requires a certain kind of social relationship between teacher and taught which we could describe as one of enhanced respect for the learner and the learner's ideas, so the only possible strategy is to accompany him or her on a journey in thought. As a teacher one needs to have rather less confidence in the obviousness and rightness of one's own way or the textbook way of explaining the phenomenon under discussion. And of course, the first task in teaching is not to arrange the subject matter, but to gather the minds of the learners, to a point where one can say:

Well, Vijay, and Alan, and Mary, what do you think these people had in mind when they put it that way?

NOTES

1 Boyle's speculations: See Marie Boas Hall (1965) *Robert Boyle on Natural Philosophy – an essay with selections from his writings*, Indiana University Press, Bloomington.

2 Is simplification of language desirable in science education? My view is that 'the language problem' of the science classroom is not adequately solved by adjusting 'readability levels' downwards, or by trying to avoid technical terms. It is more to do with an absence of encouragement for flexibility of expression, for putting the same idea in more than one way. Ideally this flexibility should be shown first in speech, and then not discouraged in writing. A word like 'elastic' means more when 'squashable', 'stretchable', 'resilient' and 'compressible' are used alongside it, rather than as a replacement for it, and of course they show that there is

something about the material which we are trying to interpret, not just to label. Teachers can show the value of this flexibility firstly by practising for themselves the habit of using both technical and less technical phrasing, and then by accepting and understanding the learner's struggles in the same direction.

Some degree of difficulty in the material to be read is actually a help in providing incentive for the learners to 'decode' it and make a restatement in their own words. To translate everything into simpler language also carries a risk of being condescending. Pupils are entitled to expect that they will be taught how to cope with technical, and even abstruse, language, and we should get them into the habit of doing so. Where pupils are very unconfident readers, the best strategy seems to me not to rewrite ideas for them, but to select more suitable written materials from real life, which are just a little above their present level of coping. If the label on the new shoe says '100% synthetic materials' or even 'polybutadiene', that is something to be grappled with, not avoided.

3 Ways of learning: Andrew Hunt (1991), personal communication. The list on which I have drawn was prepared for writers of learning episodes within the publication programme of the Nuffield Modular Science Project.

4 Professional skills for the management of interpretive activities: A programme of professional development in this field would involve workshops on the management of writing, reading, role-play, etc. The manner of focusing thought and feeling on the occasions where these activities are to work well is not the same as getting the class ready for practical work at the bench. Professional development for this work would also have to provide background in the history of ideas, which many science teachers have not got from their own higher education.

5 SATIS units are published by the Association for Science Education, Hatfield. (i) John Holman (ed.) (1986) *Science and Technology in Society: Teaching units and Teacher's Guide*, ASE, Hatfield; (ii) Andrew Hunt (ed.) (1990) *SATIS 16–19*, from the same source.

6 Structured reading activities: increasing uncertainty in order to engage the reader's active search for meaning. Two of the best-known activities which exaggerate the uncertainty to a level which will give readers' minds a more direct task to work on are:

1 sequencing a scrambled text and arguing the reasons for that sequence, and
2 reconstructing missing portions – not just odd words, but larger sections as when (say) the edge of the paper has been destroyed or 'lost'.

These and other such activities have become more widely known since the work of the Reading for Learning Project and they are called DARTs (Directed Activities Related to Text). See F. Davies and T. Greene (1979) *Reading for Learning in Science*, University of Nottingham School of Education. Both the quoted methods offer the interest of a detective hunt, and both can be powerful because they require the reader *to build up a general idea of what is being said*, and from this to predict the missing parts, or argue what the order of presentation must have been. Such devices must be used sensitively, and the reconstruction game should not be confused with the very different process of asking pupils to fill in missing words here and there, which frequently stimulates hardly any general interpretive effort. Also, because the modified passages are artificially contrived, they could quickly pall in overuse. A better long-term support to active engagement with reading would be to break the monopoly now held by informative non-fiction, and offer more science books and booklets which have a strong narrative thread, as well as more reading materials of the SATIS type which come from sources other than books.

7 Narrative prose and its effect on the reader's freedom of interpretation: See Jerome Bruner (1986) *Actual Minds, Possible Worlds*, Harvard University Press, e.g. p. 25, and also Chapter 9, 'The language of education'.

8 Support for the interpretive writer, dialogue marking, etc.: see Peter Benton (1981) 'Writing – how it is received' and Owen Watkins (1981) 'Writing – how it is set', both in C.R. Sutton (ed.) *Communicating in the Classroom*, Hodder and Stoughton, 10th impression, 1991.

Teachers' beliefs about the purposes of writing: see Yanina Sheeran and Douglas Barnes (1991) *School Writing*, Open University Press, especially Chapter 2, 'Scientific language'.

9 The many functions of language. See David Crystal (1987) in *The Cambridge Encyclopaedia of Language*, Cambridge University Press. He discusses a range of functions for language, amongst which are the following, in my order, not his: recording the facts; as an instrument of thought; as an expression of identity; for control of reality; for social interaction; emotional expression; phonetic pleasure.

Scientific language is often seen as mainly for recording facts, whereas I have been giving more prominence to its use as an instrument of thought. Its role in developing a sense of social identity for members of the scientific community, and for pupils in a classroom, deserves much more attention.

10 Language for social control: for an account of the role of attentive pausing, see Mary Budd Rowe (1973) 'Science silence and sanctions' in *Teaching Science as Continuous Enquiry*, McGraw-Hill.

Chapter 7

Group discussions in the classroom

Joan Solomon

To judge by illustrations of school science laboratories at the turn of the century[1] both practical and paper work used to be strictly solitary and silent activites. Talking between pupils was made as difficult as possible so that the deathly quiet of good discipline could be maintained at all times and at all costs! Few indeed even supposed that there were any costs.

Nowadays our science classrooms can be alive with pupil talk. Policy documents of the ASE and the DES have encouraged teachers to let children discuss together, without making any specific claims for its functions.

> reading and talking are as important to science education as listening, doing and writing.[2]

The aim of this chapter is to review the various purposes that discussion may serve for science education. It is necessary to make this specific to science, since discussion may well have different objectives for different subjects. Penny Ur,[3] speaking for language teachers, suggests the following aims:

- Efficient fluency practice
- Achieving an objective
- Learning from content
- Logical skills
- Debating skills

As part of the movement for 'language across the curriculum' we may hope that these aims are furthered by all talk in the classroom. Within science lessons, however, discussion takes on new tasks which it can carry out in special and valuable ways – for carrying out practical work, for interpreting results, and for understanding social issues.

DISCUSSION FOR PRACTICAL WORK

The commonest claim made for discussion is that it helps in the planning and design stages of practical work. The APU studies of investigation, to which science education owes so much, were too individual and research based to suggest how discussion might help; their document *Language in Science*[4] is more concerned with written work and the oral skills involved in describing – as it might be, a butterfly – than with the special purposes of group discussion. However, many practising teachers already had a strong feeling for the value of discussion, and in the run up to GCSE some of these ideas became inscribed in recommendations for preparing students for the assessment of their practical skills.

There is astonishingly little recorded evidence of how pupils profit from talk during practical work. What follows is drawn from a very patient listening and observing study of a second-year science class by June Wallace.[5] The pupils worked in pairs and she reported snippets of discussion which had value for different purposes.

1 Negotiating doing (e.g. arranging collection of apparatus and turn-taking in the experiment).
2 Removing tension (e.g. when disappointments or near quarrels have occurred).
3 Giving help and tutoring (e.g. reiterating what the teacher meant, or explaining the task).
4 Non-task talk (e.g. for greeting and 'stroking' as they settle into their pairs).
5 Negotiating knowledge (e.g. agreeing or disagreeing about what colours, measurements or tastes they perceive).
6 Constructing meaning (which will be explored separately).

It would be misleading to divide these six categories into those which seem more or less valuable. The point that Wallace makes in her commentary is that all this talk is essential. Without (1) the children would collect the wrong materials or bump into each other, and without (2) individual quarrels might break out. It is almost impossible for any two individuals to enter into such close and active proximity without a word or two of salutation (4).

The fifth category on Wallace's list is puzzling at first sight. Surely the pupils know whether it is hot, or red, or dissolving, without speaking to each other about it? The evidence from both this classroom study and from teachers' own experience insists that pupils do need to talk it over. Seeing is not quite the same as believing. Our certainty about observations is greatly increased by receiving confirmation of them from others.

PUPIL 1: 'Purple is it?'
PUPIL 2: 'Yes, sort of.'
PUPIL 1: 'Would you say purple?'
PUPIL 2: 'Yes, purple, (Pause) . . . I think purple.'
           (Satisfied at last they write it down.)

(Wallace 1986: 38)

Being sure, it seems, means being sure that others would agree with our judgement. So our pupils need to speak to each other about what they notice.

DISCUSSION FOR THE INTERPRETATION OF RESULTS

Documenting discussion of children's ideas has been a prominent feature of the CLIS project[6] and other research projects.[7,8] In some cases the general questioning area is still set by the teacher: 'What happens to food when it is cooked?', 'How do plants feed?', 'What does energy mean?' – but after that there may be more general discussion within the class. The single most important criterion for helping this to happen is that the teacher has no hidden agenda of a 'right answer' to be reached. So the concepts and theories talked about may not be what the teacher expects.

The purpose of this kind of classroom talk cannot be to learn accepted science. I sometimes doubt if it even makes the pupils' own ideas clearer as Driver and Oldham claim.[9] It does however, fulfil some very important functions:

1 It demonstrates that different interpretations do exist.
2 It encourages children to think about ideas.
3 It provides the teacher with a rapid survey, in broad brush strokes, of the variety of notions that the pupils hold.

Pupil discussion in groups

More hidden kinds of contribution to scientific knowledge take place whenever pupils talk together. As people speak, even when they are not trying to argue about the meaning of a scientific concept, the words they use, and the gestures they make, may suggest new meanings. It happens everyday through phrases like 'taking the goodness out of food' or 'leeks are heavy feeders'. It also happens serendipitously during talk in the classroom.

In a small-scale piece of research by a physics teacher[10] an unexpected happening while first-year (Y 7) groups learnt about electricity illustrated this. The course consisted almost entirely of worksheeted experiments with circuit boards. The pupils' prior notions of electric current, and their final understanding of it, were tested before and after the work. The results indicated that the overall 'progress' towards the accepted view of current was disappointingly small. But then it became clear that the pupils within each practical group had changed their ideas so as to agree with each other. They had obviously been speaking together about the experiment, what wires to put in and what connection to make, in terms of their own meaning for current. Some pupils had even dropped the 'correct' view, in order to fit in with their friends!

Similar effects can be seen in some of the CLIS transcipts:

> We had to explain why block A weighed more than B. I thought it was something to do with atoms being compressed densely in A and not so densely in B. Pete said something about air trapped in B so it made the weight lighter . . . (I said) if you get two bins and put boxes in A and compacting it and then putting more in. Then you just put non-compacted boxes in B. I think (Pete) agreed but still pressed on with his idea . . . I settled to go along with Pete's idea.[11]

The following snippet of discussion illustrates this ready acceptance of a multiplicity of meanings for a single concept.

PUPIL 1: You *get* energy from exercise.
PUPIL 2: By doing exercise.
PUPIL 3: You *lose* it by doing exercise.
PUPIL 1: You may *lose* energy.
PUPIL 4: It makes your body fit.
PUPIL 1: Yes . . . I think *both*.[12]

No possible logical contradiction between the two views about energy and exercise prevents pupil 1 from agreeing with both concept meanings, without any trouble at all.

Once the pupils are given real freedom to discuss concepts and theories entirely on their own there is no guarantee that either the right answer or the right method of argument will be used. This is *not* a strategy for instruction. Such discussion can certainly motivate children to take a more active part in the lessons and to contribute their own ideas and meanings. In both these ways it is valuable.

Social activities like small group discussion depend crucially upon collaboration and friendship. All of us, adult and child alike, need the agreement of others if we are to be comfortable with our own ideas about the world's happenings. We talk, it seems, just as much to get reassurance as to convince others. 'D'you know what I mean?' is one of the commonest phrases used. Sometimes we just hear meanings in the language that is being used. Light bulbs 'use up' electricity, and 'taking exercise builds up your energy'.

Science itself is a social process and there have been times in its history when there were groups of scientists holding different concepts. (The devotees of the One Fluid or Two Fluid theories of electric charge, in the eighteenth century, were like this. Benjamin Franklin's group even held social events, like their famous 'electric picnic' which, no doubt, reinforced concept solidarity!) Through plenary sessions in which children try to pool their group ideas they can also learn about the uncertain nature of scientific theorising, in a way which mirrors that of science itself.

DISCUSSION FOR UNDERSTANDING SCIENCE-BASED SOCIAL ISSUES

For evaluating social problems, where there can be no concealed 'right answer', most objections to free discussion evaporate. If the topic is controversial there will be different public points of view in and a cluster of answers according to personal or group interests. So it seems sensible to let the pupils' view surface in free and varied contributions. Ever since STS (Science Technology and Society) first broke in upon the school science curriculum in the late 1970s there have been calls to develop new and appropriate strategies for teaching it, and several of these have involved discussion.

Discussion within gaming and simulation

According to Ellington et al.[13] exercises of this kind can fulfil objectives such as:

> *educating through science* – interpersonal and communication skills, and *teaching about science and technology* – making political, social and economic decisions.

There is little doubt that the first of these objectives can be most valuably met by group discussion. The second objective becomes problematic only if the decisions lie too far beyond the students' experience.

Games such as *Minerals in Buenafortuna*[14] use discussion in rather contrived and restricted situations. Students work with circumscribed sets of information and find that the agenda is already set by the authors. Questions such as whether the country really wants to develop its mineral resources are taken for granted. Although the authors state that open-ended questions such as 'the consequences in terms of pollution, noise and the disruption of the local community' can be put to the group, the 'only problem of any importance', they say, is predetermined by the game makers.

The students are asked to act out particular roles in order 'to appreciate hard decisions made by others'. This creates two serious problems. The first is that most pupils will be making their own difficult decisions as citizens rather than as technocrats. Varied personal values and culture-dependent aspects that might influence a citizen are largely neglected in these games. The second problem is that acted parts call for artifical opinions. Participants who have already formed ideas on the public issue in question might be precluded from expressing what they really believe.

Discussing controversial issues in small groups

David Bridges, in his book on *Education Democracy and Discussion*,[15] argues that there are four functions for discussion when it is applied to a controversial issue. All of them begin with a sharing of personal perspectives on the topic. How and where these discussions finish indicate different kinds of achievement.

(a) sharing perspectives is a sufficient goal in itself
(b) reaching an understanding of the variety of available subjective responses
(c) making an existential (arational) choice between different values
(d) finding a rational resolution of the controversy

(Bridges 1979: 44)

Setting up such small group discussions itself presents some problems. In the first place the expression of personal values requires time and a supportive environment. There is an element of 'weighing up alternatives',[16] private or social, in any evaluation. Students who do not yet know where they stand are likely to go through a process of hesitant thinking and talking.

The second problem is the role of the teacher. S/he may be determined not to influence students, and yet trying to follow the austere prescription of the Humanities Teaching Project by being a 'neutral chair' can result in everyone's speech drying up into an atmosphere of embarrassed silence.

The third problem is the stimulus for discussion. The teacher's bidding is certainly not enough to set the ball rolling on just any cold Monday morning. There will be a need for some trigger which presents the issue as a matter for controversy.

In the *Discussion of Issues in School Science* project[17] we have had to take all three problems into account. Through the teachers we arrange for the students to talk privately in small friendship groups of just three or four pupils, we use selected video excerpts to stimulate talk, and neither we, nor the teachers, set the agenda for discussion. Indeed on the single occasion when a teacher misunderstood our instructions and set the students a list of specific questions to discuss, it proved to be a constraint. The list of questions encouraged those students who thought they had 'finished' to cut short the others' talk by going on to the next question.

VALUES, KNOWLEDGE AND UNDERSTANDING

The National Curriculum for science states in its programme of Study for Key Stage 3 (11 to 14-year-olds) that pupils

should begin to make decisions and judgements based on their scientific knowledge of issues . . .

However, the connection between the knowledge and understanding of scientific concepts, and decisions based on personal values, is not a simple one.

The DISS project is a part of a linked research programme on the *Public Understanding of Science* which is looking beyond the normal meaning of 'understanding'. The different projects are exploring how such emotive reactions as trust or distrust, fear or wishfulness, and even the glamour or status of the knower, affect how scientific knowledge is received. Recent research in this vein has examined the exchange of knowledge between Cumbrian farmers and the MAFF scientists whose task it was to communicate knowledge and regulations about radioactivity. Other projects are looking at how people in a self-help group acquire medical knowledge, or at how scientists in environmental groups perceive the contribution of mainstream science. In every case the group involved 'reconstructs' the scientific knowledge in order to see its relevance to them.

Our project is commissioned to explore how school science knowledge and media presentation of issues influence the kind of discussion that groups of students can carry out in the classroom. This category of discussion is more complex than those considered in the first two sections, and yet it has much in common with them. The category of talk that Wallace called 'removing tension' is present, as is also the search for corroboration of perception. (This was shown by the way the students talked about incidents in the video.) The social solidarity that was noticed in the context of learning science concepts also appears in the DISS transcripts. We found plenty of cases where the groups talked so closely together that they were even completing each other's sentences. They often asked each other questions, such as 'What would you do if it was your Mum?', but these were clearly not designed to find a right answer. They seemed to be posed in order to set the issue in a more familiar context. By careful deliberations and through helping each other to imagine the possible consequences, their scientific knowledge from school and the video was gradually put into a personal perspective.

Other connections between discussion of social issues and scientific knowledge appeared. One was the frequent comment that 'we need more research' which usually signalled their arrival at a point where no one in the group had relevant information.

The second effect was not so happy. Either when the group decided that they were being fed with biased or incomplete information, or when they felt powerless in the matter, they could be made angry or disaffected. At this point the discussion often abruptly changed course. Interestingly another research group in the *Public Understanding of Science* programme found a similar effect. They were investigating the views of adults who lived and worked near a chemical plant. In their report the group noted that:

where social powerlessness is perceived to be high, efforts at information dissemination may achieve low success rates.[18]

The incentive for discussing social issues constructively is not successful assessment, nor just relevance, it is the feeling that the citizen can achieve some just social objective through the combination of scientific understanding and social evaluation.

CONCLUSION

This chapter has touched upon at least five different uses for discussion within science education:

1 Negotiations before and during practical work.
2 Estimation of alternative ideas within the class about a particular topic.
3 Demonstration to pupils of different interpretations of experimental evidence.
4 Expression of values relating to social issues.
5 Exploring the reception of knowledge from television and other informal sources.

Methods of learning which depend on pupil discussion have some common features. They all require real participation. Genuine contributions will include the pupils' own experiences – relevant or not – their doubtfulness about new knowledge, and their trust in the people talking with them. All this makes the work so significant and so memorable that we have found average-ability students who were able to rehearse quite complex opinions worked out during group discussions after a gap of two or more weeks.

Science has a reputation for being exact, which can make it seem remote from everyday thinking and evaluation. Discussions between people colour its topics with human factors, making them more appealing to some of those who are not at all attracted to it at present.

NOTES

1 Jenkins, E.W., *From Armstrong to Nuffield* (John Murray, 1979).
2 ASE, *Education through Science* (Association for Science Education, 1981).
3 Ur, Penny, *Discussions that Work: Task-centred Fluency Practice* (Cambridge University Press, 1988).
4 APU, *Language in Science* (DES, 1988).
5 Wallace, J., *Social Interaction within Second Year groups doing Practical Science*, unpublished MSc thesis (Oxford University, 1986).
6 Wightman, T., P. Green and P. Scott, *The Construction of Meaning and Conceptual Change in the Classroom* (University of Leeds, 1986).
7 Solomon, J., 'Classroom discussion: a method of research for teachers?' *Br. J. Educ. Res.*, 1985, **11**(2), 153–62.

8 Caravita, S. and G. Guiliana, *Discussion in School Classes: Collective Modelling of Schemata* (Istituto di Psicologia. (Rome, 1988).

9 Driver, R. and V. A. Oldham, 'Constructivist approach to curriculum development in science', *Stud. Sci. Educ.* 1987, **13**, 105–22.

10 Kennedy, J., *Some Aspects of Children's Ideas in Basic Circuit Electricity*, unpublished MSc thesis (Oxford University, 1984).

11 Children's Learning In Science Project, *Approaches to Teaching the Particulate Theory of Matter* (University of Leeds, 1987).

12 Solomon, J., *Children's Ideas in Science and the Epistemology of Jean Piaget*, paper given at the BERA conference (University of Lancaster, 1985).

13 Ellington, H., E. Addinall and F. Percival, *Games and Simulation in Science Education* (Kogan Page, 1981).

14 ASE, *Minerals in Buenafortuna* (ASE, 1983).

15 Bridges, D., *Education, Democracy and Discussion* (NFER, 1979).

16 Kitwood, T., 'Cognition and emotion in the psychology of human values', *Oxford Review of Education*, 1984, **10**(3), 293–302.

17 Solomon, J., 'DISS – discussion of issues in school science', *Educ. Sci.*, 1988, (129), 18.

18 Irwin, A. and A. Jub, *Comments on the Manchester Project*, paper presented at the SPSG conference (Leicester University, 1990).

General

Solomon J., 'The social construction of school science', *Doing Science: Images of Science Education*, Ed. Millar, R. (Falmer, 1989).

Chapter 8

Chemical compositions

Andrew Burns and Mike Hamlin

Do we always make the most of coursework? Can standards be raised and work loads lightened by creating more effective cross-curricular links? This is one experience from a Nottingham school.

Greenwood Dale School has been involved in the Salters' GCSE chemistry project since 1987. Within this project, 15 per cent of candidates' total marks depend upon the completion of two coursework assignments. These assignments are intended to provide opportunities for schools to break out of narrow syllabus confines and to explore chemistry issues more generally.

Although we suspected that some Salters' schools would restrict their students choice of topic for fear of inadequate resources or possible lack of direction, we decided to give our students a much freer hand. We began by presenting our pupils with a wide-ranging list of topics, while also inviting them to suggest ideas of their own. Students had a week to decide upon their own topic area and, through consultation with their teacher, produce a detailed time plan for their assignment.

This approach produced a surprising variety of assignment ideas: 'The use and abuse of prescribed drugs'; 'Manufacturing hair gel'; 'The hole in the ozone layer'; 'Catalytic converters'; and even 'Is chemistry useful to Gary Lineker?' – were some recent examples. Of course, old chestnuts such as 'Acid rain' and 'Nuclear power – is it a good thing?' retain a steady following, but we feel that the widening of options has created extra interest, even excitement, for our students in completing what can sometimes be seen as 'yet another piece of coursework'.

Our students are encouraged to adopt a variety of approaches in their search for information. One interviewed local doctors and used the resultant tape recordings as reference. Another visited hairdressers in the city and through conversations with the manager of one of the salons, discovered an excellent source of research literature. Another interviewed local grocers as to the comparable advantages of plastic and cardboard egg boxes, before carrying out strength and chemical tests in the laboratory. In general we found that providing a student liaised closely with his or her teacher, an original and well-organised piece of work was likely to result.

New, whole-school management structures, established over recent years, had been designed to facilitate just such a cross-curricular approach to learning. There had been a move away from hierarchical faculty structures towards advisory and consultant responsibilities covering broader areas of experience. It was through such structures that we now sought to develop study links with other subject areas. The GCSE assignments provided a fertile starting point for this and students have completed work which links chemistry with home economics in 'The effect of different cooking methods on the vitamin C content of potatoes', with information technology in 'Using computer linked sensors to measure rates of reaction', and with geography in 'Local air pollution, problems and possible solutions'.

While these links certainly benefited a minority of our students, the possibility of also submitting such chemistry assignments as informational or factual assignments for English coursework seemed to hold even greater opportunities, as this would potentially impact on all of our pupils. We also felt that as the Salters' syllabus touches on the ethical and commercial implications of chemistry in the modern world, there would be ample scope for students to utilise a full range of presentational skills and communications media in their work.

With guidance from chemistry and English staff, students were therefore encouraged to apply consciously skills and approaches from both subjects, into their common investigations.

The markedly enhanced quality of such assignments quickly convinced us of the benefits of such a dual perspective. Language specialists did have something useful to say about organising information and argument in coherent and effective ways, and this came through very clearly.

An interesting development of this cross-curricular work arose when the Nottinghamshire Education Committee's Arts Centre (College Street) offered their video recording and editing facilities, together with the expertise of their staff. When put to the students, one group, who were making toothpaste, asked if they could use the centre to make a television style advertisement for the 'product' they were 'manufacturing' at school. This resulted in the group designing a storyboard and television script for a 60 second television commercial. They needed to create an attractive name and image for their product and to identify a target group of potential consumers.

At College Street, the students worked with the staff on scenery building, lighting, camera work, video editing and audio dubbing. The group's completed assignment was thus able to examine the chemical composition and properties of toothpaste, as well as following through into the manufacturing design, promotional and sales stages – the 60 second advertisement completing the package.

This kind of project certainly gave the students a wider perspective on how skills learnt in different subject areas are often creatively linked in the real world around them. It also had a clearly motivating cross-over effect, in that it gave the more scientifically inclined students an enjoyable experience of drama and media work, while also providing the context for a more sympathetic approach to chemistry for the more arts-based students.

Similar investigative projects looking at hair gel, cosmetics and lipstick have also been completed and last year more than twenty of our students submitted substantial pieces of coursework for both chemistry and English at GCSE.

This year, all our fourth-year pupils have started the Salters' Science GCSE course. The course explicitly requires all students to undertake investigative assignments. And the fact that all students now have a complementary science and English core curriculum has enabled us to set aside time during which the students can work on their science investigations in both subject areas. In this way students have access to expert help with the communication and language skills as well as the necessary scientific concepts.

We feel that one logical extension of this approach might be to focus on one of the assignments as a piece of science journalism – a magazine article or a newspaper feature. In this way we hope to encourage conciseness and clarity in our students' written work by providing the 'real world' discipline of a limited number of words for a known audience. This science as journalism idea could be made more realistic if the students were then able to wordprocess and page-set their assignments using desktop publishing software. In this way we would be able to save the various pages on the library computer, thereby making them available for future reference by other students.

By encouraging such joint approaches to coursework, we are deliberately moving away from the situation where students churn out huge amounts of unrelated material and instead, focusing on a smaller number of quality pieces of work which consciously link different subject areas through the joint investigation of 'real issue' topics.

Chapter 9

A variety of methods

Dorothy Dallas

LEARNING BY DISCUSSION

Class 'discussion' all too often means either a teacher talking to him- or herself with pauses while waiting for answers which never come, or the teacher and five interested pupils holding a conversation while the rest of the class go to sleep. At the other end of the continuum there is verbal anarchy, modelled on Parliament or on TV debates. If the class is already conditioned by years of experiencing such anarchy, it is hopeless for a new teacher to attempt to change it just by asking, and he or she usually descends to the irritated shouts of 'Put your *hands* up', 'I will *not* take shouted out answers!' and finally 'This class cannot discuss, I have to use worksheets'. This last is a sensible idea; the teacher can work up from well-regulated discussion in small groups gradually to a civilised discussion by a whole class – well, sometimes, anyway.

There is a case for the 'How to talk and how to listen' lesson, in the first week of the first year, giving some strong motivation for discussion, possibly during a session on laboratory safety. The ideas of the class on discussion should be actively sought, rather than imposing the teacher's ideas; the pupils usually come up with some sound suggestions for regulating it which would appear totally fascist if made by the teacher. What matters is that the teacher works towards good discussion techniques and consciously praises success in this sphere – one often hears that 2B are brighter/nicer/ nastier than 2C but rarely that 2C are so skilled at discussion that they can run one themselves.

Physical arrangement is difficult for discussion in most laboratories; in a lecture room at least pupils can turn round and discuss with those behind them, and can be in *eye contact* and *voice contact* with the teacher, although the teacher cannot move around the groups. But in a laboratory too many teachers try to discuss from behind a demonstration bench, with the class fixed in rows stretching to infinity; every answer must be repeated for the benefit of the back row, and most teachers forget to do this some of the time, so the back row loses the thread and goes to sleep or rack and ruin. The only solution to a whole-class discussion in a fixed laboratory is for the discussion leader, pupil or teacher, to stand in the middle of the room – far from the writing board so that a recorder must be appointed if needed. If possible the room should be rearranged so that bench tops form a square or a U shape, giving maximum eye contact and something to lean on and write on. Rings of chairs are favoured in some schools for discussion work, but they can provoke pools of silence and have no working surface. (See Figure 9.1A–D.)

Prepared points of discussion should appear on worksheets or on the board; unprepared questions tend to be vague, too general, or leading, unless based on years of experience – and even then . . . .! Unfortunately discussion often has to take place around a fixed oblong demonstration bench where the writing board is obscured from view, and the pupils at each end are either out of eye contact or dampening their notebooks in the sink.

Previous discussion by pupils is a useful beginning to a whole-class discussion – pupils who are embarrassed when asked to speak to everyone can then deputise another member of the group, although it is unwise to allow them to remain silent for ever. Such silent watchers may be afraid to make mistakes in public – so ensure by previous discussion that they can answer *one* question correctly in front of their class and gradually build up their confidence.

Discussion of results is a useful place to begin, with the class putting its results on the board – for example, in work on variation. But they can also be helped by wall displays where groups are responsible for explaining their work to others.

A systematic approach and critical usage of discussion is, as in all other methods, essential. Is your discussion really necessary? Do you need to lead it, or ask a pupil to lead it? Or should you try being a neutral chair – dropping in pieces of advice or evidence from time to time? This is certainly a technique to try in discussions on behaviour and attitudes, but like all other methods should not be used inappropriately or to excess.

Suggest ways of silencing those who always want to hold the floor, including yourself. Read Abercrombie;[1] his ideas are particularly applicable to sixth-form work, but the concepts are valuable for all age groups.

And with a silent sixth form as well as a riotous fourth form, you may have to concede that there are times when discussion is impossible with your class.

NOTE

1 Abercrombie, M.L.J. (1974) *Aims and Techniques of Group Teaching*, 3rd edn, SRHE Monograph 12, Guildford, Society for Research into Higher Education.

Physical arrangements for discussion work

A   Recommended

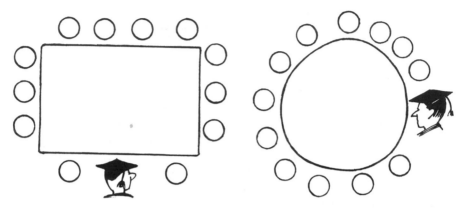

Some of these arrangements are possible in some laboratories.

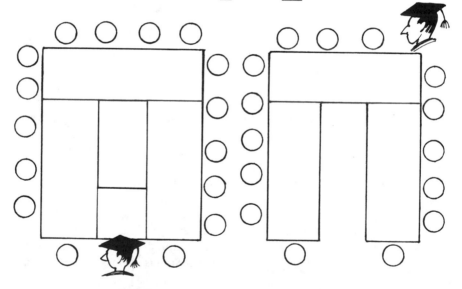

All the above arrangements:

1   Bring all the group within eye-contact — 12 is the best number to ensure maximum eye-contact and verbal involvement.

2   Provide a writing surface for all.

3   Avoid placing the teacher/leader/chairman in a dominant position.

Hypothesis — the demagogue/attention getter usually sits directly opposite the leader?

Figure 9.1A Physical arrangements for discussion work

B The following arrangements are not recommended for discussion work

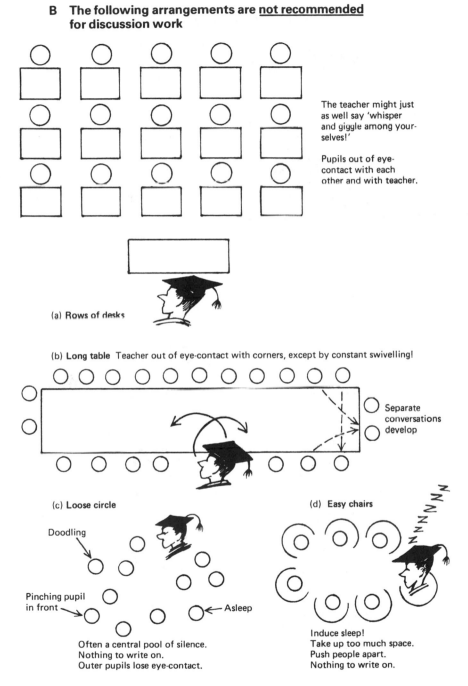

The teacher might just as well say 'whisper and giggle among your-selves!'

Pupils out of eye-contact with each other and with teacher.

(a) **Rows of desks**

(b) **Long table** Teacher out of eye-contact with corners, except by constant swivelling!

Separate conversations develop

(c) **Loose circle**

Doodling

Pinching pupil in front

Asleep

Often a central pool of silence.
Nothing to write on.
Outer pupils lose eye-contact.

(d) **Easy chairs**

Induce sleep!
Take up too much space.
Push people apart.
Nothing to write on.

Figure 9.1B Physical arrangements for discussion work

C   Discussion in a fixed bench laboratory

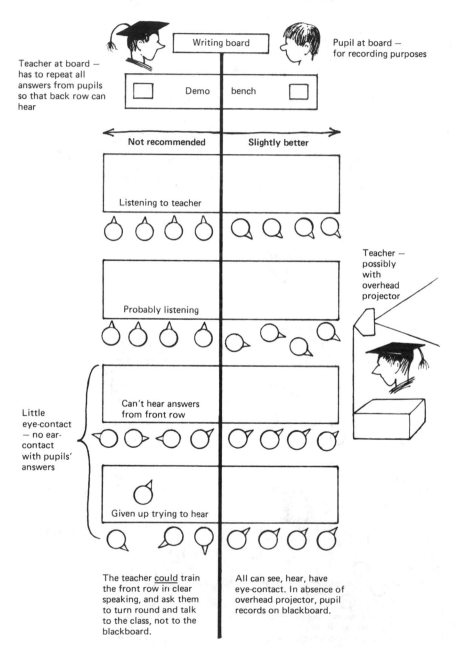

Figure 9.1C Physical arrangements for discussion work

D Discussion around a fixed demonstration bench

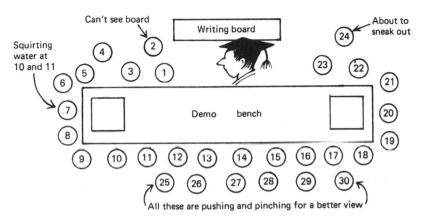

Can't see board

Squirting water at 10 and 11

About to sneak out

All these are pushing and pinching for a better view

(a) An obvious case for small group work!

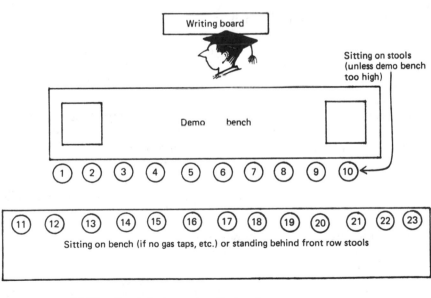

Writing board

Sitting on stools (unless demo bench too high)

Demo bench

Sitting on bench (if no gas taps, etc.) or standing behind front row stools

(b) When the whole class <u>must</u> see the board.
Where could you put nos. 24–30?
Stand on bench? Stand at sides of demo bench?
Sit on stools behind and between 1–10?
Depends on dimensions of benches, sites of gas taps, etc.

Figure 9.1D Physical arrangements for discussion work

Chapter 10

Developing pupils' skills

Terry Hudson

INTRODUCTION

The word *skill* is often used but rarely defined. It is defined in the *Concise Oxford Dictionary* as 'expertness, practised ability, dexterity and the facility for doing something'. This definition highlights the dilemma – there are different types of skill: a footballer is described as having skill on the ball, a tightrope walker shows skill and daring, a person is said to be a skilful debater and pouring a liquid is classed as a skill. All of these uses are correct, but the word skill is used differently in each case.

In answer to the question 'which skills concern the teacher of chemistry?' I have turned to three skills, (i) intellectual, (ii) motor and (iii) cognitive, listed and defined by White[1] as components of his seven elements of memory. White's seven elements (given in Table 10.1) can be interpreted as showing a progression of depth of learning, from simple recall to complex reasoning skills.

One could argue that much formal, teacher-centred teaching has concentrated mainly, though not exclusively, on the development of memory elements presented higher in Table 10.1. Competence in the recall of strings (remembered laws) and propositions (information that may be paraphrased, but is still in the form of fragments of information) is expected more than in the other elements. Many test questions are designed to test these two skills, for example

Name the three common laboratory acids.
Write down the formulae for water.
What is the ideal gas equation?

I would argue that no intellectual skill or cognitive skill is required to cope with these 'chunks' of knowledge, and that the ability to answer these questions is not a measure of understanding of chemical concepts. That is not to say that memorising diverse pieces of information, the facts and figures associated with a subject or discipline, is a bad thing, but understanding could be said to occur only when this information is used for a wider purpose.

Table 10.1 Seven types of memory element (from White)[1]

Element	Brief definition	Example
String	A sequence of words or symbols recalled as a whole in an invariate form	'To every action there is equal and opposite reaction'
Proposition	A description of a property of a concept or of the relation between concepts	The yeast plant is unicellular
Image	A mental representation of a sensation	The shape of a thistle funnel; the smell of chlorine
Episode	Memory of an event one took part in or witnessed	An accident in the laboratory; setting up a microscope
Intellectual skill	The capacity to perform a whole class of mental tasks	Balancing chemical equations
Motor skill	The capacity to perform a whole class of physical tasks	Pouring a liquid to a mark
Cognitive skill	A general skill involved in controlling thinking	Perceiving alternative interpretations; determining goals; judging likelihood of success

Images and episodes are also important elements in many chemistry lessons. Teacher demonstration and class practical work are common ways of placing these elements in the memory of the pupil. As with strings and propositions, however, recall of experiences of this type, if demanded in isolation, does not involve understanding.

The use of practical work and demonstration, possibly still amongst the most commonly used teaching and learning strategies in science teaching, brings in the elements of image, episodes and motor skills, but if the activity is passive – a sit and watch demonstration or a recipe practical – then little opportunity exists for intellectual and cognitive skill development.

Intellectual, motor and cognitive skills can be regarded as making higher-order demands on the pupil, as other memory elements must be drawn on and used consciously. To engage these elements pupils must be involved actively in their learning, with learning becoming a personal challenge, rather than the task of taking on board parcels of information for recall later. Any information encountered is analysed and reflected on – a far cry from the rote learning of chemical or mathematical formulae in isolation. How many of the pupils we have taught in the past have 'learned' the symbols of the first twenty elements of the Periodic Table without having any understanding of atomic structure, physical and chemical trends, uses of the elements or even a clear understanding of what an element was?

If we are intending to teach chemistry so that the pupils have an opportunity to come to terms with the major concepts of the discipline, I would argue that teaching strategies should encourage the learner to use the 'higher-order' elements of memory – intellectual skills, motor skills and cognitive strategy. These three elements are now discussed in more detail.

WHAT ARE INTELLECTUAL SKILLS?

White[1] subdivided intellectual skills into three main divisions: discrimination, classing, rules. This classification, though obviously artificial, is useful for looking at the types of intellectual demands made on pupils. Chemistry lessons contain numerous opportunities for allowing pupils to acquire and develop these skills. Some examples are given below.

Discrimination

Discrimination involves differentiating between different objects or substances. This is a very common occurrence in chemistry, for example discriminating between solids, liquids and gases or between organic and inorganic compounds. Interestingly White[1] states that overestimation of pupils' discrimination skills can lead to learning difficulties, as what seems obviously different to teachers may not be so to pupils.

Classing

Classing, which draws on discrimination skills, involves placing objects into groups, for example classing elements as metal or non-metal. Pupils must draw on previous experience of properties, or use observation and analysis in order to group the elements as metal or non-metal. Classing may be done instantly, as would be the case with very experienced chemists, or require the methodical analysis of a series of properties.

Rules

Rules are followed to carry out an operation. Examples would include rules for balancing chemical equations and carrying out chemical calculations. Usually rules are very specific and it would seem that anyone with certain basic skills can learn to follow rules. An example of this from chemistry teaching would be the pupil who is capable of calculating values of volume by placing numbers into gas equations, but who has no real understanding of kinetic theory. Rule following is an important skill, but unless the pupil is given the opportunity for using the skill in a wider context it is relegated to the level of a 'numbers trick'.

The difference between intellectual skills and simple recall is that intellectual skills can be adapted for use in new circumstances. For example, once a pupil can use the gas laws with one set of values, then any values for pressure, temperature or volume can be used, even if the values are previously unknown to the pupil.

WHAT ARE COGNITIVE SKILLS?

There are numerous cognitive skills, for example assessing, reflecting, goal setting, interpreting, generating ideas, evaluating, prioritising, adapting, planning and deducing. It is important that these cognitive skills, which admittedly draw on other memory elements, are developed within chemistry teaching and learning. It could be argued that without showing competence in these skills, pupils cannot demonstrate an understanding of concepts, and without such an understanding there is no meaningful learning. Teaching strategies that are active and pupil centred are more likely to develop these skills in young people than traditional teacher-led, didactic instruction, as the latter techniques make few intellectual and cognitive demands on pupils.

Referring specifically to the cognitive skills of planning and evaluation, a report from the Assessment of Performance Unit (APU)[2] states:

> Opportunities for students to design experiments, or comment critically on the design of others, are not often given in science lessons. . . . If skills of experimental design are seen to be important, then opportunities need to be given to develop these skills explicitly.

It could be argued that pupils are given too few opportunities to develop other cognitive skills. The pressure of time and external constraints, such as the examination system, can direct much teaching towards the passing on of information (filling empty pots) but the emphasis on cognitive skills within Attainment Target 1 (*Scientific investigations*) of the National Curriculum for science should mean that greater emphasis is placed on such skills in the future.

WHAT CAN WE DO TO HELP PUPILS TO DEVELOP COGNITIVE SKILLS?

Skills are developed by careful instruction and relevant practice. As cognitive skills require the manipulation and control of other memory elements, such as recalled facts, remembered episodes, images and intellectual skills, it is important that account is taken of the previous experiences and levels of skill of the pupils at the earliest opportunity. In this respect cognitive skill development and learning can be regarded as synonymous and so the approach advocated by the Children's Learning in Science (CLIS) project described below is useful.

Researchers involved with CLIS have reported that there are a range of misconceptions about scientific ideas held by pupils. Many of these ideas are central to scientific education, such as the particulate nature of matter. The researchers concluded that only a minority of pupils use accepted scientific ideas with confidence.[3–5]

The CLIS findings led to a model of learning that is now well known, and is increasingly accepted and adopted. The approach accepts that learners bring to the learning arena their own set of ideas and beliefs (schemes), and that the way that they assimilate new ideas will depend on this prior knowledge and belief.

In this sense each learner is unique. The CLIS model takes this into account and proposes that pupils will only learn new concepts if they are offered experiences that conflict with their own beliefs.

An example from chemistry (illustrated in Figure 10.1) would be to confront a learner, whose concept of matter is as one continuous substance, with practical examples of matter behaving in a manner supporting the concept of particles, for example evaporation, diffusion or dissolving.

These examples of the behaviour of matter cannot easily be explained by the pupil's continuous model of matter and, therefore, the possibility exists that new models will be searched for. It is important that the learner has been made overtly aware of his or her own ideas about matter, and has been given time to reflect on them.

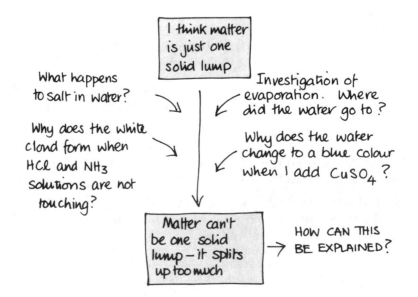

Figure 10.1 Challenging a pupil's concept of matter

The CLIS model is very important in the context of cognitive skill development as there are striking parallels between the development of understanding and the development of skills.

Classroom strategies for developing cognitive skills

Ten classroom strategies are briefly discussed below:

1 Encourage elaboration of work by allowing opportunities for pupils to paraphrase and make their own notes/diagrams. Place emphasis on pupil-designed summaries and conclusions as this creates the chance for pupils to consolidate their memory of work content and to develop vital cognitive skills such as *reviewing, evaluating and interpreting*.

2 Avoid questions, verbal and written, that exclusively demand simple recall, for example, 'Is sucrose solution an electrolyte?' *Group work responses* to more open-ended questions such as 'Plan and carry out an investigation – will sucrose solution conduct?' demand a variety of cognitive skills, such as reviewing, planning and critical analysis to be practised. Again, content is important, but an understanding of the concepts is paramount and is enhanced by engaging cognitive skills.

3 Attempt to produce *reading and writing tasks* that are active. There are many types of directed activities related to text (DARTs) but all involve the pupil in processing the text and having to adapt or use it in ways that demand greater understanding than simply reading. A simple example would be when presenting pupils with an experimental procedure. Rather than giving the procedure as a straightforward recipe that could be followed or copied with little understanding, the order of instructions could be mixed up. The pupils, individually or in groups, then have the task of reassembling the instructions in such a way as to allow the investigation to proceed in a scientifically valid and safe way. In order to do this the pupils must think carefully about the procedure and question each step. Diagrams and charts can also be presented in a form that requires processing, for example cut up as a jigsaw or with sections deleted.

4 *Analogies or metaphors* can be very powerful ways of encouraging pupils to take a wider, more reflective view of a topic. White[1] gives the example of asking pupils about the similarities between a tree and a volcano. By comparing and contrasting these two items, pupils must recall many memory elements and engage in sorting and analysing each known detail of volcanoes and trees to deal with the analogy.

5 *Spider charts and networks* can be used to promote a range of processing skills, such as generalising and reflection, as well as exercising the memory elements to do with factual recall. Pupils can be asked at the start, middle or end of a topic to draw a diagram containing as many

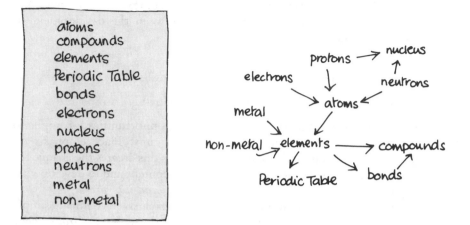

Figure 10.2 Concept mapping

aspects of the topic as they can think of. The items, words or phrases, are then linked together by arrows. Each arrow must be accompanied by an explanation of the link. This approach is a useful study technique and will be discussed later in the section on study skills.

6   *Concept mapping* is a technique similar to the one above, but in this case pupils are given a list of key words or phrases (Figure 10.2), possibly written on separate cards, and are told to order them on a table or poster in arrangements that make sense with arrows to link together words that are related. The relationships are then discussed. Pupils can be asked to write along the arrows so that a sentence is formed. For example, between elements and compounds in Figure 10.2, pupils could write 'combine to make'.

7   *Simulations* can be used to help develop cognitive skills. Not only do pupils get a 'feel' for what could be happening within a situation by actually being involved in representing part of a model, for example representing atoms during a kinetic theory simulation, but by stopping the action and asking pupils for explanations and predictions there are opportunities for developing cognitive skills. Pupils can also be asked to design their own simulations, ensuring reflection and interpretation of chemical concepts.

8   Allowing pupils to *design their own investigations* will offer opportunities for them to develop many cognitive skills. It is important that pupils unfamiliar with this approach are offered support and guidance. This can take many forms, for example clue cards, prompt questions, investigation proformas such as the action plan illustrated in Figure 10.3, and teacher intervention. Pupils will draw on previous experience and knowledge to help them to carry out investigations and this aspect can

be highlighted by considering an investigation involving acids. If asked to investigate which chemicals might be used to 'cure' indigestion, pupils would not progress far, even if practically competent, without an awareness of the acidic nature of indigestion, alkalinity, neutralisation and ways of measuring acidity (pH). In addition to the value of previous experience, it is important that pupils are encouraged to take time to perform what are possibly the most neglected phases of designing investigations – planning in the beginning and evaluation throughout. Emphasis should be placed on these elements by the teacher, even to the point of formalising the situation by asking to see plans and stopping investigations to hear feedback about progress/opinions, etc. With potentially hazardous investigations teachers should always check plans to avoid danger to pupils, but with harmless investigations it is sometimes worth allowing pupils to learn from poorly formulated plans.

9 Problem solving can be regarded as an overarching, composite skill that draws heavily on many intellectual and cognitive skills and is, therefore, an immensely important classroom strategy. Making pupils aware that they are involved in a process can be very useful, and it is possible to break down this process into stages for learning purposes. One model of problem solving developed by the *Problem Solving with Industry Project* (PSI)[6] has four stages (Figure 10.4) and it is possible to offer support at each stage.

Those pupils unable to progress from one stage to the next can be given support in the form of a written or verbal checklist of questions to act as prompt, for example

'What do the results tell you?'
'Does your solution match what you set out to do?'

In time this 'scaffolding' can be removed.

activity	time	person	equipment	variables	measure
collect apparatus	2 min	Louise Stewart	beakers thermometer water Bunsen tripod	—	—
mix water	10 min	Bill		volume	temp + time

Figure 10.3 Investigation action plan

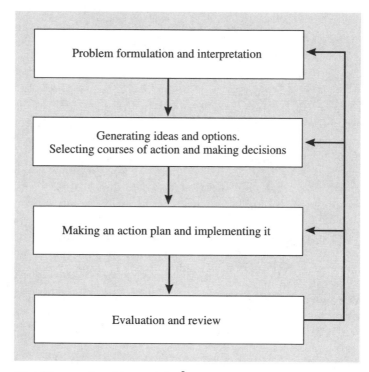

Figure 10.4 Stages of problem solving[6]

As with all effective learning the pupils must be clear about what the task is. Why are they doing it? What is the purpose?

10 Discovery learning, where pupils are given a lot of responsibility for finding out knowledge, requires a great deal of processing and analysis. In addition, participation and ownership of the learning experience can be very motivating. Pupils can very quickly become adept at carrying out research into topics and reporting back to their peers. There are some group work strategies that are designed to encourage this approach, for example the jigsaw approach.

The jigsaw approach involves the formation of 'home groups', ideally of four or five pupils. Each home group is given the same communal task, but individual group members must move away to find out essential information. To do this they work with pupils from other home groups on 'expert tasks'. At a later stage the home group re-forms, their information is shared, and the communal task is completed. The final stage is a whole-class briefing by the teacher to consolidate the main points of the investigation.

In attempting to develop intellectual and cognitive skills it is essential that the prior experiences of pupils are considered and that ample time is allowed for reflection and, hopefully, assimilation of new information. Teaching and learning strategies that are active, participative and give some responsibility to the learner make more cognitive demands than didactic methods. How many times have you heard teachers say that they did not really understand a concept until they had to teach it? It could be argued that only when planning a lesson and really analysing and reflecting on the content did learning take place with the teacher, so time for the pupil to undergo the same process should be allowed.

WHAT ARE MOTOR SKILLS?

Motor skills can be defined as the ability to carry out a whole range of physical tasks, for example pouring a liquid from one container to another. Motor skills involve memory of how the various muscles had to move to carry out a particular task. The task can then be duplicated. As with intellectual skills, motor skills are transferable – which is why those gifted in one ball sport are often very able in others. In addition, motor skills appear to be less easy to forget than other skills, but they do need to be practised to maintain good performance.

Knapp[7] states that motor skills cannot be divorced from what he calls mental skills, but that the overt part, the movement, forms the essential part in motor skills.

Motor skills are used extensively in chemistry and include those necessary for drawing apparatus and constructing charts, as well as those needed for the safe manipulation of apparatus. In terms of chemistry learning, the objective must be to be able to perform repeated actions that accurately meet a predetermined standard. Obviously the standard can be altered to make realistic demands on pupils, for example the difference between using a measuring cylinder to a tolerance of 0.1 cm^3 or 1.0 cm^3. Motor skills have predetermined goals and involve the development of sound technique.

HOW CAN MOTOR SKILLS BE DEVELOPED?

Motor skills must be learnt by 'doing' – this may be why they are so unforgettable. Learning motor skills involves repetition, so that the muscle movements can be remembered, and this takes time. If this learning process is plotted on a graph then, despite differences between individuals and variations due to the type of activity, the resultant curve would resemble the one illustrated in Figure 10.5.

There are some peaks and troughs in performance, brought about by fatigue, lack of interest, time of day, etc., but the general curve is upwards, until a plateau of performance is reached where vastly increasing the amount of practice will have very little effect on performance. It is important that this plateau does not lead to a loss of motivation. Once a pupil has mastered a skill and can carry out an operation accurately there is a danger that boredom will set in. This makes it very important to allow pupils to acquire and develop skills within an interesting and relevant context. Encouraging the practice of motor skills, even those that have been mastered, can take place within wider problem-solving activities rather than as isolated tasks. Repeated actions that have already been mastered, such as fitting specific nuts and bolts in the motor industry before the use of robots, can be done with little or no intellectual or cognitive demand; factory workers carrying out complex motor actions can quite happily talk to each other about matters totally divorced from the task.

Complex manipulations can be split down into smaller elements whilst they are being learnt. Good demonstration is a very powerful teaching tool as it is very important to give pupils a mental image of what the action is like. This must then be followed by 'hands-on' experience. A flowchart of a possible way of teaching motor skills is illustrated in Figure 10.6.

The key elements for teaching motor skills can be summarised as follows:

– take account of previous skills as motor skills are very transferable;
– break complex operations down into smaller elements;
– use good demonstrations;
– allow practice with wide tolerances initially;
– give immediate feedback about performance;
– allow skills development to take place within realistic situations when possible;

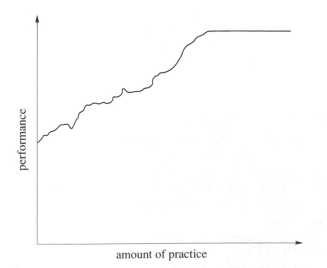

Figure 10.5 The learning process for motor skills

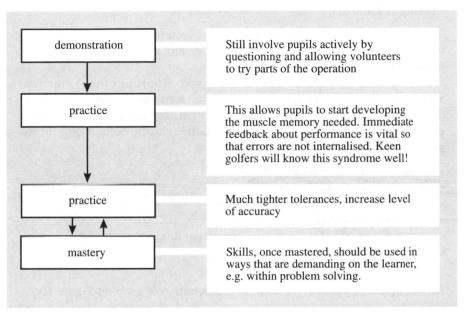

Figure 10.6 Teaching motor skills

– decrease tolerances and increase the complexity of the activity as mastery improves.

It is possible for pupils to check the motor skill performance of their peers. Providing they have a clear idea of what the action(s) should be like, they will be able to judge colleagues on these criteria very accurately. This is very useful during practical lessons, particularly with large groups, when the individual time given by the teacher to each pupil is limited.

DEVELOPING STUDY SKILLS

Improving the ways that pupils study involves the development of many intellectual and cognitive skills which are transferable rather than subject specific. Pupils will benefit from help and guidance in this area. Aspects of study skills include understanding and memorising concepts, organising work, taking notes, coping with new vocabulary and using information sources.

Making summaries

This section could have been included in the section on note taking, but as it is such an important aid to understanding, encouraging cognitive skills, it is treated separately.

Making good summaries is a very useful way of sorting out the important aspects of a topic. The act of summarising involves the pupil in making decisions about the topic covered and prioritising information, sorting it, paraphrasing it and processing it into another form. Some hints to give pupils for drawing up summaries are:

- make the summary stand out;
- do not put too much in it;
- include all the main ideas from a topic;
- use your own words;
- include drawings if it helps your understanding;
- do not introduce new ideas;
- try to draw links between the ideas.

An example of a summary drawn as a spider chart is given in Figure 10.7.

Organising work

The variety of approaches in chemistry teaching means that pupils can end up with a bewildering mixture of notebooks, files, handouts, homework sheets and practical sheets all containing vital information. It is all too easy for this collection of information to be so disorganised as to be of little value. It is important that pupils receive guidance in organising their work. Some practical hints include:

- fix handouts into your notes immediately;
- separate sections with labelled (coloured) card;
- always have clear headings and dates;
- number pages and create an index.

Pupils often have difficulty in organising their time. This is especially true of homework schedules, private study for project work and revision. Setting them tight deadlines will help, as will encouraging them to set themselves targets for completion. Revision timetables are simple to draw up and can be very motivating as each topic is crossed off the list! Interestingly, the act of designing and drawing up the timetable involves a great deal of review as pupils must consider which topics have been taught, how much 'information' is contained within each one and decide how much time to devote to each. They must also think about the sequence of revision, which involves consideration of links between the various topics.

A useful revision technique is to persuade pupils to write down or draw everything they know about a topic before they start to revise. This shows them the gaps in their knowledge. As with all revision techniques, as all teachers will know, the key is to start early, revise a little at a time and do it actively – not just reading. Twenty-minute bursts are better than three-hour marathons.

Taking notes

There are many situations in chemistry lessons when pupils will have to make their own notes. Note taking will be needed to record information from a variety of sources, for example teacher demonstration, teacher lecture, video, audiotape, practical work, literature research and class discussions. Pupils should be encouraged to:

– make their notes clear and easy to read;
– keep notes short and to the point;
– include headings and subheadings;

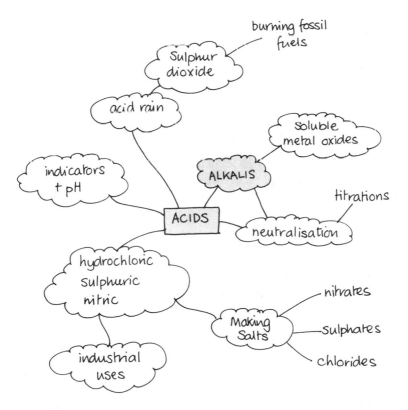

Figure 10.7 A spider chart used to summarise a topic

- highlight particularly important points;
- use their own words (especially true when using books!);
- build up a bank of new words (and meanings) and use them.

It is vital that pupils realise that notes will only be valuable if they understand them and they show up the main points. Highlighter pens or underlining may be useful for this.

Understanding and memorising new concepts

As has been stressed earlier, learning about chemistry should not simply involve the memorising of information but should encourage understanding by exercising intellectual, motor and cognitive skills. However, it is important that information about chemistry is remembered from week to week, otherwise little sense would be made of subsequent lessons and the memory elements drawn on in cognitive thought would be non-existent. Memory of ideas is linked to understanding in that recall is much easier if the facts and figures fit into an understandable framework.

Some suggestions you may wish to pass on to your classes are:

- never try to remember something you do not understand;
- try to link new ideas to ones you already understand;
- use your own words if possible, and if you have to memorise anything in a pre-set format, write your own interpretation underneath;
- use colour and underlining to highlight sections;
- try using diagrams or cartoons to explain a concept;
- keep referring back to the information – a little and often is a good rule for memorising material;
- try to fill a blank piece of paper with the information, then check how well you have done.

Researching information

There are numerous sources that pupils can use for finding out information. These include television and radio, books, magazines, newspapers, teachers, adults other than the teachers, and computers. It is well worth investing time in helping pupils to develop the skills needed for effectively using these resources.

In my experience many GCSE and A-level pupils cannot use a library efficiently and a short course of instruction on catalogue systems and a simple index is beneficial. It may be possible to liaise with the English department in this. It is also useful to keep a check on school and local libraries to find out what they keep in stock.

There are many useful and interesting articles in scientific magazines such as *New Scientist* and *Scientific American*, as well as a great deal of information and data handling in *Which?* magazine. Even if the reading age is a little high for some pupils it is possible to use DART activities to make the text more understandable, for example by giving pupils a list of headings to use for paraphrasing the article, or a simplified flowchart for them to complete if applicable.

Radio and television programmes can be excellent stimuli within classrooms, and can be used actively and imaginatively. Programmes do not have to be listened to or watched as a whole-class activity, but can form very useful small-group activities to promote discussion.

NOTES

1 White, R.T., *Learning Science.* (Basil Blackwell Ltd, 1988).
2 *Science at Age 15, Science Report for Teachers: 5*, Assessment of Performance Unit (APU). (HMSO, 1985).
3 Brook, A., Briggs, H. and Driver, R., *Aspects of Secondary Students' Understanding of the Particulate Nature of Matter.* CLISP. (Centre for Studies in Science and Mathematics Education, The University of Leeds, 1984).
4 Driver, R., Guesne, E. and Tiberghen, A. (eds), *Children's Ideas in Science.* (Open University Press, 1985).
5 Nussbaum, J., 'The Particulate Nature of Science', in R. Driver, E. Guesne and A. Tiberghen (eds), *Children's Ideas in Science.* (Open University Press, 1985).
6 *Problem Solving with Industry Project* (PSI). (Centre for Science Education, Sheffield City Polytechnic, 1991).
7 Knapp, B., *Skill in Sport: The Attainment of Proficiency.* (Routledge & Kegan Paul, 1963).

Chapter 11

Something to mop up with

J. Brophy and C. McCormick

HOW TO RECOGNISE A GOOD DAY

Lesson 1. Just wondering why the class is so late when a cheeky face appears saying ''Ello Miss – can we come in?' 'Why are you so late?' 'We were kept in to explain about the fight.' Decide it is better not to know the details and settle them into the lab. Glad to see that most of the children are clutching small bags of pasta. We are going to find out how pastas differ in the amount of water absorbed. AT 1 (Scientific Investigations) has turned us all from science demonstrators, illustrating what is already proven, into open-ended investigators. Gone are the certificates to students to celebrate the two-millionth person to confirm Faraday's laws; here should be the certificates to teachers in recognition of their proficiency in spotting opportunities to vary as many variables as possible in as many 'jolly' experiments as possible. Hopefully, the experiment captures the interest of the least motivated whilst providing opportunities to achieve the higher-level skills demanded by the National Curriculum. Spaghetti *et al.* serves as the light touch in a stodgy section of National Curriculum attainment targets. So, on with the experiment we planned last lesson. Now I need to remind them of safety aspects, making it a fair test, and, thirdly, procedure. Everyone is champing at the bit, and as soon as I say 'start', twenty-one children set up their apparatus. The lab is a veritable hive of activity. I start to visit different groups of children. 'Tell me what you have done', I ask. 'We've weighed some white spaghetti and now we are boiling it in water for 10 minutes. Then we are going to drain and reweigh it to see if it's got heavier.' 'What would that tell you?' 'How much water it's taken in, Miss.' 'Good', I say, 'could you try to calculate it as a percentage?' 'You bet', they say brightly.

I visit other groups of children, asking questions. The lesson goes quickly and it is soon time to gather them round the front bench. Overall, we have results for many different kinds and colours of pasta, which I put up on the board, and we work out the results together. I set homework and dismiss the class.

Overhear my children in the corridor telling their friends from the next class that they've just had a 'brill' lesson – bags of fun – 'our teacher is really good.' Proceed to the next lesson with a spring in my step.

The lower sixth are studying organic chemistry, and are going to nitrate methyl benzoate. All the apparatus is there, clean in matching sets – all the required chemicals are there too – even the overhead projector is there, with a clean roll and a pen that works. The lab technician smiles and tells me he is available to help. I am careful to remind the pupils about safety precautions, i.e. safety glasses, plastic gloves and lab coats to be worn, and care to be taken in the handling of corrosive or toxic substances. (Under the Health and Safety at Work Act, 1974, teachers are obliged to observe appropriate risk assessments made under the Control of Substances Hazardous to Health (COSHH)[1] Regulations before they handle a substance hazardous to health. This is checked in the LEA safety file and one or more of the following texts: *Hazcards*,[2] *Safeguards in the School Laboratory*,[3] *The Hazardous Chemicals Manual*,[4] or other.)[5] This procedure may raise one's anxiety level but it just spells out exactly what careful teachers and technicians have always done.

The pupils soon busy themselves, and I wander amongst them. They ask stimulating and interesting questions, showing that they have understood the previous lesson, and are moving forward. We have a lively discussion about possible mechanisms of reaction, good yields of product are obtained by all, a full set of homework assignments is handed in, and we all leave feeling intellectually stimulated. The pupils say how much easier it is to understand A-level chemistry than their other subjects.

Next stop the staff room for coffee – only one person in the queue, and a wide choice of sandwiches and cakes is available. I settle down to enjoy my break. My in-tray contains an invite to the maths department bash and a note from the Head telling me how pleased a parent has been with my extra help for their son – several Brownie points scored there. My free period sees off two piles of marking and the preparation of the next three days of lessons.

My afternoon class is a bubbly Year 9. We are going to plan an experiment as part of the assessment for Attainment Target 1 (Sc1) of the National Curriculum. The topic is 'rates of reaction'. I ask the class to come to the front bench, and when they are quiet I add a piece of magnesium ribbon to some dilute HCl. When it has disappeared, without a word I repeat the process using the acid further diluted. After one more repeat with yet more dilute acid I ask the class for their observations:

'The magnesium goes.'
'There is fizzing.'
'There is smoke.'
'It takes longer when you add water.'
'There is gas given off.'

I choose a vague statement and write it on the blackboard. 'When the conditions are different, the reaction goes differently.' I ask them what could be meant by 'the reaction goes differently'. Someone says, 'Could it be how long the magnesium takes to go?' Someone else says, 'Could it be how much fizzing there is?' I suggest that this might be difficult to measure, but the child replies that she could hear it. A third child suggests collecting and measuring how much gas is given off. I am delighted with their responses. We have lots of possible outcome variables.[6] I divide the children into groups of three, and give each group lots of small cards to write on. I tell them to go away and decide in their group on one outcome variable on which they all agree and to write it on one of the cards. On their other cards each person in the group writes down all the other factors that, if changed, would alter the dependent variable. They must then come to a consensus on what they mean. Each group now lays its cards on the table, and each group member chooses one of the independent[6] variables to vary, keeping the rest constant. It is so easy to see each group's progress and, where necessary, they can be prodded into more fruitful avenues. The children get 'stuck in' enthusiastically. The lesson passes quickly, and soon it is home time. No meetings tonight, so I nip off in good time, feeling well satisfied with the day's achievements. (It even carries me through the next day when the children lose their spaghetti down the sink and the photocopier goes dead.)

NOTES

1 *COSHH Guidance for Schools*, HMSO, 1988.
2 *Hazcards*, CLEAPSS, 1989.
3 *Safeguards in the School Laboratory*, ASE, 1988.
4 *Hazardous Chemicals Manual*, SSSERC, 1979, Oliver & Boyd.
5 Editor's note.
6 Input variable = Independent variable
   Outcome variable = Dependent variable.

Part IV

Assessment
A way through

Chapter 12

Assessing and evaluating in science education

John Skevington

This chapter aims to provide an outline of the organisation of assessment in the secondary phase of education in England and Wales, particularly as it applies to science, and to highlight some of the important issues (with some practical ideas) which should guide assessment if it is to make a worthwhile contribution to teaching and learning.

INTRODUCTION: WHY ASSESS?

We have been used in secondary schools to externally administered terminal examining, to provide a qualification for entry into the next stage of education or the world of work and, as a by-product, an informal indication of the effectiveness of teaching. Additionally, school-based examinations have provided a basis for decisions on pupil grouping and option choices, and class tests have been used as a means of diagnosing pupil progress on a more frequent basis.

With the introduction of the National Curriculum and its associated testing, there is a danger that a narrowly focused, externally imposed assessment system will produce an undesirable back-wash effect on school-based assessment. If this is to be avoided, teachers in science departments need to decide exactly what they believe are the outcomes of science education – which may well go well beyond the transmission of a body of knowledge and a particular set of skills – and develop the assessment system needed to reach these goals.

The ASE Policy Statement (ASE 1992) suggests three major purposes of assessment:

1 to help learners and teachers;
2 to provide relevant information to others;
3 to help institutions to perform better.

These purposes are not at odds with the statutory purposes of assessment but they should go well beyond them. Rowntree (1987) provides a useful discussion of the 'why' of assessment. In-service materials such as those produced by the Industrial Society (1989) and the Centre for Assessment Studies at the University of Bristol (1992) can provide a framework for developing a whole-school policy.

Assessment which helps teachers and learners is generally known as *formative assessment*. Its outcomes are used diagnostically. The areas of achievement and weakness of pupils are determined, so that decisions can be made about the next stages of learning and remedial action can be taken where necessary.

Assessment which is used to inform others through some form of reporting may be formative or summative. A *summative assessment* is made at the end of a learning unit or course. It provides information on the level of achievement reached by learners. The report may be teacher generated, a statement of level derived from an externally imposed system such as National Curriculum tests, or in the form of a qualification such as GCSE. However, the results of summative assessments are frequently used to assist in making choices of courses to be followed, and can thus be considered as having a formative purpose.

The use of the results of assessment in planning and reviewing teaching and learning, to improve the performance of the institution and its members, is what we shall term evaluation. This is the usual usage of the term in this country. The terms assessment and evaluation tend to be interchangeable in American publications.

AN OVERVIEW OF NATIONAL ASSESSMENT SYSTEMS

11–16

Key Stage 3

Assessment at the end of Key Stage 3 is by timed written tests, which provide the levels in Attainment Targets 2 to 4. The tests are externally set, teacher marked and externally moderated by a 'Quality Audit' process which is managed by the examination boards. The level for Sc1 is arrived at by teacher assessment and it is also externally moderated as part of the quality audit.

The levels achieved in each attainment target are averaged to provide an overall subject level. Teachers are required to provide an assessment of the levels for attainment targets 2 to 4 but, apart from pupils whose absence from the tests is authorised, no statutory use is made of these results.

Key Stage 4

Assessment at age 16 (the end of Key Stage 4) is primarily by means of GCSE. Most syllabuses provide a framework for the assessment of Sc1 which comprises the assessed coursework component of the scheme. Some are organised in a modular fashion and provide for an element of assessment during the course which, in addition to contributing to a pupil's overall summative assessment, can also be used for formative purposes.

There has been a marked increase in the development and use of modular schemes of teaching and assessment since the early 1970s, and particularly since the introduction of GCSE. For example, NEA Science (Modular) grew from 30,000 to 120,000 from 1988 to 1992. The use of end-of-module or periodic testing was felt to provide a motivation for pupils, especially the less academically inclined. The nature of such courses also matched a shift away from a content-based idea of science education towards the view that the processes and skills of science should be given an increased emphasis, because periodic assessment tended to reduce the emphasis on long-term memory. This move was accompanied by an increase in the amount of teacher assessment which contributed to the final grade, both practical skills and abilities which could not be appropriately assessed by a time-limited terminal examination, and, in some schemes, the assessment of knowledge and understanding.

The introduction of the National Curriculum and recent policy changes, which have increased the weighting of terminal assessment in GCSE, have tended to reduce some of the advantages which were claimed for modular schemes. The specification of a relatively large body of knowledge and understanding in the NC appears to have eliminated the options for choice in science courses. The contribution of teacher assessment to the final reported level has been limited to the assessment of Sc1, and the end-of-module tests are allowed to contribute no more than 25 per cent to the final level.

The teacher assessment of Scs2, 3 and 4 for formative purposes, and to provide the basis of the reports which parents are entitled to request at any time, is left to the individual school to organise. It would seem sensible to try to develop a consistent assessment programme for Key Stages 3 and 4. There are two schemes which provide 'off the shelf' assessment programmes which go some way towards meeting this need.

The *Graded Assessment in Science Project* (GASP) (ULEAC 1992) provides a five-year programme of assessment and recording of achievement which is supported by published materials. The final two years of the scheme lead to a GCSE administered by ULEAC. *The Suffolk scheme* (MEG 1992) is a GCSE syllabus administered by MEG but it includes an optional Year 9 programme which can provide the basis for teacher assessment in the final year of Key Stage 3.

Both schemes provide detailed criteria for teacher assessment of content, derived from the Programmes of Study and the Statements of Attainment, and pupils are assessed on a 'can do' basis against them. Even if a department decides to use a different GCSE course, the criteria developed by these courses can form the basis of an assessment scheme.

The GCSE will only provide certification for pupils who achieve level 4 and above. For pupils who are not likely to achieve level 4, the examining boards provide alternative schemes which involve varying amounts of teacher assessment.

Assessment post-16

The picture post-16 is much more complex than that created by the National Curriculum. It is subject to regulation and control by SEAC and the NCVQ, the two organisations which administer government policy.

In 1996, A levels are to become subject to a set of general principles which have been developed by SEAC and accepted by the Secretary of State. It is likely that a set of subject cores will be developed for the main subjects, including the sciences, and these will specify objectives and common areas of content, which must be included in all syllabuses for that subject.

The alternative 'vocational' path has traditionally been the preserve of further education colleges, although such courses are increasingly being offered in schools. There is a range of vocational courses administered by City and Guilds and the Business and Technician Education Council (BTEC). The courses are presently being rationalised by the NCVQ.

PRINCIPLES OF EFFECTIVE ASSESSMENT

Although the area of external testing and qualifications remains one of constant change and uncertainty, there are recognisable principles upon which assessment should be founded. It should:

- assess the outcomes of teaching and its associated learning;
- reflect and support the aims and objectives of a course;
- support the teaching and learning strategies employed without distorting them;
- provide sufficient evidence to enable a professional judgement of the learner's achievement to be made;
- form an integral part of the scheme of work (so should therefore be developed alongside it rather than as an 'add on').

Starting from aims and objectives

The starting point is the aims and objectives of the science course. We need to have a firm understanding of what we want pupils to achieve so that we can design methods of testing how successful they have been. Some aims and objectives may be supplied by an external syllabus, but the school ethos and the outlook of the teachers in the science department may result in further objectives being added.

The National Curriculum does not provide stated aims. The accompanying Orders state that the statements of attainment

provide the objectives for what is to be learnt in each subject.

When developing schemes of work it is useful to have a more general view of the objectives.

The overall objectives of a course are often too broad for assessment purposes. They need to be related to specific parts of the content of the course or to particular skills or processes. This involves establishing suitable criteria for assessment, often called behaviourial objectives, which specify what learners are expected to do in order to demonstrate achievement of the objective. The discussion which follows uses the context of the National Curriculum to develop these ideas, but they are equally applicable to any course.

Sometimes the statements of attainment in the National Curriculum are difficult to use as criteria for assessment because they are so broad. For example, Sc2. 6a

Pupils should be able to relate structure and function in plant and animal cells

could not be sensibly assessed by one exercise. The problem here is that there is a very wide range of cell types in plants and animals, each with a different structure and function. If pupils are to be asked:

Describe how the structure of e.g. a muscle cell and/or a nerve cell and/or a mesophyll cell is related to its function . . .

then they – and their teachers – clearly need to know, in advance, which types of cell are included on the assessment agenda. It is, however, possible to produce assessment items for which the above statement of attainment (SoA) is an adequate criterion, e.g.

*Describe how the structure of **one** type of animal cell and **one** type of plant cell enables the cell to do its job effectively.*

Alternatively, the assessment item could present information about the structure and function of particular cells – preferably cells which pupils are unlikely to have met during their course – and ask pupils to explain how their structure enables them to do their jobs.

For the purposes of formative assessment, a more sensible approach would, of course, be to collect evidence over a range of activities and over a period of time. To provide adequate opportunity for such assessment, it is important to identify the points in the scheme of work where the content implied by this statement is addressed. The appropriate assessment techniques can be related to the learning activities, and the contribution of the assessment of this particular area of the curriculum to the whole can be built up.

Other SoAs present problems as assessment criteria because they do not specify what pupils need to do in order to demonstrate achievement, a disadvantage for teacher and pupil alike. An example of this is Sc4 3b:

Pupils should know that there is a range of fuels used in the home.

A pupil writing or saying 'There is a range of fuels used in the home' actually meets the requirements of the SoA but is scarcely convincing. The statement needs rewriting before it can be used as a criterion for assessment.

One way of tackling this problem is in the *Common Themes* developed by NEAB/WJEC/ULEAC for their GCSE Science Frameworks. They comprise a comprehensive set of assessments including not only necessary interpretations of National Curriculum SoAs but also a comparable set of statements for concept areas included in the programme of study (PoS) for which there are no SoAs. For example, the section on fuels includes the following:

at level 3 *To make things hotter we can*:
– *burn gas, coal or other fuels*
– *use electricity*
at level 4 *Coal, oil, gas and wood are all fuels. They release energy when they are burned.*

The required knowledge and understanding, though still in the form of substantive statements, is now non-trivially testable as recalled knowledge, e.g.:

*Write down the names of **two** fuels people use in their homes.*

One way of heating water at home is to burn a fuel such as gas. Write down another way of heating water at home.

*Gas, wood and oil are all **fuels**. Explain what this means.*

Specifying the syllabus, wherever possible, in the form of statements, particularly ones expressed in the language which pupils are expected to understand and use, makes it clear to both teacher and pupil what is required.

Using an assessment instrument which is appropriate for the purpose

Knowledge and understanding

There is a wide range of methods of assessment by which knowledge and understanding can be assessed. The reader is recommended to consult a text such as Fairbrother (1988) for a complete discussion. The principle of 'fitness for purpose' should guide the selection of method. Decide on the purpose of the assessment and the nature of the objective which is being assessed, and then select a method which will enable you to assess that objective in as valid and reliable a manner as possible. By valid, we mean that the assessment measures what it is intended to measure, as defined by the assessment objectives; by reliable, we mean the consistency with which the assessment measures achievement.

Validity is, in part, achieved by carefully matching the design of the assessment item to the assessment objective. Using a range of appropriate assessment methods will also tend to increase it. However, this needs to be balanced against the increase in time demanded and a possible reduction in coverage of the objectives.

Reliability is increased by carefully defining the desired outcomes of the assessment; in other words having a clear idea of what aspects of pupil performance will provide the information that is needed.

(In practice there is, unfortunately, sometimes a conflict between the demands of reliability and validity. It is this conflict which underlies the disagreement about the relative contributions which coursework and terminal examinations should make to pupils' assessment at GCSE. Coursework assessment is usually based on a large sample of assignments of different types and often of a more realistic nature than is possible in examination papers, so is likely to be more valid in terms of overall aims and objectives. Ensuring that different groups of pupils undertake comparable assignments under comparable conditions, and that the criteria for their assessment are consistently applied, is, however, far more difficult with coursework than with final examinations. The introduction of GCSE saw a move towards a greater emphasis on coursework assessment. The National Curriculum attaches a greater importance to reliability than to validity and has reversed this trend.)

The assessment should be capable of being operated within the time and the resources available. This is especially important if assessment is not to make disproportionate demands and so distort teaching and learning.

The next stage is to identify exactly what aspects of pupil behaviour will allow a judgement to be made. If the objective requires recall of knowledge then the activity must involve the communication of the recalled knowledge in some form, whether oral, written, pictorial or by demonstration in some practical activity.

Many statements of attainment require that pupils understand a concept or relationship and we need them to demonstrate this understanding in some way at some level. In part, this level is set by the level and range of the concepts involved. Within the National Curriculum it is possible to identify a progression in the complexity of understanding required of pupils. This can be because of the links to other concepts which are implicit in the understanding demanded. For example, Sc4. 7d requires an understanding of 'the quantitative relationships between force, distance, work, power and time'. This goes beyond the ability to substitute the correct quantities in the appropriate formulae and carry out a calculation correctly. It embodies concepts of energy transfer, the idea that energy can be quantified, and an understanding of some of the effects of forces.

The problem is further compounded by the development of a more quantitative approach as one progresses through certain strands. We should, however, take care not to confuse the ability to use mathematics, important though this is in many aspects of science, with a comprehension of the relevant scientific concepts. For this reason, many conventional mark schemes allow for credit for the understanding and application of scientific ideas, even if the pupil makes numerical errors.

It is especially difficult to assess understanding in timed written tests. One-word or short answers are poor indicators, as are methods where rote application of techniques is possible. One way in which it can be assessed is via items which present information about situations, phenomena or devices which are not specified by the syllabus, and which are unlikely to have been used in the teaching or learning of the course. Pupils are then asked to demonstrate their understanding of science concepts which are specified by the syllabus by using them to explain, evaluate, or in some other way make sense of the presented information. Of course, the assessment of understanding lends itself to teacher assessment. A range of activities can provide evidence for understanding. Investigational work, hypothesising and the design of investigations are suitable if properly set in the context of the knowledge and understanding required by the other attainment targets.

Spider diagrams or concept mapping allow pupils to demonstrate their understanding of links between different areas of the subject. Pupils can be asked to identify the key concepts in their diagram or for the reasoning behind the links which they have made. An example of such a spider diagram is given in Figure 12.1.

Asking pupils to write questions is another technique for testing understanding. There are various ways of ensuring that the questions do not test simple recall. We can ask for questions which begin in a specific way such as 'what if' or 'how would'. A stimulus such as a diagram of a physical situation or a numerical answer with a specific context can be an effective way of starting. Pupils can be asked to produce suitable answers to their own questions as an extension to the activity.

These and other techniques are discussed in much greater detail by White and Gunstone (1992).

To complete this consideration of how effectively to assess knowledge and understanding, a number of other issues need to be considered.

Firstly, whereas formative assessment might legitimately focus attention on the specific details of the particular learning experience which pupils have encountered, this is inappropriate for summative assessment. Summative

Ideas about force and motion

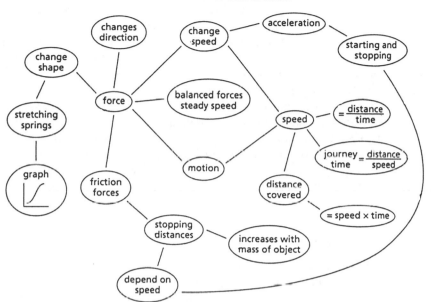

Figure 12.1 A spider diagram of force and motion

assessments should be concerned with the science concepts themselves, not with the ways in which pupils acquired that understanding. Assessing such understanding may, as indicated above, involve asking pupils to apply science concepts to specific situations but the details of these situations should be supplied in the assessment items themselves; they should not be part of what pupils are expected to recall. This principle, consistently applied, can make an enormous contribution to reducing what might otherwise be a hugely information-overloaded National Curriculum.

Secondly, the National Curriculum notwithstanding, the degree of difficulty of an assessment item depends not only on the level of the concepts involved, but also on the language used – particularly the non-scientific 'carrier' language – and on the context within which pupils are asked to demonstrate their understanding. A short paper produced by the British Association of Teachers of the Deaf offers very useful advice on the 'Language of Examinations'. Even very experienced examiners find it difficult to predict the effect of a particular context on the difficulty of an assessment item. For this reason, examining groups intend, within the limited range of levels targeted by each differentiated paper, to use marks rather than a strict criterion-referencing of items to levels. This approach will mitigate not only any unanticipated effects of context on the difficulty of items but also any inappropriate attribution of levels within the National Curriculum itself (levels which are hardly scientifically established!).

Thirdly, the requirement for differentiated papers, targeted at a relatively narrow range of levels, presents teachers with real problems about what the teaching/learning agenda for particular pupils should be. Though pupils are normally expected to follow the PoS at each key stage, the National Curriculum itself recognises that not all of the PoS for a key stage is appropriate for all pupils, and that aspects of earlier key stages may also need to be included. Furthermore, whilst it is clearly undesirable to deny pupils access to concept areas from which they might derive educational benefit, it is equally undesirable that the examinations for which they enter should provide them with no opportunity to demonstrate what they understand of concepts specified as being at a higher level than those targeted by the paper. Science teachers will not be able to avoid having to make some very difficult decisions.

Investigations and practical work

The introduction of GCSE demanded that teacher assessment of practical work be employed as the most appropriate means of measuring the achievement of laboratory and experimental skills. Syllabuses provided lists of criteria against which pupils' work could be measured, either within the context of a whole experiment or as an isolated exercise. Such skill-based assessments can be an appropriate formative tool. However, Sc1 has a particular view of the nature of the experimental work which demands that teacher assessment for the purposes of the National Curriculum is in the context of whole investigations. An investigation requires pupils to:

- *formulate questions based upon existing knowledge and understanding which they can test;*
- *put together a sequence of investigative skills (such as identification of key variables, observing and measuring) into an overall method to solve a problem;*
- *evaluate their findings in the light of the original problem;*
- *define and develop the way they tackle problems, and what they know and understand.*

(SEAC 1992)

For the purposes of assessment, the scientific knowledge and understanding which provide the context for the investigation should be of a comparable level to the investigation. Thus it is unacceptable (and probably impossible) for a level 6 or 7 investigation to be based upon an idea which is expressed in a level 2 SoA.

In the context of teaching and learning, we need to expand ideas of the purposes of practical work to embrace what to many teachers is a novel area.

Furthermore, we need to balance the demands of this new area against the need to develop more conventional practical skills, as well as knowledge and understanding, in the context of practical situations.

Managing effective assessment

Knowing why and what we need to assess is one thing. Being able to carry it out, record the results and maintain a record of the evidence used for making judgements for later use is the key to making it work.

The classroom or laboratory needs to be organised in such a manner as to facilitate assessment. This means that the teacher needs to be able to focus attention on one group of pupils whilst assessing them, yet still be able to see what else is going on, and respond to other members of the class if necessary. Pupils need to have a clear idea of the structure and pattern of their work, so that they can direct their own learning for a suitable period. To facilitate this, resource materials should be organised so that pupils are able to carry on with their work with a minimum of attention.

For some groups such self-study may not be possible. Resources may be inadequate and the nature or abilities of the pupils may not allow it. In such circumstances assessment activities will have to be restricted or adapted. The teacher has to make a decision as to what is in the best interest for the development and learning of the pupils.

Assessment is liable to be more successful if pupils understand what is expected of them, both in terms of what they have to know or be able to do, and of the performance that is needed to demonstrate their achievement. This will involve writing the assessment objectives in terms which pupils can understand. For formative assessment, this will enable pupils to participate in the process, which in itself can help relieve the burdens on the teacher. This approach can also be used to facilitate the production of a record of pupil achievement, which is a further strand in the policy of most schools.

The need to assess to externally set standards and the legal responsibilities involved in summative assessments will mean that self-assessment by pupils is unlikely to be an acceptable basis for summative assessment. At the relevant stages there is a requirement for schools to conduct a process of internal moderation and standardisation to ensure that all teachers are assessing to a common standard. This process is made much easier if the major part of this standardisation can be achieved at the stage of planning assessments. Discussions between teachers when designing assessments and their associated objectives should help ensure that assessments across the department are to a uniform standard.

Sensible record keeping

There is a risk that the conscientious and enthusiastic teacher, aided by like-minded pupils, will generate so much information during the process of assessment that much of it will be useless, because nobody will be in a position to make use of it! The key to sensible record keeping is to decide at the outset just what information will serve the purposes which the school and department policies have laid down and record only that information. Much assessment will be informal, and feedback to pupils will be verbal or by written comment against their work. In many cases it will not be necessary for the teacher to keep a separate record of this.

Sensible record keeping also requires that as far as possible the recording is done at the same time as the assessment. This reduces the time involved and makes for more reliable recording in situations which may not produce a permanent record of the pupil's work. The record must mean something in terms of the objectives of the assessment. It is unlikely that the conventional 'mark out of ten' will provide adequate information for arriving at judgements of levels.

Some activities will allow assessment of the whole class to take place during the same lesson. For others a proportion of the pupils will be assessed. It is more effective to maintain an on-going record on a whole-class sheet rather than on individual pupil records. An example of such a sheet is given in Figure 12.2. The date is there to trace the pupil's work if it is needed as evidence; the criteria provide a reminder of the basis for the judgements made by the teacher and the comments can supply further evidence for making judgements.

Relevant information can be transferred to individual pupil records at the end of a topic or as the school policy dictates. It would seem sensible to maintain and keep such records on a departmental basis and to transfer them to a central school record at the end of the year. Decisions about record keeping should be a part of a whole-school policy, but they need to be sympathetic to the problems faced by the teacher in the classroom.

EVALUATION

The assessment information derived from whole classes or from groups within classes can be used by teachers for providing feedback on their own performance, both as developers of teaching schemes and as deliverers of the different parts of those schemes. The information will be more reliable, and so more useful, if it is complemented by the views of pupils as to their own reasons for their performance. If they have a clear understanding of the learning objectives and what is expected of them in terms of performance they can usually make an honest assessment of their own contribution to learning. Again, this can be incorporated in the development of the record of achievement.

Discussions about problems and shortcomings of the scheme of work will take place as a matter of course in well-motivated departments. The head of department must ensure that time is made available in departmental meetings to ensure that these discussions have a positive outcome. They should form part of a continual review and refinement.

Postscript – some words of caution

The measuring instruments which we have at our disposal are imprecise, and what we are trying to measure is at times transient and liable to be affected by the measuring process. Models of the curriculum and its assessment are human constructs just like the models which scientists have created to explain the Universe. The difference is that the curriculum and its assessment rest on a very slim research base. Most of the foundations are the stuff of personal and political prejudice. Like most (or all?) human constructs these things are not immutable and they are not eternal. It would be at best unwise, and at worst wrong, to grant assessment the status of the measure of

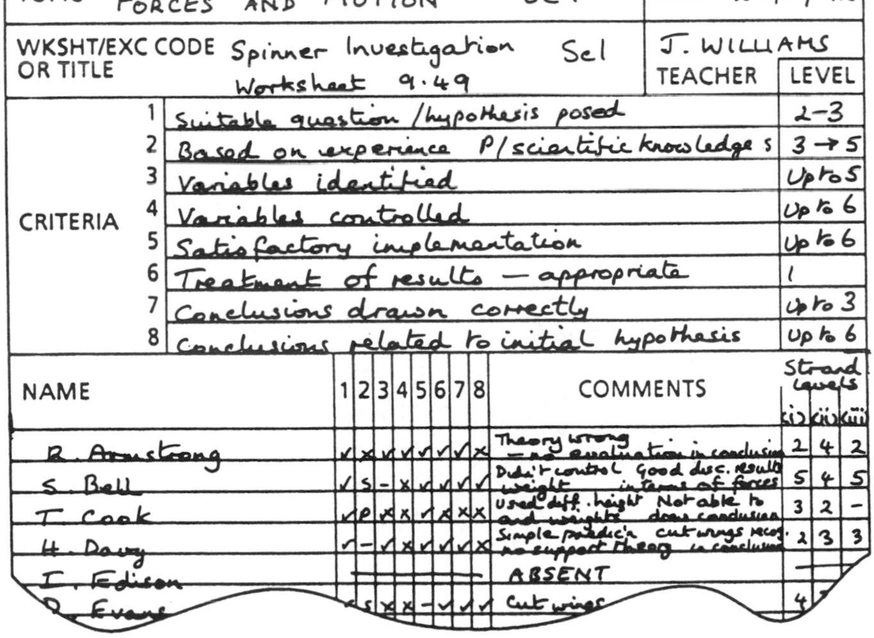

TOPIC Forces and Motion Sc4	DATE 22/1/92
WKSHT/EXC CODE OR TITLE Spinner Investigation Sc1 Worksheet 9.49	J. Williams TEACHER

CRITERIA		LEVEL
1	Suitable question/hypothesis posed	2–3
2	Based on experience P/scientific knowledge S	3 → 5
3	Variables identified	Up to 5
4	Variables controlled	Up to 6
5	Satisfactory implementation	Up to 6
6	Treatment of results – appropriate	1
7	Conclusions drawn correctly	Up to 3
8	Conclusions related to initial hypothesis	Up to 6

NAME	1	2	3	4	5	6	7	8	COMMENTS	Strand levels (i)	(ii)	(iii)
R. Armstrong	✓	✗	✓	✓	✓	✓	✓	✗	Theory wrong – no evaluation in conclusion	2	4	2
S. Bell	✓	S	–	✗	✓	✓	✓	✓	Didn't control weight. Good disc. results in terms of forces	5	4	5
T. Cook	✓	P	✗	✗	✓	✗	✗	✗	Used diff. height and weights. Not able to draw conclusion	3	2	–
H. Davy	✓	–	✓	✗	✓	✓	✓	✗	Simple prediction no support theory. Cut wings recog. in conclusion	2	3	3
I. Edison									ABSENT			
D. Evans	✓	S	✗	✗	–	✓	✓	✓	Cut wings	4	[illegible]	

Figure 12.2 A class sheet for pupil records

the quality of an education or a school, as some seem to want. There are plenty of examples of successful people who were 'failed' by the education system in the past because they 'failed' its assessment system. We need to maintain a sense of balance, building on those aspects of assessment which seem to be useful in assisting the progress of pupils and treating the others with the caution that they demand.

REFERENCES

ASE (1992) *ASE policy present and future*, ASE.

British Association of Teachers of the Deaf, *The language of examinations*.

Fairbrother R.W. (1988) *Methods of assessment*, Longman.

Industrial Society (1989) *Managing assessment*, The Industrial Society.

MEG (1992) *GCSE Coordinated Science syllabus: The Suffolk development*, Midland Examining Group.

NEAB, WJEC and ULEAC (1992) *GCSE Framework Common Themes*.

Rowntree D. (1987) *Assessing students: How shall we know them?*, Kogan Page.

SEAC (1992) *KS3 school assessment folder Part 2*, School Examinations and Assessment Council.

ULEAC (1992) *GCSE science syllabus: Graded Assessments in Science Project*, University of London Examinations and Assessment Council.

University of Bristol (1992) *A whole-school assessment policy*, NFER-Nelson.

White R. and Gunstone R. (1992) *Probing understanding*, Falmer Press.

Part V

Making science accessible to all

Chapter 13

Gender differences in pupils' reactions to practical work

Patricia Murphy

INTRODUCTION

The low number of girls studying physical science after the age of 13 has been the subject of world-wide concern since the 1970s. The change of status of science from an optional to a compulsory subject in the curriculum of many countries is an attempt to alter this situation. This can only be effective, however, if the reasons for girls' avoidance of science can be identified and counteracted. Much is known about the differences in attitudes, experiences and achievements of girls and boys as they relate to science. What currently concerns educators is the way these factors inter-relate to create gender differences.

Recent curriculum innovations in science typically include an increased emphasis on 'active' learning. To ensure that such innovations are beneficial to all pupils it is important to consider how gender differences operate in the practical context. Unfortunately, there is a confusion of messages coming from the literature about girls' and boys' attitudes to, and performance on, practical activities. Omerod (1981), for example, found that 'liking of practical work' was a significant discriminator for boys in all three science subject choices, in that it was an added incentive to study science. This was not true for girls. Yet recent studies looking at classroom intervention strategies have recommended practical work, or 'active' work, as a way of combating gender differences (see, for example, Hildebrand 1989). Some national science surveys have shown large differences in favour of boys on practical tests (Kelly 1981), others either no differences or a trend in favour of girls (Department of Education and Science 1988). Girls' lack of confidence in practical contexts and fear of practical equipment has also been commented on in several studies.

To understand these apparent contradictions it is necessary first to explore the nature of gender differences and the factors that determine them.

GENDER DIFFERENCES IN ACHIEVEMENT – THE INTERNATIONAL SCENE

Outside the UK the well-known survey programmes of educational achievement are those of the International Association for the Evaluation of Educational Achievement (IEA) and the National Assessment of Educational Progress (NAEP) in the United States. The first wave of surveys for these programmes took place in the late 1960s and early 1970s. The questions used were almost all multiple choice and the majority were strongly content based. The UK programme of the Assessment of Performance Unit (APU) started later (1980–4) and used quite different measures of achievement. The science surveys included: three practical tests, measuring skills, observation skills and practical investigations; tests of science content; and other process skill measures (Murphy and Gott 1984).

The IEA survey found that on average boys scored considerably better than girls in science achievement tests in all nineteen countries surveyed. A study by Kelly (1981) explored this finding further. The study focused on the 14-year-olds in the IEA sample from fourteen developed countries. The IEA science tests were written tests which included measures of chemistry, biology and physics content; laboratory practice, that is knowledge of apparatus and experimental procedures; and attitudes to science. The results again showed boys ahead of girls in every branch of science. The largest differences were for physics and the practical subtest. The smallest difference was for biology, with chemistry intermediary. Girls in some countries did achieve higher scores than boys in others. However, the nature and magnitude of the gender differences were consistent across the various countries. The NAEP (1978) programme in the United States similarly found boys ahead of girls at ages 9, 13 and 17 on tests of physical science content, and only small differences in favour of boys in biology.

The cross-cultural uniformity of gender differences in science achievement suggests that cultural factors alone cannot account for them. Kelly (1981) identified the 'masculine' image of science, common to all countries, as a contributory factor. She argued that as girls and boys have learnt to respond to gender-appropriate situations, then a 'masculine' science will alienate girls and discourage their engagement with it. Kelly's study also showed that internationally boys had a greater liking for, and interest in, science. There were considerable variations between countries, indicating to Kelly that cultural expectations did influence attitudes, particularly girls'. She did note, however, that boys achieved better in science than girls with equally favourable attitudes.

The UK APU science surveys of 11-, 13- and 15-year-olds included tests of both the skills and content of science. Only a small number of the test questions used were multiple choice. The results of the surveys are given in Table 13.1, along with the related information from the IEA and NAEP

Table 13.1 Some international survey results

APU test	Results from APU	Results of other surveys		
		IEA	NAEP	BCSS
Use of graphs tables and charts	$B_{15} > G_{15}$			$B = G$
Use of apparatus and measuring instruments	$B_{15} > G_{15}$		$B > G$	$B > G$
Observation	$G > B$			
Interpretation	$B_{13,15} > G_{13,15}$			$B = G$
Application of:				
Biology concepts	$B = G$	$B > G$	$B > G$	$B = G$
Physics concepts	$B > G$	$B > G$	$B > G$	$B > G$
Chemistry concepts	$B_{15} > G_{15}$	$B > G$	$B > G$	$B = G$
Planning investigations	$B = G$	$B > G$		$B = G$
Performing investigations	$B = G$			

B denotes boys' performance, G that of girls; B_x denotes the performance of boys aged x. The symbol '$>$' should be read as 'better than'.

surveys already discussed. In some cases there is a subscript to indicate the age at which the gender difference emerges. Where there is no subscript this indicates that the difference or similarity in scores occurred across the ages tested. The APU results demonstrate that gender differences in favour of boys increase as pupils progress through school.

Table 13.1 also refers to the results of another regional survey, the British Columbia Science Surveys (BCSS) (Hobbs *et al.* 1979). This is included because, like the APU surveys, pupils' achievements on both the skills and content of science are assessed. However, like the IEA and NAEP surveys, the tests were in written, not practical, mode and the questions were largely multiple choice. The British Columbia results show boys' superiority to be restricted to tests of physics content and of measurement skills.

The IEA results found that boys continued to outperform girls even when their curriculum backgrounds were similar. This was not the case in the APU surveys. When pupils with the *same* curriculum backgrounds are compared all performance gaps at age 15, except those for applying physics concepts and the practical test-making and interpreting observations, disappear. The results show that even when able girls continue to study physics they do not achieve the same level as boys as a group. The gap in physics achievement between girls and boys established at age 11 increases with age (Johnson and Murphy 1986), a finding also reported in the other survey programmes.

The 1984 APU survey looks in some detail at pupils' interests and attitudes to science. The results show a polarisation in the interests of boys and girls across the ages. Girls' interests lie in biological and medical applications, boys' in physics and technological applications. The same polarisation is evident in the pastimes and hobbies reported by the pupils. Girls also saw science as having little relevance to the jobs they might choose, unlike boys. Indeed, the proportion of girls selecting a job drops if they perceive a high science content in it. At age 15 a markedly higher proportion of girls than boys describe physics and chemistry as difficult. These findings replicate the IEA survey results.

At the time of the last APU surveys the second round of IEA testing was being carried out (1983–4). Some of the results for different countries have been published which provide further information about the nature of gender differences in science. For example, the second international science study (SISS) for Japan and the United States (Humrich 1987) again showed 14-year-old boys ahead of girls for each science subject. However, Japanese girls outperformed boys and girls in the United States in physics whereas Japanese boys achieved lower biology scores than boys in the United States. Japanese scores were lower than US scores on tests of knowledge but substantially higher on tests of comprehension and application. The differences in levels of achievement for girls and boys between the two countries appear to reflect the different curricular emphases. For example, in Japan there is an early focus on the development of reasoning skills. Mathematics, which is particularly influential in physics learning, is a highly valued subject for all pupils. Biology, on the other hand, is accorded relatively low priority. Clearly the educational objectives of a culture can influence gender effects.

The SISS results for Israel (Tamir 1989) showed a similar pattern of differences to the first IEA study. However, by age 17 the gender differences in biology and chemistry had disappeared for science majors and the difference in practical laboratory skills evident at age 14 was not present at age 10 or 17. The study found that girls specialising in physics did less well than boys in all science areas, whereas female chemists and biologists only did less well in physics. It is evident from these results that girls' learning in physics is an international problem.

National survey results have consistently shown boys ahead of girls on physics tests. Recent research in Thailand, however, provides an exception to these findings (Harding et al. 1988). Seven sets of tests were used in the study: three practical tests (of manipulative skills, problem solving, and observational skills) and four paper-and-pencil tests (on the links between practical work and scientific knowledge; sources of evidence; scientific knowledge; and scientific attitudes). The results show girls at age 16–18 performing at least as well as boys in physics and better than boys in chemistry. In laboratory tests girls outperformed boys in both physics and chemistry. The researchers posit several reasons for these uncharacteristic results, among them that science in Thailand is compulsory; the teaching approach is practical; chemical tasks have a 'feminine' image, as do some of the practical physics tasks; there are no differential expectations of pupils; and females participate in all levels and fields of employment.

It appears possible to alter girls' underachievement in physics by reconsidering the cultural expectations of girls and boys and how these are reflected in the organisation and values underpinning the school curriculum. There are indications from each of the national surveys that in certain circumstances tasks in biology and chemistry can favour either boys or girls. To understand these results it is necessary to examine the effects of particular features of the tasks – for example, the degree of openness; the type of solution sought; and the manner of response expected.

The polarisation of pupils' out-of-school experiences, as evidenced in their chosen hobbies, pastimes and choice of reading and television (see Johnson and Murphy 1986, for a discussion), indicates some of the ways in which perceptions of gender-appropriate behaviours are constructed. Such perceptions lead girls and boys to develop the different interests and attitudes to science demonstrated in the surveys. These in turn affect how they engage with school science and their subsequent achievements in it. How pupils interact with science also depends on the image of science that is represented to them in their culture. The uniformity of gender differences across countries gives support to the contention that science has a masculine image in many cultures. The Thai results reinforce this.

Messages about girls' and boys' liking for and achievement in practical work remain unclear. The APU results indicate that girls are well able to handle a range of practical situations and indeed do better than boys in practical tests of observation. The Thai research also demonstrates girls' competence in practical work. The difficulties girls appear to have relate to more traditional curriculum approaches to experimental science. For girls the approach to practical work, the purpose it is seen to serve and the types of problem addressed by it all influence their performance.

The factors which influence gender effects operate throughout pupils' schooling and appear to be particularly critical for their learning in the intermediary school years (ages 13–14). We now take a closer look at the research results to try to establish potential sources of gender differences in science achievement.

DIFFERENCES IN EXPERIENCE

Kelly (1987) found little relationship between previous science-related experience, subject choice and achievement. The APU results paint a different picture. In the APU science surveys boys and girls at ages 11 and 13 perform at the same level on assessments of the use of apparatus and measuring instruments. These tasks were practical and pupils' performance was judged largely by their actions. When performance on individual instruments is considered, girls as a group do significantly less well than boys on certain ones. Boys are better able than girls to use hand lenses and stopclocks at all ages, and microscopes, forcemeters, ammeters and voltmeters at ages 13 and 15. Pupils in the surveys were asked what experience they had, out of school, of the various measuring instruments used. The results show that boys' performance is better than girls' on precisely those instruments of which they claim to have more experience. The different experiences of pupils affect not only the skills they develop but also their understanding of the situations and problems where their skills can be used appropriately. To plan effective classroom strategies it is necessary to focus on both the nature of the differential experiences and their consequences. For example, boys are better able to use ammeters and voltmeters yet they do not have experience of these outside of school. They do, however, play more with electrical toys and gadgets than girls. Such play allows boys to develop a 'feel' for the effects of electricity and how it can be controlled and manipulated. This is an essential prerequisite for understanding how to measure it. For girls to overcome this lack of experience they need to be faced with problems whose solutions, as they perceive them, require certain measurements to be taken. In this way girls will select instruments themselves and engage with them purposefully. This is a very different curriculum strategy to simply encouraging practice with instruments.

Another example of the influence of different pastimes relates to girls' well-documented lack of experience of tinkering and modelling activities. A common strategy employed to overcome this is to provide young children with Lego to play with. Teachers, however, are often discouraged by girls' apparent failure to engage with it. When boys play with Lego they do so in a purposeful way. Their play allows them to establish the link between their purposes and the potential of Lego to match them. It is this relationship that girls need a chance to explore. To facilitate this teachers have to identify the problems that girls find motivating in which Lego can serve a useful function. The same holds true for other areas of girls' inexperience. Erickson and Farkas (1987) investigated gender differences in 17-year-old students' responses to science tasks. They found that females only drew on their school experience whereas males were able to draw on a combination of formal experience linked to their everyday 'common-sense' knowledge. This gave the males an advantage in generating scientific explanations. They also report on females' negative responses to science tasks related to their lack of confidence and fear of handling practical equipment such as bunsen burners and electrical circuits. Girls' aversion to electrical matters is a well-established phenomenon which persists beyond schooling.

When faced with unfamiliar situations it is natural to feel uncertain about them. Girls' lack of certain experiences means that they approach some learning situations in science with diffidence and fear. In the APU surveys one assessment included open-ended practical problem-solving tasks set in a variety of contexts. More girls than boys react negatively to overtly scientific investigations. They express a low opinion of their scientific ability and feel generally unable to respond to such tasks. If the same problem is set in an everyday context and such scientific equipment as measuring cylinders and beakers are replaced with measuring jugs and plastic cups these same girls feel competent to tackle it (DES 1989).

However, such a strategy has its drawbacks. Faced with an apparently everyday problem both girls and boys, quite reasonably, seek everyday solutions. Consequently they tend not to control variables or to collect quantified data. This suggests that the confidence of girls in practical work might be enhanced by working initially in everyday contexts but with problems that can only be solved using some degree of rigour. Hence there is a need, understood by the pupil, for scientific equipment.

DIFFERENCES IN WAYS OF EXPERIENCING

Research into gender differences (Chodorov 1978) has related the different patterns of nurturing that many girls and boys receive to the different values and view of relevance that they develop. These lead them to look at the world in different ways. As a result children come to school with learning styles already developed and with an understanding of what is and is not appropriate for them. What they judge to be appropriate they tackle with confidence; what they consider alien they tend to avoid.

Although girls outperform boys overall on practical observation tasks they do less well than boys on observation tasks which have a 'masculine' content – for instance, classifying a variety of different screws. The same situation was noted in pupils' performance on practical investigations. When offered a choice of investigations, girls who were competent problem solvers rejected the one with an electrical content as they 'did not understand electricity'. This was in spite of assurances that the solution did not depend on any specific understanding of electricity. Boys, on the other hand, tended to reject the domestic-orientated tasks. They did so not because they regard the tasks as outside their domain of competence but rather outside science. They have a restricted view of the purposes that their knowledge can and should serve.

The results of the APU science surveys show that, irrespective of what criterion is being assessed, questions which involve such content as health, reproduction, nutrition and domestic situations are generally answered by more girls than boys. The girls also tend to achieve higher scores on these questions. In situations with a more overtly 'masculine' content – for example, building sites, racing tracks, or anything with an electrical content – the converse is true. Similar content effects are clear in other survey findings (see, for example, NAEP, SISS and BCSS). Alienation ultimately leads to underachievement as girls and boys fail to engage with certain learning opportunities.

Evidence available from classroom interaction studies indicates that the differences in the nature of the feedback that girls and boys receive about their classwork lead girls to have lower expectations of success and affect the way pupils interpret future experiences (Dweck *et al.* 1978). For example, when girls and boys were presented with an investigation based on content they had already met in class the boys felt confident that they knew the answer, while the girls were inhibited by the belief that they should know the answer.

Girls and boys do appear to experience practical work differently. Randall (1987) looked at pupil–teacher interactions in workshops and laboratories. She found that girls had more contacts with the teacher and of longer duration than boys. However, the girls' contacts included many requests for help and encouragement about what to do next. Randall found that teachers, rather than building up girls' self-confidence, accepted their dependence on them and thus reinforced their feelings of helplessness. The combination of girls' timidity and boys' bravado leads to girls being marginalised in laboratories. Effects of this kind will lead to a real lack of skills in girls and to a substantial problem in future motivation.

DIFFERENCES IN PROBLEM PERCEPTION

An outcome of children's different images of the world and their places in it is that the problems that girls and boys perceive are often very different given the same circumstances. Typically girls tend to value the circumstances that activities are presented in and consider that they give meaning to the task. They do not abstract issues from their context. Conversely, boys as a group do consider the issues in isolation and judge the content and context to be irrelevant. An example of this effect occurred when pupils designed model boats to go round the world and were investigating how much load they would support. Some of the girls were observed collecting watering cans, spoons and hairdryers. The teachers assumed that they had not 'understood' the problem. However, as the girls explained, if you are going around the world you need to consider the boat's stability in monsoons, whirlpools and gales – conditions they attempted to re-create.

In another situation pupils were investigating which material would keep them warmer when stranded on a mountainside. They were expected to compare how well the materials kept cans of hot water warm. Again, girls were seen to be doing things 'off task'. For example, they cut out prototype coats, dipped the materials in water and blew cold air through them. These girls took seriously the human dilemma presented. It therefore mattered how porous the material was to wind, how waterproof and whether indeed it was suitable for the making of a coat.

These examples of 'girls'' solutions are often judged as failure either because their problems are not recognised or because they are not valued.

Such responses to girls' perceptions of problems mean that not only do they typically not receive feedback about their actions but any feedback they may receive will require them to deny the validity of their own experiences. This is a deeply alienating experience.

Another consequence of boys' and girls' different outlooks on the world is that they pay attention to different features of phenomena. A review of the APU item banks reveals that boys more often focus on mechanical and structural details, which reflects their greater involvement with modelling and handling mechanical gadgets both in and outside school. Girls attend to colours, textures, sounds and smells, data boys typically ignore. Consequently, girls always do better than boys, for example, on tasks concerned with chromatography irrespective of the scientific understanding demanded. It is easy to see how these differences go some way to explaining pupils' levels of achievement in physics and chemistry. Girls can deal with mechanical details just as boys are able, for example, to distinguish smells, but their different experiences result in alternative values and perceptions of relevance. When observing or interpreting phenomena pupils will deal with different selections of data unless teachers are alert to these effects.

Earlier mention was made of pupils designing model boats to go round the world. This task, along with one asking for the design of a new vehicle, was given to pupils aged from 8 to 15. The pupils' designs covered a wide range but there were striking differences between those of boys and girls. The majority of the boats designed by primary and lower secondary school boys were powerboats or battleships of some kind or other. The detail the boys included varied but generally there was elaborate weaponry and next to no living facilities. Other features included detailed mechanisms for movement, navigation and waste disposal. The girls' boats were generally cruisers with a total absence of weaponry and a great deal of detail about living quarters and requirements, including food supplies and cleaning materials (notably absent from the boys' designs). Very few of the girls' designs included any mechanistic detail.

The choice of vehicle design and purpose also varied for girls and boys. Many boys chose army-type vehicles, 'secret' agent transport or sportscars. The girls mainly chose family cars for travelling, agricultural machines or children's play vehicles. The detail the pupils focused on was generally the same as before. Where boys and girls chose the same type of vehicle they still differed in their main design function. For example, the girls' pram design dealt with improving efficiency and safety. The boys' pram was computerised to allow infants to be transported without an accompanying adult.

These very different perceptions of the same problem reflect the way girls are encouraged to be concerned with everyday human needs. It was noteworthy that when the pupils had to focus on an aspect of their design the boys had few difficulties abandoning their initial design details. The girls, however, retained their details, which often made it difficult for them to pursue the teachers' focused investigation.

If a problem is perceived to be about human needs then it is not a simple matter to reject that perception and to focus on a more artificial concern, that is the learning of a specific subject outcome. Yet this is commonly assumed to be unproblematic in science. Furthermore, an ability to do this may only reflect a limited and uncritical view of problems and problem-solving strategies. All pupils will benefit if some attempt is made to relate the focus to the larger problem and to discuss individual perspectives of relevance.

PUPIL-FRIENDLY PRACTICAL WORK?

Rennie (1987), reporting on a study of 13-year-olds in Western Australia, found that the relative inexperience of girls can be overcome in an activity-orientated style of science teaching. Similarly, the science curriculum of Thailand which appears to support girls' learning is described as activity-based, learner-centred, and focused on novel aspects of enquiry and discovery. Girls performed at a higher level than boys across the ages on the APU observation tests. The tasks used in these tests also tend to be novel and allow pupils to test out their own hypotheses before reaching a conclusion. It was found that girls' performance was significantly higher than boys' on such tasks, but particularly so when the tasks were both active and open. Furthermore, the nature of the task can override the content effects discussed earlier. For example, an observation task involving various electrical components in a circuit was popular with boys but not with girls. Boys' performance was also significantly higher than girls. Yet when the performance of girls who liked the type of task, in spite of the content, was compared with boys who similarly liked the task there were no gender differences in performance. These findings lend some support to the view of what a gender-inclusive science curriculum might be like.

It is often concluded from discussions of gender differences that girls need to address problems that reflect their social concerns. Yet the observation tasks described are not untypical science examples. It is important here to distinguish between accessibility and conditions for learning generally. The tasks used in the APU study are accessible because they allow pupils to formulate and test their own hypotheses. It is up to the pupils to accept or reject them on the basis of their own data. It is the pupils' views of relevance that prevail. However, in learning situations, if the new knowledge pupils acquire is to be linked to their existing knowledge then problems do need to be set in the context of human experience and needs. These provide the framework for girls to make sense of the problems posed and the motivation and purpose they need to continue with the complexity of learning in science. Of course, the same should obtain for boys.

SUMMARY

Practical work can play a crucial role in combating gender differences. As the discussion has pointed out, it matters what type of practical work is encouraged. Strategies for changing the aims and nature of science learning to take account of gender differences must be applied thoughtfully. There is little point in attempting to extend the accessibility of science if in the process other groups of pupils become alienated. Classroom strategies will have to take account of boys' and girls' present preferred styles of working and interests as well as providing opportunities for them to reflect critically on them. Many of the tactics that need to be employed to facilitate girls' scientific learning are merely examples of good teaching practice anyway – for example, setting tasks that allow all pupils to express their interests and understandings in a manner that is appropriate for them. However, it follows that tasks of this kind must be fairly broad and general, and therefore that pupils will perceive different problems and different solutions within them. Of course, this has always been the classroom reality but the intention now is to make it an explicit and understood aspect of teaching practice. Consequently, there will be a need to adopt a more flexible approach to curriculum planning. A much broader view of the potential learning outcomes in any one lesson or module will have to be accepted by teachers. Similarly, consideration will have to be given to the numerous learning pathways that pupils can follow in acquiring particular scientific understanding. This is necessary because teachers have to focus pupils' learning and need to be aware of when and how to do this in a way that enables pupils to see the point of the focus and thus continue with their learning. The teacher's role will be even more demanding than at present if such strategies are adopted. On the plus side they will be rewarded by the commitment and achievements of pupils who hitherto have found it difficult to make sense of science.

REFERENCES

Chodorov, N. (1978). *The Reproduction of Mothering*. Berkeley, University of California Press.

Department of Education and Science (1988). *Science in Schools Age 15. Review Report*. London, DES.

Department of Education and Science (1989). *Science in Schools Age 13. Review Report*. London, DES.

Dweck, C. *et al*. (1978). 'Sex differences in learnt helplessness: the contingencies of evaluative feedback in the classroom', *Developmental Psychology*, **14**, 268–76.

Erickson, G. and Farkas, S. (1987). 'Prior experience: a factor which may contribute to male dominance in science'. Contributions to the Fourth GASAT Conference 2, Michigan, USA.

Harding, J., Hildebrand, G. and Klainin, S. (1988). 'International concerns in gender and science/technology', *Educational Review*, **40**, 185–93.

Hobbs, E.D., Bolt, W.B., Erickson, G., Quelch, T.P. and Sieban, B.A. (1979). *British Columbia Science Assessment (1978)*, General Report, Vol. 1. Victoria, BC, Ministry of Education.

Humrich, E. (1987). 'Girls in science: US and Japan'. Contributions to the Fourth GASAT Conference 1, Michigan, USA.

Johnson, S. and Murphy, P. (1986). *Girls and Physics*. London, DES.

Kelly, A. (1981). 'Sex differences in science achievement' in Kelly, A. (ed.), *The Missing Half*. Manchester, Manchester University Press.

Kelly, A. (1987). 'Does that train set matter? Scientific hobbies and science achievement and choice'. Contributions to the Fourth GASAT Conference 1, Michigan, USA.

Murphy, P. and Gott, R. (1984). *Science Assessment Framework Age 13 and 15*, Science Report for Teachers: 2. ASE

National Assessment of Educational Progress (1978). *Science Achievement in the Schools*. A summary of results from the 1976–77 National Assessment of Science, Washington Education Commission of The States, Washington DC.

Omerod, M.B. (1981). 'Factors differentially affecting the science subject preferences, choices and attitudes of girls and boys' in Kelly, A. (ed.), *The Missing Half*. Manchester, Manchester University Press.

Randall, G.J. (1987). 'Gender differences in pupil–teacher interactions in workshops and laboratories' in Weiner, G. and Arnot, M. (eds), *Gender under Scrutiny*. Milton Keynes, Open University Press.

Rennie, L.J. (1987). 'Out of school science: are gender differences related to subsequent attitudes and achievement in science?'. Contributions to the Fourth GASAT Conference 2, Michigan, USA.

Tamir, P. (1989). 'Gender differences in science education as revealed by the Second International Science Study'. Contributions to the Fifth GASAT Conference, Haifa, Israel.

Chapter 14

Teaching chemistry to pupils for whom English is a second language

Maggie Farrar

INTRODUCTION

The science laboratory is a linguistically rich environment. Not only are pupils exposed to a wealth of vocabulary they are also engaged on a process of discovery which requires them to hypothesise, predict, observe, describe and draw conclusions. Much of what goes on in a chemistry lesson is observable and therefore concrete. The language used to describe chemical processes and the new vocabulary used by pupils in a chemistry laboratory means that science is in fact a second language to most pupils.

This chapter will demonstrate how placing language at the forefront of your science teaching will lead to an enhanced learning experience for all pupils including those who are bilingual.

Let us begin by looking at the pupils. Who are our bilingual learners and what are their needs? Pupils who are bilingual learners may or may not have studied science in another country. They may or may not be literate in their first language and their individual competence in speaking, reading and writing in English will probably be at dissimilar levels.

Before a bilingual pupil joins your class you need to find out:

- how long the pupil has been in England;
- what the pupil's previous educational experience is;
- if the pupil is literate in his or her mother tongue;
- what the pupil's level of English is.

I will use as examples three bilingual children who are at differing stages in their language development and look at how their needs might manifest themselves in the laboratory and how we as teachers can support them.

SUPPORTING THE PUPIL

Asma

Asma is a 12-year-old pupil who has just arrived in this country from Bangladesh. She has completed two classes in primary school in Bangladesh. She speaks Sylheti, a dialect of Bengali, and is not literate in Bengali. She knows how to write her name, the name of her school, and she can count up to twenty in English. She is beginning to become familiar with basic classroom vocabulary 'pen, pencil, bag, diary, etc.'. She will speak Bengali in a small group and has therefore been placed in a working group with another Bengali speaker. She is not confident about using English.

Many pupils go through a 'period of silence' when they first come to school in England. She should not be forced to speak until she is ready, but teachers need to be aware that the process of language acquisition has begun – she is already assimilating all the language patterns she is hearing around her.

Supporting Asma's learning in science

It is very easy as a teacher with a large demanding class to disengage from a pupil such as Asma who does not speak to you or demand your attention. During the lesson ask her to give out paper, clean the blackboard and collect homework. Opportunities for a non-verbal response will enable her to communicate with you without speech. It will allow her to feel she belongs. When she begins to respond verbally she may do so with one- or two-word requests. Always give her the model of the language she is seeking. For example, if she comes up to you with a request 'paper Miss', say to her 'You want another *piece of paper* Asma, here you are, here's another piece of paper'. *Every linguistic exchange is an opportunity to teach language.*

Similarly when she begins to answer questions give her the opportunity to respond by simple yes/no answers. Asking other pupils to think of and ask these questions is a useful learning exercise which involves the whole class.

Find ways of reinforcing new language. Put labelled pictures or photographs of apparatus on the wall. Give her five new words on cards to take home to learn for homework. Let her match the words with the apparatus when she comes to the next class. Let her build up this stock of cards and when she becomes a little more confident let her:

- turn over one card at a time and look at it for a few seconds;
- encourage her to look at the whole word and take a picture of it in her mind;
- then ask her to turn the card face down and to write the word from memory;
- she can then look at the card and check her attempt.

Reading

If the class are reading a complex text, give her five to ten vocabulary items (words) on cards and ask her to go through the text and see how many times she can find them. This is a useful exercise to help her to recognise the shapes of letters and words. If the text is disposable ask her to underline certain words in certain colours – a useful strategy for teaching and reinforcing colour. Talk to her about the text, using questions such as:

'Where is the title? Can you point to it?'
'How many words are in it? Write the number down.'
'How many paragraphs are there? Number them.'
'In which paragraph can you find this sentence . . .?'

It will be useful at this stage to build-up your own store of texts on tape. Another pupil could tape a text for homework. This is a useful learning activity, especially if you ask them to tape their own summary at the end of the tape giving the gist of the text or the main learning points of the lesson. If Asma has a cassette player at home let her take tapes home. Even though not all the language will be comprehensible she will still be having exposure to language patterns and scientific terminology which she can listen to over and over again. It may be worth investing in a personal stereo for class use also. Let her listen to the tape when the rest of the class are involved in a silent individual activity.

Speaking

Use what she is doing to reinforce language. Take care to use consistent language and when you ask her questions initially you will need to supply both the question and the answer, e.g.

'What are you doing Asma? I'm boiling water.'
'What is this? It's a Bunsen burner.'

She may want to repeat this and speak with you. At this stage pupils can get very confused with the 'I'/'you' distinction and will repeat whatever you say. It is important that what they say is true *for them*, so as the teacher I usually stand behind the pupil and thus become *part of them* as I say, 'I'm boiling water'.

Remember, however, that the best models of language use she will have contact with will be her English-speaking monolingual and bilingual peers. Make sure she is not isolated from them.

Writing

Give her plenty of chances to do some writing and therefore record what she is learning. At this early stage in language development simple copying will be most appropriate. You can check her level of scientific comprehension by giving her, for example, diagrams and labels to match and copy, or sentences to copy with gaps to fill in. This can be made more controlled by giving her the number of dashes to indicate the number of letters in the missing words, with the missing words given under the sentences, e.g.

Today I boiled _____ .
First I put on my safety _____ .
Then I put the _____ _____ on the mat.

water   Bunsen burner   goggles

She can be supported in making a record of the lesson or writing up an experiment by giving her the sequence of events jumbled up on paper. Then give her the ordered sequence on a tape. By using the sounds of the words on the tape and matching the sound to the word she can make a record of her learning.

It would be useful at this stage to ask Asma to begin her own personal dictionary of scientific terms (so helping her to learn the alphabet). Any words she has located in a text or used in writing can be added to it.

Teacher expectations

At this stage Asma should understand about safety in the laboratory. She should understand the geography of the laboratory and where to find things. This can be reinforced by always making sure she collects her own equipment and puts it away. She should be learning the names of basic apparatus and basic vocabulary associated with the area of the syllabus she is working on.

Tho

Tho is a Vietnamese speaker who has been at secondary school in England for one year. He is literate in Vietnamese and studied science at school in Vietnam before coming to England. He can communicate quite well orally, but he will discuss work more readily in a small group than in a class. He will need support to comprehend scientific texts and his writing, if freely set, will contain many grammatical and spelling errors.

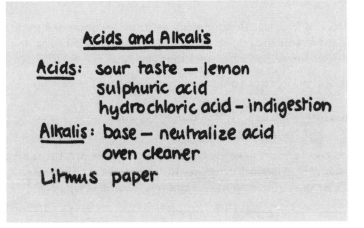

Acids and Alkalis

Acids: sour taste — lemon
        sulphuric acid
        hydrochloric acid - indigestion
Alkalis: base — neutralize acid
        oven cleaner
Litmus paper

Figure 14.1 Introducing a topic on acids and alkalis

Supporting Tho's learning in science

When he listens to you presenting a new topic it will help him if key phrases are written on the blackboard to guide his listening. If you are introducing a topic on acids and alkalis the blackboard summary might look like Figure 14.1.

Another day you might begin a new topic by asking pupils to brainstorm all the things they already know about a particular topic. It will also help Tho if your exposition is broken up into 3 to 5 minute slots. This will give the class a chance to articulate new information and put it in their own words.

After presenting or reinforcing new concepts, or summing up after a practical lesson, ask the class to 'retell' what you have been saying. Put keywords on the blackboard as the class reflects on what they have learnt. One member of the class can then use all the keywords to give a summary, or pupils can have a go at doing this in a less exposed environment, e.g. a small group.

Repetition and retelling will help Tho to make new knowledge 'his own', so he will be more likely to internalise and remember it. This also helps him with new vocabulary items whose pronunciation may be problematic. The keywords and phrases could then be copied down by all the pupils and a summary written for homework.

Speaking

At this stage in language development, your observation of a pupil's practical work gives you the opportunity to stretch the pupil's manipulation of language structures. Ask basic questions such as:

'What do you think is going to happen?' (future tense)
'What's happening?' (present continuous)
'What's just happened?' (present perfect)
'Did the same thing happen last week?' (past)

The laboratory gives teachers the perfect context for practising some of the more difficult grammatical structures for a pupil such as Tho to grasp. When he responds, your role is to model and reinforce new language:

TEACHER: 'What's going to happen?'
THO: 'It change colour to blue.'
TEACHER: 'That's right, it's going to change colour from white to blue, isn't it. What's going to happen?'
THO: 'It's going to change colour from white to blue.'

Reading

It will help Tho if the reading he has to do is about an activity he has just done so he can place it in a concrete framework in his mind. Tho should also be given strategies to help him to read the text with comprehension. Ask him to think about the title and to predict what the text might be about. Perhaps a group may like to brainstorm all the words they think might appear in the text. Then ask him to locate the words in the text. Give him the text cut up into paragraphs/phrases and stuck on to cards and ask him in his group to resequence the text. If the text is very complex, give each member of the group the piece of text and ask them to tell each other what their piece is about before sequencing it. This strategy is perfect for giving bilingual learners like Tho access to a whole text while only requiring them to read a small part of it. This activity can be made more complex by writing keywords from the text on the back of each card (as illustrated in Figure 14.2) and asking pupils to share the information on their card using these keywords only.

Once the text has been reassembled, his understanding of it can be checked by the following strategy:

– Formulate a number of true and false sentences and ask him to mark them 'T' or 'F' according to his understanding of the text.
– Ask him to locate key sentences and vocabulary in the text which answer questions such as:
     'Which sentence tells you that . . .?'

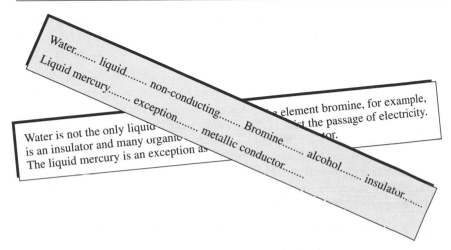

Figure 14.2 A piece of the text with keywords on the back

'Which word means . . .?'
'Which is the most important sentence in the text?'
'Which sentence do you find the most difficult?'

His scientific vocabulary can be increased by asking him to write down five new words from the text and to place them in order of how difficult he thinks they are to (i) explain, (ii) spell, (iii) say, etc.

Writing

If Tho is expected to write freely his work will contain errors. His writing can be supported by the following:

1 Ask him to sequence sentences (or skeleton sentences) to form the basis of the write-up of an experiment.
2 Give him a substitution table (such as the one illustrated in Figure 14.3) to enable him to write scientifically and linguistically correct sentences. Substitution tables are useful as they give the pupil all the words they need to write sentences, but the correct choice of words depends on their understanding.
3 Give him a model which he can then use as a basis for doing his own writing. In the following example a text which describes how to make salt from rock salt is used as a model for writing up the process of an experiment.

   In order to make salt from rock salt we used the following apparatus. A pestle and mortar, a measuring cylinder, a spatula, a Bunsen burner, a beaker, a filter funnel and filter paper. First of all we took a piece of rock salt and ground it to powder with the pestle and mortar. Then we placed the ground rock salt in a beaker. Next we measured 100 cm³ of water into a measuring cylinder and added this to the beaker. After that we . . .

Pupils in a class, as well as Tho, can be asked to underline all the verbs in one colour and all the words that sequence events (first of all, then, next, after that, etc.) in another colour. They are then asked to use these words when they write up their own experiment. If the pupils are doing a different experiment they can be asked to underline all the words in the model text that they think they will use when writing up their own experiment. This is especially useful when pupils are beginning to use the passive voice when writing up experiments. When Tho writes freely, his writing (as illustrated in Figure 14.4) can be responded to positively in a number of ways.

As a science teacher you could comment on:

- his degree of scientific understanding (tick and note correct descriptions of scientific processes and use of terminology);
- his ability to sequence events in a logical order;
- how accurately he has copied language from the board, text or worksheet;

Sugar Orange juice	are	
Sand Glass	is	soluble in water.
Tea leaves Wood	isn't	
Coffee Chalk	aren't	

Figure 14.3 A substitution task

First I put water in to a beaker about ¾. Then I burn the bunsen burner or on and put place the beaker on and leave it for to boil it. When it start to bubble, I turn the bunsen burner off and with a tweezers I clip the leaf into boiling water for a few second to kill.

Figure 14.4 An example of Tho's writing

– his use of grammatical structures when writing up an experiment – how many can he manipulate?

Teacher expectations

In many ways a pupil like Tho is more vulnerable to underachievement than Asma. Because of the emphasis on practical work Tho will probably be exhibiting more understanding in science than in other areas of the curriculum. It is easy for teachers to presume that pupils such as Tho are competent because of their oral ability. They overlook the fact that support and help is still needed, particularly in the areas of reading and writing. A lack of support at this stage in these areas can lead to progress in reading and writing reaching a 'plateau' and in particular for errors in writing to become internalised through habitual use.

Yesim

Yesim is a Turkish speaker who has been in England for four years. She is fluent in Turkish and her oral ability in English is approaching that of her English-speaking peers.

Supporting Yesim's learning in science

All the strategies described previously for Asma and Tho will help Yesim. As a more fluent language user, she should be able to internalise and remember more complex new language and concepts but will need to have them reinforced and be reminded of them. Some strategies which are useful for developing the scientific vocabulary of all pupils in a class are as follows:

1 Write new vocabulary items on the blackboard and ask pupils to shut their eyes while you rub one off. When they open their eyes, ask them to guess which item is missing. This can be varied by asking the class to look at the blackboard for 15 seconds, and then covering it up. Then ask the pupils to work in groups to see how many items they can remember.
2 Write vocabulary from the previous lesson on the blackboard. As pupils come in, ask them to underline any word they have forgotten the meaning of. This helps you to see at a glance how much revision you need to do.
3 Some pupils benefit from words being broken up into syllables, especially the names of elements which many pupils, not only bilingual pupils, find difficult to read. Syllables can be printed on to cards which are used by pupils to build up the names of elements, and then these are matched with their symbol, as in the illustration overleaf.

Each of these activities can be used as a quick warm up at the beginning of a lesson, or to finish a lesson. Their value is that they ensure pupils are repeating vocabulary over and over again as they get caught up in the activity.

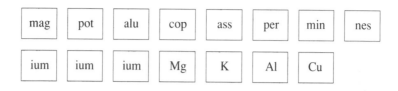

Reading

When Yesim is reading she will benefit from exposure to complex texts but with support available. She will be unable to 'read and make notes' without resorting to a degree of copying. The following strategies will support her note taking.

Give Yesim headings and keywords with which to make notes, e.g. ask her to read a text about reactivity. When she has finished, ask her to close the book and give her headings and keywords to use to make notes on what she has read. When she has finished ask her to read the text again to see if there's anything she's missed out.

Headings	*Keywords*
Reactivity – what is it?	metals / corrode / don't magnesium / reactive gold / unreactive / water pipes
Reactions with water	magnesium / steam oxygen / steam / hydrogen gas
Reactions with air	magnesium / zinc / layer / oxide damp air / iron magnesium / white magnesium oxide iron filings / sparklers

Another way to facilitate note taking is to ask her to read a section of the text and pick out the ten most important words. Take the text away and ask her to use the keywords she has chosen to make a summary. Alternatively, ask the class to pick out keywords for each other. This can lead to a lively debate about language and meaning as the pupils ask each other why particular keywords were chosen and not others.

Writing

It is sometimes assumed that pupils such as Yesim should be able to write without support. Teachers then spend a large amount of their time correcting errors in the writing. The writing support previously suggested will help Yesim, as will the following strategies which focus on spelling.

Ask Yesim to look at her own work and to:

- underline in blue all the sentences/words she is sure are correct;
- underline in red all the sentences/words she is not too sure of, but which she thinks are almost right;
- underline in green all the sentences/words she thinks she has got wrong.

When Yesim is given new vocabulary, e.g. the names of elements, ask her to:

- underline the section of a word she thinks is going to 'trip her up', e.g. *hydr*ogen;
- think of words with the same spelling pattern, e.g. sodium, potassium, magnesium;
- look for words inside words, e.g. sul*phide*/va*pour*.

CONCLUSION

Having looked at strategies for accessing scientific language let us now summarise what kind of chemistry lesson is most accessible to a bilingual learner and thus encourages the development of language.

As teachers we need to plan chemistry lessons that:

- are group orientated;
- encourage talk;
- encourage pupils to 'talk about' their learning throughout the practical activities;
- value the use of the mother tongue;
- give bilingual pupils access to monolingual peers' language;
- break up teacher presentation and allow pupils to 'make it their own';
- have a variety of reading and writing tasks which are accessible for all pupils;
- focus on language, especially new vocabulary, and actively teach and reinforce it;
- allow for language experimentation lessons where making errors is an acceptable part of learning.

Glancing down this list you will probably be saying to yourself – but surely this is just good teaching? Yes, it is. A good lesson, well delivered with the above elements in it, *is a good language lesson*. It will deliver what all bilingual pupils need – the opportunity to develop their English language competence within the context of other learning.

SUPPORTING THE TEACHER

Teaching large groups with differing needs can sometimes seem like a daunting task. What other support is available to you and your pupils?

The learning environment

Are you making the most of your learning environment? Look round your laboratory and ask yourself:

1 Where is my blackboard? Can all the pupils see it? What does it look like at the end of the lesson? Is there an area of my blackboard specifically reserved for new language? After I've given oral instructions do I write them up on the blackboard as *visual reinforcement*?
2 How are the benches grouped? Where do I place myself in relation to them during the presentation stage/the practical stage? Where are the bilingual pupils sitting? What kind of language do they have access to in their groups?
3 What's on the walls?
   – keywords?
   – an *aide-mémoire* for the pupils of common errors?
   – models of good work?
   – visual reinforcement of new ideas?
   – language used regularly for hypothesising and predicting, e.g. 'I think', 'perhaps', 'maybe', 'what if'?
4 What's on the benches besides equipment? Are there dictionaries or a thesaurus?
5 Is there a common code of conduct that is visible to the pupils? For example, 'Always ask at least three other people in the room your question before you ask me.'
6 Is a marking scheme for both written and practical tasks displayed to allow pupils to comment on each other's work?
7 Is the lesson agenda on the wall? Do pupils know what the purpose of the lesson is? Is your lesson plan displayed? Do the pupils know what's going to happen in the lesson and how much time they have for particular activities?

Pupils internalise a lot of language as they gaze around the room. The more you can use this to reinforce the language you expect them to use in chemistry, the more beneficial it will be.

The department

Does your department have a policy on supporting bilingual pupils? As a member of a department you need to be able to draw on the support of your colleagues. A discussion about policy could centre on the following questions:

1 How do we identify the needs of bilingual pupils? How do we find out about their past learning experiences in science?
2 How do we ensure that beginner bilingual pupils understand enough basic scientific vocabulary and have the basic skills to operate safely in a laboratory? (A member of the department could be given specific responsibility for assessing bilingual pupils' basic scientific skills on entry, as well as devising and operating a short induction course to science.)
3 What is our grouping policy? Is it by ability, by language, by friendship/pupil choice?
4 What other support can we draw on in school and how do we wish to work in partnership with these staff, e.g. ESL teachers/teachers responsible for pupils with special needs?

   Setting up partnership teaching with members of the learning support departments is a very rewarding experience for both departments if it is done effectively. For it to succeed, it is vital that discussion between the teachers involved, to clarify roles in the classroom, takes place before the work begins.

   - Will you wish to work collaboratively with both teachers being equally responsible for presenting the lesson, setting and marking homework, discipline and classroom management, etc.?
   - Do you want the support teacher to focus on a number of individuals in the classroom only and therefore to work in a support capacity making sure that the curriculum is accessible to these targeted pupils?
   - Who are the pupils who will be targeted by the support teacher and what learning targets will be set for them?
   - What is the aim in working together? Is it to develop a particular skill, e.g. writing up experiments, developing vocabulary or developing language skills to enable the pupils to take part in pupil-centred investigative work?
   - How will the partnership be evaluated and at what stage – after half a term or a full term?
   - How will the materials you have devised in partnership and the new insights gained in teaching and learning in science be fed back to your respective departments?
   - What is the agreed procedure if either of you are dissatisfied with the partnership?

5 What does it mean for us as science teachers to say that *all* pupils are our responsibility? What staff development needs emerge from this? How can we share ideas and strategies for supporting bilingual pupils in the laboratory?

How you teach and how you engage pupils in their own learning is central to how accessible the curriculum is for those pupils. A school and a department can either produce or reduce language and learning difficulties. Thinking about the above questions will give you a starting point.

Part VI

Science education
A debate

Chapter 15

Redefining and reorienting practical work in school science

Derek Hodson

LEARNING ABOUT SCIENTIFIC PRACTICE

It is generally agreed that one of the major goals of science education is to bring about an understanding of the processes of science. In this context, 'processes of science' does not mean the skills of carrying out particular laboratory operations (such as using a burette, microscope or potentiometer), but the skills of carrying out the 'strategic' processes of science (such as hypothesising, inferring, designing experiments, interpreting data). In recent years there has been a tendency, in some quarters, to give such priority to the processes of science that content has come to be regarded as relatively unimportant. Underpinning such an approach to the teaching of science are a number of assumptions:

1 Scientific processes are clearly definable and discrete. They can be used independently of each other.
2 Processes are content free. They precede concepts, in the sense that their use leads to the discovery of new knowledge.
3 Process skills are generalisable, transferable from one context to another and readily applicable in any context.

Consideration of the philosophical and psychological issues raised by the process-led science movement, discussed at some length by Millar and Driver[1] and in the fairly recent collection of essays edited by Wellington[2] is outside the scope of this chapter. What is under consideration here is the assumption that the goal of understanding the processes by which scientists generate new knowledge is best achieved by engaging children in conventional practical work. Careful perusal of the lists of processes of science generated by curriculum projects such as *Warwick Process Science*[3] and *Science in Process*[4] reveals that many might be better learnt and developed by methods other than laboratory work. Teaching techniques employing computer simulations and databases – and any other methods that enable attention to be focused on abstract conceptual issues – may be better suited to the fostering of such aspects of scientific creativity as hypothesis construction and experimental design.

Computer simulations provide a 'safe environment' in which students themselves can engage in these more creative aspects of science. Through such experiences, students learn much more about the concepts and phenomena under investigation (because they have more opportunity to manipulate ideas), they acquire some of the planning and design skills of the creative scientist, and they learn that science is about people thinking, guessing and trying things that sometimes work and sometimes fail. For example, experiments in genetics require the selective breeding of several generations of an organism in order to observe the appearance, or not, of certain characteristics. Even with rapidly maturing insects like fruit flies, a real investigation lasts several weeks and requires experimental skills that are only incidental to the course as a whole. Computer simulations enable several genetic variations, in several species, to be studied within a single lesson. CATLAB,[5] for example, enables students to generate a series of hypotheses relating to the inheritance of coat colour and pattern in domestic cats, and to vary the 'experimental conditions' for a breeding programme in order to produce data for testing their hypotheses.

Computerised databases allow students to make predictions or to speculate about relationships, and to check them against the 'facts' quickly, reliably and in a secure and private learning environment. They provide opportunities for students to explore ideas, to construct and reconstruct knowledge, to hypothesise and test *for* themselves and *by* themselves, free from the restrictions of worksheets and teacher directions. They have made it possible – maybe for the first time – for learners to investigate thoroughly their own questions about a whole range of things, without the constraints imposed by inadequate laboratory facilities, underdeveloped practical skills, insufficient time and materials available, or considerations of personal safety. For example, PERIODIC PROPERTIES[6] enables learners to hypothesise about trends in chemical behaviour, across periods and down groups, and to check out their predictions quickly and reliably. All distractions and pedagogic noise are eliminated. There is no need to struggle with difficult apparatus and wayward materials! By investigating the periodicity of various properties, students develop a deeper understanding of electronic structure and the factors affecting chemical reactivity and bonding.

By using the computer as a tool to find answers to their own questions, students begin to develop real problem-solving and enquiry skills. They learn to identify problems that are significant, worth investigating and susceptible to systematic enquiry. They learn to plan investigative strategies and to check and refine procedures. At the same time, they learn that some questions and problems do not have a unique solution or right answer. Some solutions are tentative and in need of refinement, requiring further information or demanding further enquiry; some are compromises between conflicting values and considerations. Thus, computer databases have the potential, in the hands of skilled teachers, to assist students to develop a wide range of cognitive skills, enquiry procedures and attitudes that are exceedingly difficult to teach in other ways.

Database management systems, which enable students to construct and manipulate their own databases, may furnish even more powerful learning opportunities than those provided by pre-compiled databases. As soon as students begin to compile and use their own databases, they begin to address questions such as 'What information should we record?' 'How should we code it and present it?' 'What means of cross-referencing should we employ?' Questions such as these highlight conceptual relationships that might otherwise remain hidden, and impress on learners that successful classification of information depends on the utilisation of theoretically valid criteria, and that the same things can be classified in several different ways, according to purpose. Database construction is all about decision making, and the decisions are made in the light of theoretical considerations that heighten and deepen conceptual understanding, as this comment from a student involved in the construction of a database on New Zealand birds reveals.

> The books we use can only give us the facts and don't muddle the information up. When we use the computer we can get different information and see how everything fits together. We'd never be able to find out this sort of stuff if we only had books.[7]

It's 'muddling the information up', in ways that the student considers significant, that is the key to learning. To achieve that, learners must engage in certain activities.

- Decide on significant criteria for categorising entities, phenomena and events – i.e. establish theoretical priorities.
- Locate sources of data.
- Gather data and resolve conflicts and discrepancies.
- Organise and enter data, paying attention to format, screen layout, etc.
- Test, debug and revise the data files to ensure easy, flexible and appropriate access to data.

In constructing databases, students gain real insight into the way knowledge is structured and organised. By redirecting attention from the collection of 'raw data' towards the organisation of information, students are required to identify criteria they believe are scientifically significant and relevant to the purposes they have in constructing the database. Thus, they engage in a kind of theory building – the very pinnacle of scientific creativity.

What is unique to this kind of CAL is that there is no 'hidden knowledge' in the computer program. On the contrary, knowledge is located in the mind of the learner, and the computer is used by the learner to explore, modify and develop that knowledge. In other words, the starting point is the learner's existing knowledge, and the learning process is the reconstruction of that personal understanding in the light of feedback from the database. Viewed in this way, database learning fits perfectly into a constructivist psychology of learning and the current emphasis on affective goals and student control of learning. In the past, we have often constrained the development of conceptual insight and curtailed the development of problem-solving skills and scientific creativity by guiding students too closely through learning tasks, by identifying problems before students encounter them and by frequently supplying the 'best' solution. Databases provide a unique opportunity for allowing students to proceed unfettered into the world of scientific problem solving and the exploration of ideas.

In many respects, then, computer-based practical work is superior to bench work, which is expensive (both in terms of capital investment and consumables), needs a lot of laboratory space, requires a large time allocation and is often dirty. To be effective, bench work requires technician support that is often not available to science teachers in countries outside Europe and North America. Most important of all, it frequently 'doesn't work', in the sense that inexperienced children obtain erroneous and confusing results that do little to enhance understanding, especially if the various possibilities have not been thought about in advance. Often the demands on students' manipulative and organisational skills are such that they act as a considerable barrier to learning. Students are frequently put in the position where they have to understand the problem and the experimental procedure (neither of which they have been consulted about), assemble the relevant theoretical perspective (with only minimal assistance from the teacher), read, comprehend and follow the experimental directions, handle the apparatus, collect the data, recognise the difference between 'results obtained' and 'results that should have been obtained', interpret the results, write an account of the experiment (in a curiously obscure and formal language), and all the time ensure that they get along well with their partners. In short laboratory work – as presently practised – has too many unnecessary barriers to learning (too much pedagogic noise). Often that noise can be reduced by better planning, or eliminated altogether by the adoption of alternative active learning methods.

WHITHER LABORATORY BENCH WORK?

None of the foregoing is intended to be an argument for the total replacement of laboratory bench work by alternative learning methods. The key question is not so much whether laboratory bench work should be employed, but how it should be used to best effect. Just as there are aspects of science education for which laboratory work is unsuited, so there are aspects for which bench work is ideally suited and for which there is probably no sensible alternative. One of the more obvious concerns the acquisition of laboratory bench skills. Clearly, CAL is no substitute for hands-on experience with real apparatus. No one becomes proficient in the use of a burette by running a computer-simulated titration! A much more significant role for bench work concerns concept development, understanding of the nature of scientific enquiry and the key issue of personalisation of learning which constitutes both a complex prerequisite for engaging students in doing science for themselves and the educational outcome that justifies doing so. Prior to that, however, and a crucial part of laying a solid foundation of personal experience, is what Woolnough and Allsop[8] refer to as 'getting a feel for phenomena'.

If education in science is about making sense of the physical world in which we live, a first step in the process must be familiarisation with that world. Bench work may be the only way of experiencing at first hand the attraction and repulsion of a magnet or the smell of a gas. The direct experience of chemical changes (such as burning magnesium), the handling and care of living organisms, and the use of instruments that extend our senses (such as telescopes and microscopes) are other aspects of familiarisation with the world around us that cannot be achieved in any other way. So, in this respect, bench work is crucial. It is not enough just to read about green gases and blue crystals, about light bending as it passes through a prism, about electric currents creating magnetic fields. Learners need to see these things, to experience phenomena directly, to handle real objects for themselves. White[9] argues that the provision of such first-hand experiences (which he refers to as 'episodes') is the principal purpose of practical work and the means whereby learning is enhanced by establishing crucial links to 'the propositions and intellectual skills that are acquired in more teacher-centred lessons'.

NOTES

1 Millar, R. and R. Driver, 'Beyond processes', *Stud. Sci. Educ.*, 1987, **14**, 33–62.
2 Wellington, J. (ed.), *Skills and Processes in Science Education* (Routledge, 1989).
3 Screen, P., *Warwick Process Science* (Ashford Press, 1986).
4 ILEA, *Science in Process* (Heinemann, 1987).
5 Simmons, P.E. and V.N. Lunetta, 'CATLAB – a learning cycle approach', *Am. Biol. Teach.*, 1987, **49**, 107–9.
6 PERIODIC PROPERTIES is available from Hodder & Stoughton.
7 Anderson, B., 'A database at school', *CCDU Newsletter*, 1985, **6**, 30–3.
8 Woolnough, B. and T. Allsop, *Practical Work in Science* (Cambridge University Press, 1985).
9 White, R.T., 'Episodes, and the purpose and conduct of practical work', in B.E. Woolnough (ed.), *Practical Science* (Open University Press, 1991), 78–86.

Chapter 16

What is 'scientific method' and can it be taught?

Robin Millar

INTRODUCTION

The emphasis on science as process is endorsed by the Department of Education and Science Policy Statement which asserts that 'the essential characteristic of education in science is that it introduces pupils to the methods of science' (DES 1985a: 7). It goes on to outline this method as a series of steps beginning with observation, leading via classification to the drawing of inferences and the formulation of hypotheses ('seeking patterns'), and culminating in experimental testing.

This view of science method as a set of discrete 'processes' underpins several recent curriculum packages. The Introduction to *Warwick Process Science* (Screen 1986a, b) lists the processes 'made explicit' in the course as: observing, inferring, classifying, predicting, controlling variables, and hypothesising. *Science in Process* (ILEA 1987) draws attention to the following 'process skills': applying, interpreting, classifying, investigating, evaluating, observing, experimenting, predicting, hypothesising, raising questions, and inferring. *Nuffield 11–13* (1986) distinguishes 'processes' and 'skills', listing as 'skills to be developed': handling equipment, observing, patterning, communicating, designing investigations and experiments, and mental modelling. Notes on what is meant by 'patterning' indicate (*Nuffield 11–13, Teachers' Guide I* 1986: 17) that it includes classifying and predicting; 'designing investigations' incorporates raising questions, hypothesising, and controlling variables.

Despite the variations in terminology (processes, skills, process skills), there is clearly substantial common ground here. Many of the 'processes' occur in all the lists; some which are separate in one list are subsumed into broader categories in another. I will use the term 'process' to refer to such activities as observing, classifying, inferring, hypothesising, and so on. I will not use it to refer to more general activities like 'approaching problems scientifically' or 'taking a scientific approach', nor for more specific ones such as 'reading a thermometer to within 1 °C', where the term 'skill' may be more appropriate.

Teaching 'processes'

It is important to be clear that 'processes' are not seen simply as organising elements or categories in many of these new curriculum projects but as a major part of what is to be taught. *Science in Process* talks of the 'acquisition and use of process skills' and of processes being 'taught'. *Nuffield 11–13* speaks of 'the skills to be developed'. *Warwick Process Science* argues that 'a knowledge-led curriculum has little relevance' because of the explosion in information and the ease with which it can now be accessed. The process alternative focuses on 'the qualities of science education which might be termed "the primary or generic qualities" which will be of value when the facts are out of date or forgotten'. It goes on to say: 'If any qualities or generic skills are transferable then the processes must form a substantial proportion, and any preparation of young people must take into account the transferable skills which they will need to succeed' (Screen 1986a: 13).

The aim then clearly is to develop the processes through teaching. This leads naturally to the idea of *assessing* the extent to which pupils can use them. Assessment objectives for GCSE, as laid down in the various National Criteria (DES 1985b), include substantial elements grouped under the heading 'skills and processes'. Process objectives are set alongside those relating to content and concepts as though these were comparable. Grade descriptions outline what is meant by different levels of performance on process tasks. Processes, then, are seen not merely as providing the *means* of instruction and motivation but also its *ends*.

Summary of argument

I want to argue

1 that it is superficial and misleading to portray the method of science in terms of discrete processes;
2 that many of the so-called processes have no special association with science but are common to systematic thought in all formal disciplines and, indeed, to informal common-sense reasoning; that is, that they are general cognitive skills which we all routinely employ throughout our lives, without any need for formal instruction;
3 that there is no evidence that we improve on our performance of any of these (content-independent) processes and that the onus of proof that such improvement *is* possible lies firmly with those who advocate a 'process approach'.

To do this, I will look briefly first at the idea of a 'method of science' and then turn to consider a number of the science 'processes' in turn, focusing on the issue of teaching and learning as it applies to each of them. (Fuller accounts of some of these arguments can be found in articles by Millar and

Driver 1987 and Finlay 1983.) I will end by proposing an alternative to the process view of science method and try to explain why the choice between images of science is more than just a matter of choice or of fine academic distinctions, but may be of some importance for the public understanding of science as it impinges on our everyday lives.

WHAT IS SCIENTIFIC METHOD?

Current views of science processes, including those cited above, present an image of the method of science as a *hierarchy* of processes, beginning with observing and leading on via classification to inference and hypothesis. This is essentially an *inductive* view. Criticisms of induction as an account of how scientific enquiry proceeds are commonplace in the literature of philosophy of science (Popper 1959; Hempel 1966; Chalmers 1982). In an educational context, the *discovery learning* approach, which is modelled on the inductive view of science, has also become largely discredited. The practical difficulties which it poses for the teacher, as pupils fail to 'discover' what was intended, have been extensively documented (Atkinson and Delamont 1977; Solomon 1980; Harris and Taylor 1983). These problems do not stem from any incompetence on the part of teachers but from fallacies in the assumptions underlying the approach (Koertge 1969; Stevens 1977; Wellington 1981; Driver 1983). Knowledge, in the form of useful generalisations ('patterns'), does not simply emerge from objective and detailed observation.

An alternative is to remain agnostic about the origin of hypotheses and generalisations and instead to identify the scientific method with the testing of these hypotheses by experiment. This is the *hypothetico-deductive* view of science. As an account of science, it too has been found to need much development and qualification. There is little support from philosophers or historians of science, for example, for the idea that a hypothesis is ever conclusively falsified by an experiment. Some argue that the current hypothesis is never rejected until an alternative is available (Lakatos 1970); then a 'crucial experiment' can decide between the two. Even this is poorly supported by the historical record. Theory choice seems less like following rules of procedure than the exercise of skilled judgement, frequently influenced by other interests and commitments. In the classroom, the hypothetico-deductive approach (see, for example, Leicestershire Education Authority 1985) also has its problems; teachers faced with ambiguous experimental results from 'difficult' experiments tend to rely on the 'second-hand' authority of the textbooks rather than the 'first-hand authority' of the experiment (Millar 1985, 1987). The nature and sophistication of classroom experimentation and equipment means that established theory cannot be seriously tested (Koertge 1969).

Fuller accounts of these arguments are readily available in the literature (e.g. Chalmers 1982; Newton-Smith 1981; Lakatos and Musgrave 1970;

Hodson 1982). To summarise, we can safely say that amongst historians, philosophers and sociologists of science there is no general agreement about whether science has a method or, if so, what it is. But within this uncertainty there is substantial agreement on several points. Most accounts agree, for example, that scientific enquiry cannot be portrayed as rule following but involves the exercise of skill: in deciding what to observe, in selecting which observations to pay attention to, in interpreting and drawing inference, in drawing conclusions from experimental data, even in replicating experiments (Collins 1985: ch. 2). Decisions about all these things cannot be pinned down by sets of rules; they cannot even be seen after the event as having been guided by the intuitive possession of sets of rules 'in the head'. Much of scientists' knowledge of the method (or methods) they follow is tacit; doing science is like practising a craft (Polanyi 1958: ch 4; Ravetz 1971). And this, of course, has implications for the way science and scientific enquiry can be taught.

PROCESSES OF SCIENCE

Even if we accept the need for caution in talking of a 'method of science', there can be little doubt that scientists do observe, draw inferences, propose hypotheses, devise experiments. The argument of the previous section is that these are not linked by a set of rules and procedures into a method which will guide scientists as to how to tackle a new problem or how to reach agreement on what a set of experimental results mean. I want now to argue that these 'processes' have no special link with science but are simply convenient labels for the general approaches which we all use all the time in making sense of the world. It is not just that the method of science is more than the sum of these parts, but rather that the essence of what it means to 'do science' lies elsewhere. I will develop this argument by looking at several of the proposed processes in turn. In doing this, I want also to focus particular attention on the question of what it would mean to try to improve a learner's performance on these processes, that is of what it would mean to make the claim that one was *teaching* the processes. Here it is important to keep in mind that the idea of teaching processes depends fundamentally on the notion of transferability of learning – the inference that improved skill in observing, or classifying, or hypothesising is transferred to new areas of application. The claim is that by making these processes the focus of instruction (either explicitly or implicitly), pupils will develop very general skills which they can then apply to new problems in new areas, either within science or beyond. This latter claim is, for instance, evident in the DES Policy Statement's argument that 'each of us needs to be able to bring a scientific approach to bear on the practical, social, economic and political issues of modern life' (DES 1985a: 2–3).

Observing

We all observe. There is a certain peculiarity in suggesting that it is something we need to be taught. Of course what is meant is that children should be taught in science lessons to observe closely, to notice detail, to make relevant observations. But that is just the problem. What is relevant? Without a hypothesis or some kind of prior expectation there is no means of deciding what is, or is not, relevant to observe. This is part of what is meant by the now generally accepted view that all observation is theory laden (Hanson 1958).

Any teacher who has taught children to use a microscope knows about the theory-ladenness of observation. Imagine a group of children who have not previously seen diagrams of onion cells being asked to follow instructions on preparing a slide of a piece of onion skin and then to observe it under the microscope and draw what they see. Obvious but 'irrelevant' features, like air bubbles between slide and coverslip, are likely to dominate many drawings. Few will show a neat pattern of cells like 'bricks in a wall'. But now imagine giving the same prepared slides to a group of children who have already seen the standard textbook drawing of onion cells. Their drawings of the same view down the microscope will be very different. An interesting series of studies along these lines asked children to observe biological specimens such as stained sections of a twig (Bremner 1965; Hainsworth 1956, 1958). Amongst other findings, it was noted that the children made and recorded significantly more 'correct' observations following teaching about the general structures present in plants.

What does all of this tell us? Does it mean that the children do not, in some sense, see features of the magnified onion cells or twig sections before instruction? We must surely acknowledge that the visual information falling on the child's retina is not altered by the knowledge he or she brings to the task; but rather that, as Hanson (1958) has observed, 'there is more to seeing than meets the eyeball'. There is always more information available to our senses than we can attend to. Even if we consider only the sense of sight, this remains true; the visual field is so rich and detailed that we cannot simply 'observe everything'. We have to be selective and hence we need a basis of background knowledge about what we are looking at to guide the process of selection.

One further point about observation is also worth making. Much of the emphasis on observation in science education is based on the notion that scientists are good observers. Tycho Brahe's years of painstaking observation of planetary positions which made Kepler's work possible are held up as an example of good scientific practice; so too are Fleming's and Becquerel's 'chance' discoveries of penicillin and radioactivity respectively – images of the openness of mind to unanticipated observations. What is less often noted is that these examples embody two entirely different meanings of 'observant'. As Hacking (1983: 167) comments:

> Sometimes persistent attention to an oddity that would have been dismissed by a lesser experimenter is precisely what leads to new knowledge. But this is less a matter of . . . observation-as-reporting-what-one-sees, than the sense of the word we use when we call one person observant while another is not.

It seems altogether less clear that this is the sort of thing that anyone could teach.

Classifying

Like observing, classifying is something we have all been doing since birth, if not, indeed, even earlier. Infants classify the oval shape with two eyes, nose and mouth as a face, and respond differently to it than to other visual stimuli. They quickly learn to recognise the particular 'face shape' that is their mother's. All of this involves classifying, noting similarities and differences. So too, at a slightly later stage, does the acquisition of language. We need the ability to classify in order to make any sort of sense of the world. In principle every moment, every object we observe, is slightly different from anything else we have encountered. But we do not see it that way. Instead we recognise familiar objects behaving in familiar ways. The ability to classify is something we all possess and classifying is something we do unconsciously and routinely. All learning depends on it (Kuhn 1977).

How then could we make a claim to *teach* classifying? If the infant is an expert classifier (and he or she must be to make sense of the constant bombardment of sensory data), how can science teachers possibly claim to teach anyone to classify? The answer is that we do not teach classifying but rather two somewhat different, though related, things. We teach children something of the conventional scientific classifications; and we encourage them to make some aspects of the intuitive process of classifying explicit, by articulating the criteria on which their particular classifications are based. In doing so we demonstrate that unlike the propensity to classify, the actual classifications we use are conventional, and dependent on the purposes which we have in mind.

Scientific classification involves learning the particular classifications which scientists employ and which are established as productive for pursuing scientific ends. Pupils may be reluctant to classify a human as an animal (Bell 1981; Munby 1982), or wish to classify a whale along with fish rather than mammals, and be able to specify the criteria they are following in doing so. This reflects not a failure of the 'process' of classifying, but a failure to grasp or appreciate the usefulness of the particular classification system which scientists use in these cases. In other words, the decision that the criterion 'bears and suckles live young' takes priority over the criterion 'lives in the sea' is a matter of choice. It is not, in any sense, *obviously* more correct. The choice of relevant criteria depends on what the purpose of the classification is. If you want to look at evolutionary links between species, one criterion will work better; if you want to catch a whale, you will do better with the other!

Any activity in the science classroom involving classifying, or 'pattern seeking', is inextricably linked to a basis of knowledge and commitments (purposes). Whatever we may think, it is these that we are teaching about, not the 'process' of classifying.

Inferring

At first sight the idea of a distinction between observation and inference may seem a straightforward and useful one. It links up with things we might want to teach children about respect for evidence, and about the need not to push one's conclusions beyond the available information. Pupils are given some data and asked to distinguish which of a number of statements are observations based on the data, and which are inferences, consistent perhaps with the data but going beyond it. The moral of these stories and activities is always the same; good scientists make only those claims which their data support. That simply isn't true; if it were, science could never have got off the ground.

The difficulty lies in the idea (discussed above) that all observation is necessarily theory laden. Any statement reporting an observation carries, concealed within it, theoretical ideas. To take an example, imagine a girl pupil investigating the cooling of water in two flasks, one surrounded by insulating material, the other not. The water in both flasks starts off at the same temperature. After 10 minutes, she measures the temperature in the flasks and reports: the water is warmer in the lagged flask than in the unlagged one. Is this an observation or an inference? Perhaps we treat it as an observation, hoping to press on to the inference that insulation slows down energy losses from hot objects. But the girl's report is already an inference, based on the observation: the temperature reading on the thermometer in one flask is higher than in the other. This in turn is also an inference, based on some observation such as the mercury thread inside the glass tube in one of these instruments is longer than the thread inside the other. Is this an observation or an inference? We are in a situation of potentially infinite regress. We cannot say anything useful about the experiment except by making statements which contain theoretical ideas, and are therefore to some extent inferences.

The same is true of all of our experiments. We do not observe that electric current is the same at all points around a series circuit; we notice (if we do it carefully) that the pointer on an instrument stops at the same point when we connect the wires leaving the instrument and several other components in a number of different ways. Norris (1984) makes a similar point in discussing a textbook exercise inviting pupils to write down their observations while watching a candle burn. He argues that it is rational to regard the statement that there is liquid wax (and not just liquid) on top of the candle as an observation, rather than an inference. He argues that scientists typically make the strongest claim which is not subject to reason to doubt (Shapere 1982), and that 'the mere fact that it is *possible* to doubt that the liquid is paraffin is not sufficient *reason* to have such doubt. It is possible to doubt anything' (Norris 1984: 133, his emphases).

To follow rigorously a policy of scepticism, then, is not to do good science. Gaining scientific knowledge is more like pulling oneself up by one's bootstraps, building an edifice of ideas on best guesses and hunches, which can be tested for their usefulness in explaining and predicting. This is skilful work, not rule following; and that is the message about science we need to give our pupils.

Hypothesising

As a final example, let us consider the 'process' of hypothesising, the activity of making an imaginative leap beyond the data to try to account for observed regularities. Again I want to suggest that this is not something which can be taught, but is something we do all the time. The boy who reports that he 'catched' the ball is making a hypothesis: that the past tense of all verbs is formed by adding '-ed' at the end. So language is acquired, not only by simple observation and copying, but also by hypothesising, followed by the test of using the hypothesised word in conversation. Abercrombie (1969: 13) shows how the act of crossing the road, which we all routinely accomplish, involves making hypotheses about the future positions of cars and other road-users, based on observations and generalisations from past experience.

As anyone who has closely observed young children carrying out investigations will confirm, even 5-year-olds are expert hypothesisers. It is not at all clear that the 'process' of hypothesising as deployed by young children is any less sophisticated than research scientists' hypothesising – as a content-independent cognitive achievement. What does differ is rather the complexity and sophistication of the database and conceptual ideas available to the expert. What we teach is not hypothesising, but *scientific hypothesising*, that is forming hypotheses which employ scientific concepts and have the purpose of seeking to provide general explanations about how the world behaves.

INTERIM SUMMARY

This is a good point to take stock of the argument so far. I have suggested that the 'processes' of science are features of general cognition and that we all use them routinely without instruction. Consequently I have argued that there is a major problem inherent in any claim that we are teaching these 'processes' to children, and that they are the essence of what science contributes to the curriculum. The 'processes' have no special link with science. Artists observe closely, librarians and supermarket managers classify, historians and television repairmen infer and hypothesise. If these 'processes' are not what makes science distinctive, what *is* the method of science? What, exactly is special about science?

I will take up that first question in the final section. As to what is special about science, I would suggest, with Munby (1982), that science is a human invention which uses language in a particular fashion to describe the world. It differs from the other formal disciplines in the sorts of 'constructs' (that is, concepts, principles, theories) that it uses and in the purpose that they serve (to provide general explanations of how the world is).

CLAIMING TO TEACH 'PROCESSES'

My central aim in the discussion of 'processes' above has been to illustrate just how problematic it is to maintain seriously the view that we can *teach* these processes, as content-independent strategies and activities, to children; that is, that we can design classroom activities which will result in children becoming better at the performance of tasks involving these 'processes' which are different from the context in which they were originally taught. This claim of transferability is implicit in all the literature on science 'process'. If we claim to teach observing, or classifying, or hypothesising, we are claiming that we can teach children to become better at these, to perform better in tasks which involve these 'processes' but which are quite different in content and context from those we used for instructing them.

But what would this mean? We would need to have some idea of progression in these 'processes'; we would need to know that one task is an 'easy' observing or hypothesising task, while another is 'harder' or 'more advanced'. What could such a claim mean? What is 'elementary' classifying as opposed to 'advanced' classifying – independently of content? How do we turn a 'poor' observer into a 'good' observer – across *all* observation tasks? If the arguments above are accepted, the onus is now firmly on those who advocate a 'process approach' to identify much more clearly than they have done to date precisely what it is that they are claiming that children will learn from such an approach, and what empirical evidence they can present to support their claim. At present such evidence is conspicuous only by its absence.

WHY 'PROCESS'?

Why then, given these objections and a virtual absence of empirical support, has the 'process science' bandwagon developed such a head of steam? One obvious explanation is that the 'process' emphasis is a reaction against a content-dominated transmission model of science teaching. Those who argue for 'process' seek to involve pupils more actively in science. This is a welcome development and some of the work it promotes is a great improvement on previous practice. The flaw in the 'process' approach, however, is that it confuses means and ends – it fails to see that active learning approaches are the *means* of engaging pupils' attention and interest in science lessons, but are not themselves the *ends* or goals of instruction.

Does this means–ends confusion matter, if the actual classroom work is stimulating and worth while? I want to argue that it does not matter, for two reasons. The first is to do with assessment. If processes cannot in fact be taught and if pupils' performance on content-independent processes cannot be improved, it is absurd, as well as deeply unjust to pupils, for these to feature prominently in schemes of assessment. The second is that the image of science which the 'process' approach presents is a seriously misleading one when it comes to understanding social issues and controversies which involve science. The 'process' approach subtly shifts the emphasis from science as reliable knowledge towards scientists as reliable knowers. The outcome is to encourage learners to invest authority in the scientist, whose knowledge is derived by following agreed rules. Within such a perspective, the only way to interpret disagreements between scientific 'experts' about nuclear power, radiation risk, environmental issues, food additives, and so on, is as evidence either of bias or of incompetence (Collins and Shapin 1986; Millar and Wynne 1988). A less rule-bound view of scientific and techno-logical practices, where data and results are always open to negotiation before the community accepts them as 'facts', provides a more adequate basis for interpreting the science–society relationship.

A WAY FORWARD

Towards attainable goals

How can science education now free itself from an unhelpful and distorting emphasis on 'process'? First, I think, we need to identify a much clearer separation between specific skills which can be taught and improved (and may therefore be assessed) and more general processes which cannot. Second, if we wish to use the language of general processes, we need to become clear that it is 'scientific observing' (rather than 'observing'), 'scientific hypothesising' (rather than 'hypothesising') and so on, that we should be aiming to develop and promote through school science, and recognise that the exercise and development of these skills depend crucially on a basis of science content and concept knowledge. Third, we need to clarify the stages in developing these science skills. The work of Norris (1983, 1984) on scientific observation is a pointer to the sort of work which is required. Similarly thoughtful and detailed analyses are needed to replace the current superficial rhetoric of 'process' if we are to make any progress towards separating the attainable from the illusory.

Science as craft

More fundamentally, however, we need to take stock of the current situation in which science curriculum rhetoric propounds a view of scientific enquiry almost totally at odds with current thinking. Amongst philosophers and sociologists of science it is now generally taken for granted that scientific enquiry cannot be seen as a set of rules or standard procedures which can be applied unproblematically to all situations and which can provide simple and direct means of acquiring new knowledge or of confirming proposed explanations. Science does have characteristic ways of working and characteristic standards of judgement and appraisal, all of which are governed by current conceptions in the field of study as well as by available technologies and are influenced by the purposes for which the enquiry is undertaken. But these can never be fully encapsulated in a set of rules. They contain many tacit elements which can be communicated only through the interaction between the learner and a more experienced practitioner. Doing science is more like the skilful exercise of a repertoire of 'craft skills' (Polany 1958; Ravetz 1971) than the following of an algorithm. The training of scientists involves the process of coming to internalise these tacit canons of procedure and judgement. Oakeshott sums up this view in the following terms:

> the coherence of scientific activity [does not] lie in a body of principles or rules to be observed by the scientist, a 'scientific method'; such principles no doubt exist, but they . . . are only abridgements of the activity which at all points goes beyond them, and goes beyond them, in particular, in the connoisseurship of knowing how and when to apply them. Its coherence lies nowhere but in the way the scientist goes about his investigation, in the tradition of scientific enquiry.
>
> (Oakeshott 1974: 103)

In teaching children science, we are helping them to internalise the procedures and standards of the scientific community. We are assisting the child to construct for him- or herself a mental representation of the scientific ways of working and judging. Stenhouse (1975) argues for a model of teaching, in all subjects, in which the teacher guides the learner towards an appreciation of the standards of judgement inherent in a discipline, through the process of day-to-day correction and critical comment on the learner's work.

The worthwhile activity in which teacher and students are engaged has standards and criteria immanent in it and the task of appraisal is that of improving students' capacity to work to such criteria by critical reaction to work done.

(Stenhouse 1975: 95)

The science teacher's judgements are governed by 'faithfulness to the knowledge we have of how to conduct the specific activity we are engaged in' (Stenhouse 1975: 101–2). This acknowledges the tacit dimension to all knowledge; applied to science, it would perceive instruction as seeking to inculcate elements of an approach – the practice of a 'craft' – the art of doing science.

This is what good science teachers have always done. It is what science teachers should be encouraged to do, rather than spending an ever-increasing share of classroom time on making 'process-based' assessments of doubtful validity.

REFERENCES

Abercrombie, M.L.J. (1969) *The Anatomy of Judgement*, Harmondsworth: Penguin.

Atkinson, P. and Delamont, S. (1977) 'Mock-ups and cock-ups: the stage-management of guided discovery instruction', in P. Woods and M. Hammersley (eds) *School Experience: Explorations in the Sociology of Education*, London: Croom Helm.

Bell, B. (1981) 'When is an animal not an animal?', *Journal of Biological Education* 15, 3: 213–18.

Bremner, J. (1965) 'Observation of microscopic material by 11–12-year-old pupils', *School Science Review* 46: 385–94.

Chalmers, A.F. (1982) *What Is This Thing Called Science?*, 2nd edn, Milton Keynes: Open University Press.

Collins, H.M. (1985) *Changing Order*, London: Sage.

Collins, H.M. and Shapin, S. (1986) 'Uncovering the nature of science', in J. Brown, A. Cooper, T. Horton, F. Toates and D. Zeldin (eds) *Science in Schools*, Milton Keynes: Open University Press.

DES (1985a) *Science 5–16: A Statement of Policy*, London: HMSO.

—— (1985b) *General Certificate of Secondary Education – The National Criteria: Science*, London: HMSO.

Driver, R. (1983) *The Pupil as Scientist?*, Milton Keynes: Open University Press.

Finlay, F.N. (1983) 'Science processes', *Journal of Research in Science Teaching* 20, 1: 47–54.

Hacking, I. (1983) *Representing and Intervening*, Cambridge: Cambridge University Press.

Hainsworth, M.D. (1956) 'The effect of previous knowledge on observation', *School Science Review* 37: 234–42.

—— (1958) 'An experimental study of observation in school children', *School Science Review* 39: 264–76.

Hanson, N.R. (1958) *Patterns of Discovery*, Cambridge: Cambridge University Press.

Harris, D. and Taylor, M. (1983) 'Discovery learning in school science: the myth and the reality', *Journal of Curriculum Studies* 15, 3: 277–89.

Hempel, C.G. (1966) *Philosophy of Natural Science*, London: Prentice Hall.

Hodson, D. (1982) 'Is there a scientific method?', *Education in Chemistry* 19, 4: 112–16.

ILEA (1987) *Science in Process*, Ten Units and Teachers' Guide, London: Heinemann.

Koertge, N. (1969) 'Toward an integration of content and method in the science curriculum', *Curriculum Theory Network* 4, 1: 26–44.

Kuhn, T.S. (1977) 'Second thoughts on paradigms', in *The Essential Tension*, Chicago, IL: Chicago University Press.

Lakatos, I. (1970) 'Falsification and the methodology of scientific research programmes', in I. Lakatos and A. Musgrave (eds) *Criticism and the Growth of Knowledge*, Cambridge: Cambridge University Press.

Lakatos, I. and Musgrave, A. (eds) (1970) *Criticism and the Growth of Knowledge*, Cambridge: Cambridge University Press.

Leicestershire Education Authority (1985) *Science as a Process: Encouraging the Scientific Activity of Children; Assessment of Science Process: a Criterion-Based Approach*, Leicester: Leicester Education Authority.

Millar, R.H. (1985) 'Bending the evidence: teachers' reactions to "difficult" experiments', paper presented to the British Sociological Association Science Studies Group Conference on 'The Uses of Experiment', Newton Park College, Bath, August.

—— (1987) 'Towards a role for experiment in the science teaching laboratory', *Studies in Science Education* 14: 109–18.

Millar, R.H. and Driver, R. (1987) 'Beyond processes', *Studies in Science Education*, 14: 33–62.

Millar, R.H. and Wynne, B.E. (1988) 'Public understanding of science: from contents to processes', *International Journal of Science Education*, 10, 4: 388–98.

Munby, H. (1982) *What is Scientific Thinking?*, Ottawa: Science Council of Canada.

Newton-Smith, W.H. (1981) *The Rationality of Science*, London: Routledge & Kegan Paul.

Norris, S.P. (1983) 'The philosophical basis of observation in science and science education', *Journal of Research in Science Teaching* 22, 9: 817–33.

—— (1984) 'Defining observational competence', *Science Education* 68, 2: 129–42.

Nuffield 11–13 (1986) *How Scientists Work, How Science is Used, Teachers' Guides 1 and 2*, London: Longman.

Oakeshott, M. (1974) 'Rational conduct', in *Rationalism in Politics and Other Essays*, London: Methuen.

Polanyi, M. (1958) *Personal Knowledge*, London: Routledge & Kegan Paul.

Popper, K.R. (1959) *The Logic of Scientific Discovery*, London: Hutchinson.

Ravetz, J.R. (1971) *Scientific Knowledge and its Social Problems*, Oxford: Oxford University Press.

Screen, P. (1986a) 'The Warwick Process Science Project', *School Science Review* 68, 242: 12–16.

—— (1986b) *Warwick Process Science*, Southampton: Ashford Press.

Shapere, D. (1982) 'The concept of observation in science and philosophy', *Philosophy of Science* 49: 485–525.

Solomon, J. (1980) *Teaching Children in the Laboratory*, London: Croom Helm.

Stenhouse, L. (1975) *An Introduction to Curriculum Research and Development*, London: Heinemann.

Stevens, P. (1977) 'On the Nuffield philosophy of science', *Journal of Philosophy of Education* 12: 99–111.

Wellington, J.J. (1981) 'What's supposed to happen, sir? Some problems with discovery learning', *School Science Review* 63, 222: 167–73.

Chapter 17

Practical work in science
A task-based approach?

Richard Gott and Judith Mashiter

We suggest that there are several key aspects to the problem of pupil failure in that the aims of the science curriculum are deficient in a number of ways. First, they are too abstract in terms both of the ideas themselves and of the contexts in which those ideas are usually taught. The difficulty of the ideas for many pupils means that their experience of secondary school science is one of repeated and demoralising lack of success resulting in a vicious circle of failure, demotivation and more failure. Second, they are not sufficiently motivating, in that they lack perceived relevance to pupils' own lives. Third, they rely on practical work as a means of enhancing 'conceptual learning rather than acting as a source for the learning of essential skills' (Fensham 1985). Finally, they are based (wrongly) on the premise that pupils will be able to use ideas, spontaneously, in a wide variety of situations. (The reader is referred to Fensham's (1985) reflective essay for a detailed and well-argued discussion of these issues.)

By examining the nature of the 'traditional' science curriculum and then considering some recent innovations attempting to change the curriculum and its teaching, an argument for a task-based approach will now be developed.

THE KNOWLEDGE TRANSMISSION MODEL

The preoccupation in the 1960s and 1970s was with conceptual understanding, culminating in the influential Nuffield schemes. The pupil was seen as having a mind empty of preconceptions. The aim of science education was to fill that mind with the 'truths' of science. The scientist was portrayed, often quite explicitly, as a man (and very occasionally a woman) in a white coat in a 'high-tech lab' engaged in incomprehensible but, by implication, extremely difficult and important work. By studying science pupils could avail themselves of the opportunity to become members of this elite. Indeed, the course frequently suggested that pupils be allowed to become 'scientists for the day', as if being a scientist is something that one casts off before returning to the real world. The underlying philosophy of science was, and often remains, inductivist in origin. That is to say, pupils were introduced to a topic via experiments during which neutral observations were made. Hypotheses could then be generated from these neutral data and pupils would subsequently 'discover', or be helped to discover, the particular concept to be acquired.

With particular reference to the nature of *practical* work within this view, the purpose was to illustrate concepts so that pupils could 'see' them in action. 'The aim does not lie in the discovery process . . . [but in] the understanding of certain basic concepts' (Woolnough 1988a). In practice, the Nuffield approach became very didactic in the hands of teachers not well versed in its philosophy. (For a fuller discussion of the Nuffield schemes see Woolnough 1988.)

The pertinent point here is that all of this practical work had one aim only – that of introducing, illustrating or refining *concepts*. The consequence, in terms of pupil learning, has been that many pupils acquire fragments of knowledge which they can recall only in the context in which they were taught or reinforced. 'Good' pupils collect more knowledge fragments than their 'weak' peers. Opportunities to put science to use in relevant situations were limited since the practical work was so tightly defined and often used purpose-built and 'pupil-proof' (in theory!) apparatus.

THE KNOWLEDGE REFINEMENT MODEL

Most courses aimed at knowledge transmission have an implicit view of learning centred on the premise that pupils have an empty mind into which a body of knowledge, called science, is to be transferred. An alternative view is based on the constructivist model of learning and teaching which emphasises the alternative frameworks, or naive preconceptions, which research suggests that pupils already hold (Millar and Driver 1987). Essentially, the alternative frameworks view supposes that pupils have their own perceptions of the environment involving language, beliefs and relationships and that these personal perceptions are frequently in conflict with the 'correct' concepts of the agreed body of scientific knowledge. Indeed, these perceptions are often referred to as preconceptions, as the intention is that they will be supplanted by the 'proper' concepts.

The constructivist approach focuses on the bringing about of change through revised teaching strategies but the overall objective is still the acquisition of the concepts that traditionally constitute school science. The challenge of teaching is then seen to be the effecting of change from preconceptions to the 'correct' conceptual understanding by providing experiences which either prevent pupils developing *mis*conceptions or which force them to confront the mismatch which exists between their ideas and the actual behaviour of the environment.

This approach suffers from two major drawbacks. First and foremost, its basic aim is identical to that of the concept approach – the acquisition of more, and more powerful, concepts. We are still primarily concerned with pupils' ability to explain, for example, the phenomenon of evaporation with the 'powerful tool' of the kinetic theory. Evidence suggests that many, and probably most, pupils are not able to do this. Whether alternative teaching strategies will remedy this remains a matter of doubt. Several years' experience of various programmes for accelerating development have produced little in the way of success. It could be dangerous to rest our hopes on this as a solution. And second, the approach still allows concepts to drive and steer the curriculum. All attention is directed towards concept illustration, the logical conclusion of which is the devising, often contriving, of methods, including experimental work, for doing this. The cleaner and more clinical the experiment can be, by the removal of the messy clutter which is reality, then the greater the chance of pupils understanding the underlying idea. As a consequence, and with the best will in the world, the opportunity for choosing a context which is relevant to the pupils' experiences, rather than our own, is very limited.

Practical work can reveal the mismatch between pupils' preconceptions and the concept which is the desired learning objective. Thus its purpose is more than simple illustration and has more structure and direction than enquiry or discovery. Nevertheless, its role is primarily to facilitate the change in conceptual understanding and it therefore exists for and is driven by that collection of concepts to be acquired. This is not to suggest that such practical work has no value but rather to note its restricted and restricting role in the curriculum.

The point at issue here, as Fensham (1985) comments, is that 'the majority of the school population learns that it is unable to learn science as it has been defined for schools'. We think the problem is even deeper in that public perception of science almost *requires* that it be incapable of understanding; it only becomes science when it is not understood.

THE 'PROCESS' MODEL

Over the past few years several courses have emerged which have been given the label 'process science'. Often the 'process approach', as epitomised in such curriculum developments as *Science – A Process Approach (SAPA)* (American Association for the Advancement of Science 1967), *Science in Process* (Wray *et al.* 1987) and the *Warwick Process Science* project (Screen 1986), has been understood by teachers in a rather vague, ill-defined way as being somehow 'active', 'practical', skills based and student centred. *SAPA* arose from work in the United States on a study of what eminent scientists do as part of their everyday activity. It is interesting to note, in passing, the reliance on this high-status view of science. Why do we not examine the use that 'ordinary' people have for science – the nurses, plumbers and intelligent laypeople?

Putting this to one side for now, let us examine the nature of a 'process approach' in more detail. The premise of the approach is that science should place more emphasis on its methods rather than focusing exclusively on its products. This is a challenge, at least in principle, to the accepted endpoint of science education as a body of conceptual knowledge. The processes include observing, classifying, describing, communicating, drawing conclusions, making operational definitions, formulating hypotheses, controlling variables, interpreting data and experimenting.

In practice, the 'process approach' has come to have two strands. In the early years of secondary school science, the processes acquire a metacognitive role in which lessons are *about* 'observing', 'classifying', and so on. The processes assume the status of goals which mirror the concepts of the traditional or the constructivist approaches in importance. A lesson may focus on 'observation' and proceed to illustrate what it is to observe. But do pupils need to know that they are 'observing' or 'inferring'? The question as to whether or not metacognition will assist *pupils*, as distinct from teachers, to *use* the processes does not have an obvious answer. That does not mean that making such terms explicit to the teacher, so that they become part of teaching and learning, is not important. But perhaps they are better seen as a checklist to ensure that varieties of cognitive processes are included. Simply learning a definition, rather than being made aware of the 'correct' term for an activity with which they are already familiar, is unlikely to advance pupils any further in their understanding of science.

Typically, courses in the later secondary school years then deal with processes as a more efficient means to acquire concepts; they become the means rather than the ends of instruction. This is the viewpoint adopted by the constructivists who claim that processes are 'the vehicles by which children develop more effective conceptual tools. . . . For science, we would argue, is characterised by its concepts and purposes, not by its methods' (Millar and Driver 1987). So we find that the redefinition of science is only partial. While acknowledging that the methods of science are important, the methods are those of induction and operate within a concept acquisition framework. It is not likely, therefore, that the problems of relevance and motivation will be tackled effectively.

PROCEDURAL UNDERSTANDING IN SCIENCE – THE MISSING ELEMENT

Gott and Murphy (1987) have suggested that science is about the solving of problems in everyday and scientific situations. They chose to define a problem as a task for which the pupil cannot immediately see an answer or recall a routine method for finding it. To investigate and solve any problem, be it practical or not, there are a set of *procedures* which must be understood and used appropriately. In brief these procedures include:

- identifying the important variables
- deciding on their status – independent, dependent or control
- controlling variables
- deciding on the scale of quantities used
- choosing the range and number of measurements, their accuracy and reliability
- selecting appropriate tabulation and display.

Such activities are sometimes referred to as practical skills and as such are often taught in isolation. How many courses have 'circus'-type experiments involving the use of measuring instruments or the creation of tables, graphs and charts? Procedural understanding is not simply a collective term for such skills. The *Non-statutory Guidance* for the National Curriculum in science (DES 1989) describes procedural understanding as an 'understanding of how to put all these specific skills together' via the identification and operationalisation of variables and the display and interpretation of data.

Parallels occur in non-practical problems. The idea of deciding which are the independent and dependent variables and which variables must be controlled applies equally to multi-column tables such as those found in *Which?*-type magazine reports (comparing the relative strengths and weaknesses of different makes of some commercial device) or in complex data on environmental effects, for example, as it does to planning and performing practical investigations; interpreting such tables often means 'cutting' the data – holding one or more variables constant, while looking at the effect of one variable on another. Data on the effects of pollution, for instance, can be accompanied by details of wind strengths and directions, maps showing the location of factories, farming patterns, and so on, which require a hypothesis to be formulated which can be tested, not necessarily conclusively, against the data.

We must beware of a temptation to think that such understanding is trivial. APU evidence suggested that, for instance, well over half of 13-year-olds were unable to manipulate two independent variables successfully (Gott and Murphy 1987). Pupils must have considerable practice before they can apply procedural understanding with confidence.

As we argued in an earlier section, most of the practical work in which we ask pupils to engage involves the illustration or 'discovery' of concepts. We ask pupils to follow instructions or 'do as I have done', fill in a table and display the data in a certain standard way. This is acceptable, even necessary, in experimental work designed to deliver a concept. But in a broader, task-based view, such a narrow conception of practical work must be rejected. The extra element of procedural understanding comes into play if this recipe of instructions is removed. It follows, as a natural corollary, that the science can be more 'open'.

THE STRATIFICATION OF THE SCIENCE CURRICULUM

To summarise the discussion so far, practical work has been used for a variety of purposes. Most commonly, it has been used to illustrate *concepts* on the basis that 'seeing is believing'. More recently, it has become fashionable to argue that practical work can be arranged in order to disturb and refine preconceptions – the idea of illustrating concepts has been replaced by the idea of active confrontation of preconceptions. The third approach, of 'process science', takes the elements of a 'scientific method' and elevates them to the same status as that given to concepts in the traditional approach. It may become necessary to add to that list the procedural approach to open-ended investigative work, which, through its influence on the National Curriculum, will begin to inform curriculum development in the short and medium term.

We wish to suggest that there is an underlying problem here of stratification which is distorting, even artificially polarising, the curriculum. In each of the above views, the key elements of science are extracted and taught in isolation. One stratum is represented by the powerful concepts of, for example, energy transfer. Another stratum consists of the processes of inferring, and so on. (Yet another could, in the future, be the procedures of investigational science.)

Learning experiences, even models of learning itself, are then tailored to deliver these strata, often in deliberate and clinical isolation from each other. So, to take heat transfer as an example, experiments are selected *because* they will, we hope, deliver an understanding of the concept as efficiently as possible; the choice of context is secondary, at best. The process stratum, usually taught before the harder concept stratum, is designed to equip pupils with the tools necessary to deal with these concepts. On leaving school we expect the understanding from each stratum to merge spontaneously, enabling pupils to solve a problem such as identifying and remedying those areas of a house which are not energy efficient. The advantage claimed by this approach is one of economics; the ideas are applicable to any example in any situation, so we do not need to cover all situations, or indeed any of them. As Tobin (1984) points out in the context of a process approach:

> Process skills are not separated from science content when problems are encountered in real life situations. However, in classroom contexts, it is often convenient to isolate the processes so that activities can be planned to provide students with intensive practice on the skills.

The argument seems very logical and quite attractively neat and tidy. We know that it has worked for us, the controllers of the curriculum. But, of course, we have defined science from our inherited viewpoint. And, more importantly, the majority of pupils cannot share this perspective. Far from being powerful ideas for solving a variety of problems, science becomes an attachment of status and power for the few and fragments of disjointed knowledge for the many.

As Layton *et al.* (1986) note in connection with the historical development of science education and in the context of concept-driven curricula:

> Schools and colleges, in so far as they incorporated science in the curriculum, adopted a canonical version marked by abstraction and social disconnection. . . . As science had succeeded in establishing a place in education for the people, so it had become insulated within the contexts of knowledge generation and validation and withdrawn from the contexts of use. . . . In short, science for specific social purposes was replaced by science for science's sake.

Perhaps even more crucially, such a stratified approach denies the way pupils learn. It assumes that they will take on trust our assurance that all this knowledge will be useful to them, even as we deny them the opportunity to put it to use, there and then, in relevant situations. Such an abstract and deferred gratification is unlikely to motivate and encourage the majority of pupils. Indeed, evidence is accumulating which suggests that, to take one example, 'process skill learning appeared to be more effective when process skill lessons were infused into the regular science curriculum . . . rather than teaching the process in a brief topic as is often done' (Tobin *et al.* 1984).

A TASK-BASED APPROACH TO CURRICULUM DESIGN

What sort of science should we be teaching? What role should practical work play? How can concepts, processes and procedures be brought together in a more relevant and effective manner? How is science to be made at once less abstract, more relevant and more motivating?

Our first step must be to re-examine the definition of procedures and processes, since there is some overlap. If we take procedures to be concerned with operations on variables (in a heuristic sense), then some of the 'processes' will come under such a definition, most obviously such ideas as 'controlling variables'. Those which remain under the process banner sit happily with the definition of Tobin *et al.* (1984) in which 'processes' are concerned with different modes of thought or 'intellectual operations involved when solving problems encountered in science and, more generally, in everyday life situations'.

The view to be advanced here is one which attempts to move away from a stratified and, to the pupils, fragmented position to a holistic approach in which processes weld together and refine both procedural and conceptual understanding. We believe that the way forward is to construct a curriculum

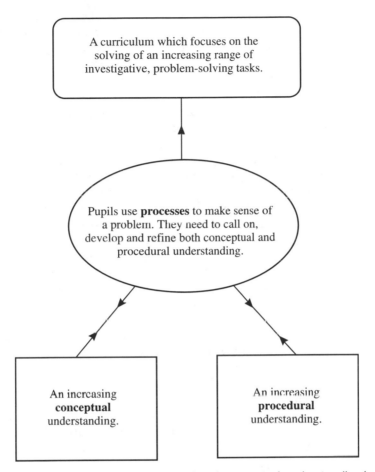

Figure 17.1 Processes mediate procedural and conceptual understanding in the solution of a task

around a series of tasks that have within them the elements of motivation that stem from confidence in a sense of ownership of the activity by the pupils (see Figure 17.1).

It may be useful to consider an example of such an approach. The first requirement is to identify a context in which the task is to be set. For younger pupils, in primary schools (age 5–11), this may well be an everyday situation such as road safety. A task might involve them initially in investigating how Plasticine models are deformed in collisions with toy cars of various masses travelling at different speeds. It may develop these ideas using published data on accident statistics with a view to creating a news sheet about the dangers on our roads.

For pupils in secondary school a series of tasks may involve the investigation of structures for cars which compress on collision, or how one such structure crushes under different forces. (Other non-practical tasks may involve the collection and analysis of secondary data on stopping distances, manufacturers' data on the construction of collapsible box sections or steering columns, or data on the effectiveness of safety belts at different speeds and restraining bodies of different masses.)

The role of 'processes', as defined earlier, now becomes apparent. The *processes* are the various 'ways of thinking' that will be needed to coordinate the pupils' conceptual and procedural understanding into an overall plan for the task. As the task develops, they will *use and develop concepts* such as strength, force and deceleration *while utilising and refining the procedural elements* of the task – the strategies of deciding what to vary, measure and control and how to do it effectively to give valid and reliable results.

Would such activities be too hard, too abstract? Experience suggests that problems can be selected that are within the reach of the vast majority of pupils. It is true that there are differences in performance. Some pupils will carry out more sophisticated investigations in response to a particular task than others; but all will feel that they have achieved something. So motivation is enhanced because it depends so crucially on success. Moreover, the setting of the activities within meaningful contexts provides probably the best chance of encouraging the transfer of procedures and concepts since the stratified elements of understanding are no longer divorced from purposeful problem-solving activities but are contained within them.

The key to such an approach would lie in the selection of appropriate tasks. They would need to be both practical and written. They would need to be selected for their intrinsic interest and motivation and would have to require pupils to draw on their increasing understanding of concepts and procedures, thus continuously refining them.

PROGRESSION WITHIN A TASK-BASED CURRICULUM

Progression can be defined for a curriculum more easily than it can for assessment purposes. A curriculum, unless we are attempting to create an individualised learning package, can prescribe progression by reference to group behaviour, which is likely to be a little more predictable than that of any individual. Assessment, on the other hand, is by definition personal and subject to all the idiosyncrasies of the individual's interests, experience out of school, home background and so on, which we know to be so influential in pupil attainment. Given the limitations of space here, we will consider only progression in the curriculum.

The evidence to hand suggests that a large number of factors are influential in determining task difficulty. We consider three of the most important.

The first of these is *context*. Evidence exists from a variety of sources that the context in which a task is set may be one of the most important determinants of pupil success. Clearly a pupil with a particular interest in gardening, say, will be motivated and knowledgeable in a task involving the investigation of the effectiveness of weedkillers. Pupils' interests and background knowledge will broaden as they grow older, influenced by peer pressures and the immediate environment of home and school. It is against this increasingly complex and diverse contextual background that tasks should be set.

A second influential factor is *conceptual understanding*. Concepts interact with tasks in complex ways which require further investigation before we can begin to predict task difficulty with any confidence. Two examples may help to illustrate that complexity.

If the task requires pupils to work with concepts with which they have some acquaintance (heat and temperature, say), then they are likely to make progress – to the point where those implicit ideas can become clarified as they evaluate their solution against the demands of the task. If, on the other hand, the concepts are not available even in an implicit form (electrical current, say), then pupils will have no basis on which even to begin the task and, what is more, little motivation to do so.

Once started on a task, the need to control variables becomes apparent in those circumstances where the pupils have sufficient understanding of the underlying concept to recognise its importance. For instance, in a comparison of the insulation properties of two thermos flasks, the need to control the initial temperature of the liquid relies on an understanding that the rate of cooling will be dependent on the instantaneous temperature. Many pupils who control other more obvious variables – the volume of the liquid, for example – fail to see the necessity for controlling the initial temperature. Add to this picture the fact that concepts themselves present gradients of difficulty which may well be pupil specific, and the problems of progression through concepts become all too apparent.

A third factor is *procedural understanding*. Although gradients of difficulty in procedural understanding are largely a matter for conjecture in the face of a dearth of evidence, there is a small amount available from Gott and Murphy (1987) and Foulds and Gott (1988). We suggest that one way to begin the structuring of investigative work centres on the procedural aspects of the number and complexity of the variables involved.

Thus a *Which?*-style test involving independent and dependent variables, both of which are categoric, serves as a starting point (for instance, younger children, set the task of finding out which of two sorts of jelly dissolves more quickly, may simply watch them and 'see which is fastest'). A second level would be a *Which?*-style test in which the dependent variable is continuous; we would be expecting pupils to quantify the rate of dissolving. Pupils would need to deploy the additional element of procedural understanding represented by the recognition and measurement of such a variable.

The next level would involve the move from categoric to a continuous independent variable. Pupils would now need to decide how many values of that variable to use, over what range and at what intervals: for instance, how does the rate of dissolving depend on the temperature of the water? The resulting data is best represented in a line graph, rather than the bar line chart appropriate to the preceding level.

Increasing the number of independent variables to two adds another level of complexity which, through research in the Piagetian tradition, we know to present difficulties to a significant minority of pupils at all ages in the secondary school phase (about a third of 16-year-olds). Pupils would be asked to find out whether the temperature *or* the size of the jelly pieces affects the rate of dissolving. The two independent variables would be categoric (the temperature of the water and the size of the jelly pieces, given two fixed temperatures and sizes, for instance) while the dependent variable, the rate of dissolving, would be continuous.

Once the idea of separation of these independent variables is mastered, the task can be changed by presenting pupils not with two sizes and temperatures, but with a packet of jelly and a source of heat. The task would ask pupils to determine how the temperature and the size of the jelly pieces affect the rate of dissolving and becomes a complex one involving them in decisions as to number and range of measurements for independent variables, both of which are now continuous.

Given this complex picture, how is task progression to be defined? We have argued in this chapter that a key issue in motivating pupils is that of relevance – the choice of a context which sustains that motivation while catering for the development of the concepts that constitute a realistic curriculum is clearly, therefore, a vital element of curriculum design.

As to the more complex issue of procedural and conceptual understanding, we have suggested that to separate out the two would be a mistake; that to progress wholesale along first one stratum and then another is ineffective and demotivating. But that does not preclude an emphasis on one or the other in a particular task.

In structuring such a curriculum it may be useful to select an initial series of tasks, set in an appropriate context, in which pupils are asked to advance only along one of the strata (for example, working with a familiar concept, but advancing procedural skills). Once familiar with the procedural skills of *Which?*-style tasks, say, it may then be appropriate to deploy those procedural skills in contexts which involve less well-understood concepts – dissolving jelly might become linked to rates of reaction. The concepts can be developed within investigations, providing that pupils have some initial ideas which will allow them some purchase on the task. Other concepts which are very new to them may require an explicit introduction along more traditional lines before the ideas can be refined through use in investigative situations.

The trick will be to sequence the tasks so that the motivation derived from the relevance and completeness of the activity is not subverted by the need to control progression in concept and procedure, whether that need derives from assessment purposes or the structuring of schemes of work. Such a curriculum is, at present, not much more than a gleam on the horizon, but still a gleam worth striving towards.

REFERENCES

American Association for the Advancement of Science (1967). *Science – A Process Approach*. Washington, DC, Ginn & Co.

Department of Education and Science (1989). *Science in the National Curriculum*. London, HMSO.

Fensham, P.J. (1985). 'Science for all: a reflective essay', *Journal of Curriculum Studies*, 17, 415–35.

Foulds, K. and Gott, R. (1988). 'Structuring investigations in the science curriculum', *Physics Education*, 23, 347–51.

Gott, R. and Murphy, P. (1987). *Assessing Investigations at Ages 13 and 15. Assessment of Performance Unit Science Report for Teachers: 9*. London, Department of Education and Science/Welsh Office/Department of Education for Northern Ireland.

Layton, D., Davey, A. and Jenkins, E. (1986). 'Science for Specific Social Purposes (SSSP): perspectives on adult scientific literacy', *Studies in Science Education*, 13, 27–52.

Millar, R. and Driver, R. (1987). 'Beyond processes', *Studies in Science Education*, 14, 33–62.

Screen, P. (ed.) (1986). *Warwick Process Science*. Southampton, Ashford Press.

Tobin, K. (1984). 'Student engagement in science learning tasks', *European Journal of Science Education*, 6, 339–47.

Tobin, K., Pike, G. and Lacey, T. (1984). 'Strategy analysis procedures for improving the quality of activity oriented science teaching', *European Journal of Science Education*, 6, 79–89.

Woolnough, B.E. (1988). *Physics Teaching in Schools 1960–1985*. Lewes, The Falmer Press.

Wray, J. *et al.* (eds) (1987). *Science in Process*. Ten units and Teachers' Guide. London, Heinemann.

Chapter 18

The overselling of science education in the 1980s

Bryan Chapman

J.K. Galbraith made a distinction between 'institutional truth' and reality.[1] Institutional truth is 'what serves the needs and purposes of the large and socially pervasive institutions that increasingly dominate modern life'. As examples, he cited the 'institutional truth' about Russian imperialism which (up till now!) has had to be accepted before employment with the Pentagon could be contemplated; the 'institutional truth' of the financial world that 'the pursuit of money by whatever design within the law is always benign' before a graduate could be accepted for employment on Wall Street; a total belief in the curative power of bran-filled breakfast foods before joining Kellogg's, not to mention the fundamentalist fervour demanded of potential employees of the Coca-Cola Corporation. It goes without saying that, at the end of his damning indictment of 'institutional truths', he urged the graduands, against all preferment and advancement logic, to choose reality.

Other 'institutional truths' that now have to be embraced by anyone seeking preferment or advancement include the value of industrial experience; the importance of education for entrepreneurship; the overriding importance of record keeping and assessment; progression; and that the educational needs of all children are identical and therefore they all have to jump through the same curriculum hoops. Woe betide those who have a different view of reality.

One 'institutional truth' embodied in the National Curriculum is that 'science' is so important that all future citizens should have it delivered to them throughout all their years of compulsory schooling. Quantitatively, education in the sciences is now twice as important as either literacy or numeracy. Whether the ability to measure wind speed; to describe how a microphone works; to name the major organs of flowering plants; to give a simple explanation of electrolysis or any other of the many 'trivial pursuits' enshrined in law, actually justifies this position of supremacy does seem open to question. Does this 'naming of parts' approach to learning science have any connection with the reality of doing science? Or is conforming to the 'institutional truth' of the National Curriculum all that now matters? For whose benefit is science being made compulsory, anyway? Is it the individual child who is expected to benefit from this science, or society? The logic of the labour market suggests that if the policy is only moderately successful we will have far more scientific and technologically competent young people than that market needs. Economically aware young people will be well able to draw their own career conclusions about this. Indeed, even without the National Curriculum, they already are.

Evangelical enthusiasm for science is not new. In 1854 Herbert Spencer posed the question 'What knowledge is most worth?' His answer:

> For direct self-preservation, or the maintenance of life and health, the all important knowledge is Science. For that indirect self–preservation which we call gaining a livelihood, the knowledge of greatest value is   Science, for the due discharge of parental functions, the proper guide is to be found only in – Science. For that interpretation of national life, past and present, without which the citizen cannot rightly regulate his conduct, the indispensable key is – Science. Alive for the most perfect production and present enjoyment of art in all its forms, the need for preparation is still – Science, and for the purposes of discipline – intellectual, moral, religious – the most efficient study is, once more – Science.
>
> *Education: Intellectual, Moral and Physical*

Twelve years before this George Stephenson had, in his lectures to Mechanics Institutes, been warning that 'British Industry was in danger of falling behind its competitors'. His successors are still saying more or less the same thing, ever more stridently.[2] Sir George Porter, showing his frustration years on, has asked: 'Should we not force science down the throats of those that have no taste for it? Is it not our duty to drag them into the twentieth century?' His rhetorical answer: 'I'm afraid that it is'.[3]

But is he right? It is after all the twenty-first century for which today's young people are being educated, not the twentieth century. Whether the educational priorities of what, for most young people, will be a post-industrial society really require such an emphasis on science as exists in the National Curriculum is, to put it at its mildest, debatable.

How is it that science education has become a core element of the National Curriculum? Stuart Sexton, one-time education adviser to Sir Keith Joseph and now Director of the Institute of Policy Studies, has argued that the statutory assessments associated with the 1988 Act should have been confined to 'an assessment of the child's achievement in literacy and numeracy.'[4] He went on to affirm that it was self-evident that there is more to education than these 'but that all such (other) aspects of education should be subject to constant external, statutory assessment seems to me to be non-sense'. It seems clear from this that a less prescriptive view of education would have prevailed had not Sir Keith been 'retired'.

It is arguable that the role of science education in schools has been grossly oversold over the last decade. The claims made for it have been of a proselytising nature owing more to politics than to argument. Does every-one need science education through to 16+? Will it make any difference to this country's future economic performance? Will young people be happier because, for example, they 'understand pyramids of numbers and biomass', are able to 'use bistable circuits' and 'know that things can be moved by pushing them'? Just what is it about science – or any other subject for that matter – that makes it so necessary to prescribe in such detail what should be taught and how long it should take to teach it?

THE CLAIMS FOR COMPULSORY SCIENCE EDUCATION SCRUTINISED

That the sciences are, or can be made to be, of direct employment relevance to young people

At best this claim only applies to the small, and reducing, percentage of young people going into employment requiring scientific knowledge or skills. Such employment is extremely vulnerable to deskilling through auto-mation. Within this group the numbers who have to use their scientific knowledge, as distinct from operating technology based on that knowledge, are minimal.[5] Can the compulsory study of any subject be justified on the grounds that a minority may eventually find some aspect of it relevant to their employment? If so, why not compulsory ballet classes?

That industry requires scientifically competent school leavers

When potential employers complain that school leavers lack employment skills, it should not be assumed those skills are scientific or, for that matter, technological in character. Early in 1990, at yet another conference con-cerned with the demographic skills crisis facing British industry, the Director-General of the government's training agency acknowledged that 75 per cent of the growth of employment forecast for the current decade would be in management and the professions followed by construction, leisure and tourism. Unless manufacturing industry is able to compete £ for £ and perk for perk with the burgeoning financial sector for the services of able young people it will be whistling in the wind no matter what we teach in our schools.[6] In any case, surveys of employers' requirements of school leavers consistently place personal qualities and basic numeracy and literacy way above any specific subject requirements. If a science qualification is demanded it is much more likely to be for reasons of selection rather than content. If this is so, it follows that the more young people who gain such a qualification the less its selection value becomes.

That compulsory sciences will lead to an increased uptake of science
subjects at A level which will, in its turn, lead to an increased output of
scientifically and technologically qualified graduates entering industry

This claim is unproven. Early claims for the newer double certification schemes have to be seen against a background of other changes related to the introduction of GCSE. HMI report[7] that, so far, the introduction of balanced science has, even in those schools where it is well-established, only led to 'a modest increase in the proportion of pupils going on to study A-level science courses'. Given the increase in uptake of 'balanced science' courses that coincided with the introduction of GCSE, the 1990 A-level results would appear to confirm this minimal influence.[8]

The continued, ever more strident, complaints of industrialists that we do not produce enough qualified engineers, scientists and technologists must also be seen in the context of rapidly changing employment patterns throughout the developed world. The 1989 OECD Employment Outlook survey noted that all its member states were experiencing a move away from manufacturing into service employment. Only in the United States (11.1 per cent) is the proportion of the workforce engaged in finance, insurance, real estate and business services higher than in the UK (10.6 per cent) and our rate of increase is greater. Given the rewards accruing in this sector, scientists and technologists are as likely to be found there as anyone else. It may be that we do not need to train more engineers, scientists and technologists: all we have to do is to ensure that those we do train do not migrate into careers which are perceived as offering better prospects than engineering or science. If the business and financial sector pays better, offers more security, more perks, better career structures, better provision for mothers and married women returnees than do industries employing scientists and engineers then the remarkable thing is not that so few of our brightest young people are being attracted into these fields but that so many, despite everything, continue to study them. Finding a solution to this problem, assuming it is a problem, has virtually nothing to do with education and almost everything to do with society. But even in Germany and Japan, countries in which, incidentally, a rigorous formal approach to education in the sciences has never prevented them producing creative engineers and technologists in the past, there is a growing trend for their most able graduates to opt for careers in financial and related services rather than engineering and technology. Despite all the rhetoric, the reality is that, globally as well as nationally, careers in engineering, science and technology are beginning to look like second-best options to today's career-conscious, financially aware young people.

The global nature of economic activity and the single European market suggest:

1 That economies of scale are going to reduce significantly the overall requirement for scientific/technological manpower.
2 That this manpower will be recruited on a pan-national basis rather than on a national one.

Not only does this make national concerns for the production of scientists and technologists irrelevant, it also suggests that the best scientists and technologists will, as they always have done, gravitate to where they perceive the opportunities and rewards to be greatest, no matter who educates them. There is nothing new in this except perhaps the focus of migration.[9] Within Europe the high-tech focus seems much more likely to be Rhone–Alps than M4, with all the implications that will have for R & D in this country.

That compulsory education in the sciences will give those taking non-science/technological degrees a better perception of science/technology and hence lead to a more favourable commercial/financial environment for scientific/technological enterprises

Two somewhat tenuous reasons advanced for the decline in this country's manufacturing base are:

1 The lack of engineers and scientists at boardroom level.
2 Boardroom – and financial institutional – ignorance of the sciences leading to an unwillingness to invest in science-based enterprises.

By ensuring that everyone has an education in the sciences to 16+, the 'institutional truth' is that this state of affairs will be changed.

Even if this anti-science/anti-technological bias does exist, it does not follow that a causal relationship exists between it and British industry's comparative failure to invest in science-based enterprises. It is economically naive of us to believe that industry is about making products; it is about making money.[10] As Galbraith comments 'merger and acquisition mania . . . have on occasion brought to the command of our business enterprises owners who did not know what their newly acquired firm produced' – apart, that is, from returns on capital invested. If returns on investments in services are greater than returns on investments in manufacturing, why make? Japan is in the process of relocating much of its low value-added manufacturing capacity outside Japan since, by doing so, the return on Japanese investment is increased. Reinvestment of Japanese manufacturing profits in Australasian, European and US real estate, *rather than in manufacturing*, should also be noted.[11]

Arguably, it is our governments' ideological unwillingness to underwrite the development of 'near-market' technology – e.g. financing a national fibre optic network or high-speed rail links to the Channel Tunnel – that is the most serious disincentive to industrial investment in science and technology in the UK today. France takes a very different view of such investments. The United States has always used its defence procurement budget as a *de facto* state subsidy for commercial non-military exploitation of high-technology products.

That the sciences have a particular role to play in developing 'technological capability', deemed to be an essential element in the preparation of young people for life in an advanced technological society

Whether education in the sciences is important in developing the 'technological capability' of young people is only worth discussing if the premise behind the statement is accepted. In fact, technological advances reduce rather than increase the overall need for 'technological capability' within society. Washing clothes on the banks of a river requires far more 'technological capability' than does the pressing of the correct sequence of buttons on a programmable washing machine. In the 1930s Maynard Keynes[12] highlighted the deskilling nature of technology and the impact this would have on employment long before the advent of the micro-chip. In the electronics industry the need is increasingly for software rather than hardware skills. IBM's 1990 milkround recruitment target was for 200 electronics engineers with software skills but only 10 with hardware expertise. Arguably the formal logic of the classics provides a far better grounding for the disciplined logic of software engineering than does the National Curriculum in science.

That education in the sciences develops skills which have applications in many other areas of human activities

Claims made for transferable skills are always suspect. Those made on behalf of the sciences are no more – or less – suspect than those made on behalf of many other areas of the curriculum. Furthermore if a skill has general applicability it is clearly illogical to specify an area of experience through which it must be delivered. Instead of referring to scientific skills it would be more accurate to refer to those general human skills which find applications within the sciences. This distinction is important. If the aim of education is to develop process skills – whatever they are – there is no evidence that we need a science curriculum to deliver them. Whether there is any legitimacy to thinking of the sciences as a collection of skills, given that the nature of science is itself regarded as problematical, is another matter.

That because of the pervasiveness of science and its applications, education in the sciences is a vital element of education for a democratic society

This is the traditional liberal educationalist's claim. Of all claims made for compulsory science education it is at one and the same time the most appealing and the weakest. To justify it, it would be necessary to show that those already educated in the sciences have significantly different views on societal issues related to science and technology than their non-scientifically educated contemporaries have. Indeed, some, following Herbert Spencer, would go further and make claims for science education which extend way beyond science. Only if we are convinced of the first could the second be a possibility. I am unaware of any evidence which convinces me that scientists are less likely to have car crashes, more likely to be concerned about the environment, less prone to catch AIDS than their non-scientifically educated peers. When a societal issue does emerge – Chernobyl, ozone layer depletion, environmental degradation, nuclear/fossil fuel energy production, powerline health hazards *et al.* – it is clearly adult, rather than school, scientific education that matters. It is an educational task that, up to now, public service and independent television has served well and the majority of the press badly. What the deregulated future holds in store is another matter; those involved appear deeply pessimistic about their future. It needs also to be recognised that, outside their own specialisms, few scientists are any better equipped to make judgements on scientific matters with which they are unfamiliar than any other intelligent lay person. Very few scientists are, or indeed aspire to be, scientific polymaths.

That compulsory education in the sciences will encourage more young women to take up careers in engineering, the sciences and technology

The issue of compulsory sciences for girls is, of course, emotionally bound up with broader gender-related issues. Equality of opportunity should not, however, be confused with identity of opportunity.[13] Whether the 'under-representation' of women in engineering and the physical sciences arises as a direct result of their opting out of these subjects at school is questionable. It is, perhaps, worth observing that career-minded young women are already attracted to the same prestigious business, legal and financially related careers as are attracting their male contemporaries. One reason for this is that they have been made aware that many companies in these fields have taken positive steps, through the provision of career breaks, creches *et al.* both to retain them and provide career progression. A combined degree in Business Studies and European Language(s) must seem a far better career bet to young people of both sexes, not just young women, than, say, a degree in Chemical Engineering.

That an education in the sciences is a vital component of everyone's general education

It is difficult to argue against this one. Kenneth Baker gave as one of his reasons for making science education compulsory that 'all young people should be encouraged to see science as a vital – and enjoyable – part of their cultural heritage'.[14] Splendid sounding. But is there not an almost explicit contradiction between the terms 'encourage' and 'enjoyable' on the one hand and 'compulsion' on the other? And does it really require around 20 per cent of curriculum to provide this component? After all, godliness only gets 2.5 per cent!

SCIENCE AND TECHNOLOGY: A SYSTEMS APPROACH?

Most of the utilitarian reasons advanced for compulsory science education blur the distinctions between science and technology, and hence scientific and technological education. The fact that there is a close symbiotic relationship between the sciences and many technologies should not be allowed to obscure the essential differences between them. These differences are important on both intellectual and pedagogic grounds. In brief, the sciences, ultimately, are about understanding nature; technologies are about the application of reliable knowledge, some, but not all, of which has been derived from science. Much traditional science that relates to technology only does so in a *post hoc* sense – pulley systems may be explainable scientifically but they were in use long before this explanation existed. Even when scientific understanding does lead to application, as is increasingly the case in areas of high technology, it does not follow that understanding the science of a technology is a necessary prerequisite for applying it. A *Wireless World* editorial has posed the question 'Engineering – or Dominoes?'[15] Having first reminisced about doing 'interminable experiments on the latent heat of vapourization and the laborious plotting of magnetic fields' in his 1940s school physics course the editor continued:

> It is, it goes without saying necessary for the modern pupil to have the use of advanced modern equipment. . . . A micro, given the correct data, will do exactly what is expected of it very efficiently . . . but where is the striving? And, without the striving, where is the learning? Is there a danger of producing a great number of people who call themselves electronic engineers but whose knowledge of electronics stops short at an ability to program and an awareness of the cheapest supplier of interfaces?
>
> The only answer to all these weedy, half-baked questions is that undoubtedly that is exactly what engineers will be like, and quite soon too: there is no reason why they should be any different. It has been said for years that the microprocessor is a component, to be used as any other

component. There can be little advantage to a user in knowing the precise details of the internal working of a micro – it can be regarded as a machine which will do its job when asked. It is not necessary to know the finer points of oscilloscope design to use it to its fullest extent: neither is it absolutely necessary to know more than the capabilities and characteristics of a micro, or any other i c to obtain maximum performance from it. And when the remaining parts of a circuit are also integrated, there will be no pressing need to understand the use of power transistors or passive components, either, unless one has to design the i cs. 'Systems engineering' will be supreme.

We have to recognise that most users of science and most scientists, most of the time, are systems engineers. They do not need to understand the science of which they make use. A surgeon does not have to understand the science of lasers and of fibre optic transmission in order to use them in his work; nuclear magnetic resonance does not have to be understood by the technician taking a brain scan; a gardener does not need to understand the chemistry of soil and the biochemistry of plants before taking advantage of the work of horticultural scientists. Sometimes the underlying science of a technology is irrelevant to the practitioner. Nigel Kennedy does not have to understand the physics of a violin in order to make it sing; Steve Davis' skills owe very little to his understanding of Newton's laws and the Roux brothers' ability to create classic dishes has not been gained through studying culinary chemistry.

Perhaps the role of science education as a necessary precursor to a career in engineering and/or technology is less universally important than institutional truth commonly assumes? However, the editorial concludes:

> This is not, of course to say that all engineers will be satisfied without a detailed knowledge of exactly what happens inside the i cs. Perhaps these people will be the originators – the ones who, because they know more of the internal operation, will be able to apply i cs with a greater imagination. But do not decry the simple user of modules: he will know all he needs to know.

In this context the 'simple users of modules' are the technologists who create the deskilling artifacts of modern life. The overwhelming majority of us do not even need to know there is a 'module' in our artifacts, let alone understand them. All we need to be able to do is to read, *and make sense of,* the instruction manual! The inescapable conclusion which follows from this is that, for the vast majority of young people, neither the employment nor utilitarian cases for science and technology education have much substance. But then, apart from 'basic literacy and numeracy' is this not true of the other core and foundation subjects of the National Curriculum?

The case for technology education for all is probably much stronger than that for science education. (Whether that applies to technology as it appears in the National Curriculum is another matter.) To make progress in the sciences an ever-increasing level of sophisticated and abstract thought is generally deemed necessary. Practical work, no matter how motivating, is of no scientific relevance if the theoretical framework in which it is embedded is not understood. By contrast technological activities are accessible at many levels. Much work can be done on and with circuits without being concerned with, or needing, any theories of electrical conduction; the physics of expansion does not have to be understood before a bimetallic strip can be deployed; an understanding of the quantum mechanics of field effect transistors is not a necessary precursor to the use of calculators stuffed full of them and a condom worn by, or inserted in, a materials scientist is not made more effective because of his/her knowledge of the elastic properties of polymers. What technologists are concerned about is making use of reliable knowledge. It is learning how to make use of the input/output characteristics of a system that matters, not the science responsible for those characteristics.

This 'systems approach' to the use of reliable knowledge is totally in tune with the Information Technology Society which today's young people are entering. It is, in fact, the way mankind has always operated. Not 'normal science' so much as 'normal technology'. Education *aimed at providing competence in the sciences* only makes sense for those who have the potential and the curiosity to become the originators of the future. Perhaps, for the others, there are more important educational priorities.

SCIENCE FOR CITIZENSHIP

If employment priorities are misplaced, what of Science for Citizenship? David Layton[16] challenged science education many years ago when he suggested that:

> Just as the classicists have questioned the extent to which a knowledge of the language and literature of Greece and Rome is necessary for the achievement of an understanding of the influence of classical on European civilisation, so scientists might ask a similar question. 'How much knowledge of the procedures and conclusions of the various sciences is necessary in order to achieve an understanding of the relations of science to technology and society?'

Clearly for the majority of young people who are not going to use science, it is this kind of understanding that matters. Whether a science education that gives so much time and emphasis to practical 'can do' activities is the right way to achieve this is another matter. Being able to read an analogue scale; use a pipette; make a microscope slide are no more the stuff of democratic decision making than they are, for that matter, of modern scientific practice. David Layton argues persuasively for the use of historical case studies to achieve such an understanding. Whether understanding the role that science and technology played in the past will help young people put them into twenty-first-century global economic context is, to put it at its mildest, unproven. Whereas Kay's flying shuttle, Hargreaves' spinning jenny and Crompton's mule still required workers, mostly unskilled, to produce cotton goods, the application of the microprocessor to production removes even that requirement unless, of course, the cost of labour is held below the cost of investment in automation. Only in Third World economies, or economies based on very unequal distribution of wealth, such as the UK's, is this the case.[17]

What role will science and technology have in the kind of societies that seem likely to exist as we enter the next century? Science and technology servicing a global economy rooted in free-market competition and consumption would seem to have very different priorities to those that would exist in a global economy based on cooperation and conservation. Do we really want to educate young people so that they can deploy their scientific and technological skills on the trivia of affluence? Developing new scents to help sell otherwise identical soap powders; four-colour striped toothpastes; elliptical teabags; production lines to convert cows into beefburgers even faster than McDonalds do at present? Or do we want to educate them for a world in which, if they do eventually become scientists and technologists, their science and technology will be directed to the somewhat more worthy end of ensuring, or rather attempting to ensure, the survival of Planet Earth? Is effective science education for world citizenship possible within the context of a world economic system which clearly depends on maintaining global inequality for its metastability?

Equity demands that a child born in China, or Ethiopia, or Bangladesh has the right to the same standard of living as one born in the United States or Germany or Japan. China currently consumes energy at a rate of less than 0.8 kW per person. In the United States consumption is 10 kW per person.[18] The global warming and environmental consequences of any Chinese government exploiting its fossil fuel reserves, however efficiently, so that its citizens have the same standard of living as the United States is only too obvious. Yet we have an economic system which depends on ever-increasing consumption for its survival. When people buy less clothes the effect on the employees of Next, Laura Ashley, their suppliers et al. is disastrous. Clothes and cars that lasted would be an economic disaster for manufacturers and their employees alike. For the existing economic system to function we need to fill wardrobes with clothes we never wear and to have cars that fail their MoTs. Alec Guinness's White Suit[19] is a nightmare our economic system cannot afford to come true. It really is doubtful if a science education for citizenship which called into question the twin shibboleths of growth and free-market economics which the National Curriculum is designed to inculcate would be permitted if it had any chance of being effective. What would a science and technology education for world citizenship look like? How would its priorities differ from one based on national self-interest? The stark contrast between the rich and the poor nations of the world is well documented. In the context of the present global economic system, better science and technology actually makes it easier for the rich to exploit the poor. Satellite surveillance of crop development and the movements of locust populations in Africa is not carried out for the benefit of Africans; it is commissioned by those who operate on the world commodity markets.

Perhaps it is all too late anyhow. Irreversible damage may already have been done to the environment. Ben Elton[20] has chronicled the efforts of the unimaginably rich to escape to the Moon when they realise the catastrophic consequences that their exploitation of Planet Earth has had on the environment. As Professor Durf, their scientific adviser, puts it:

> I can think of no better illustration to underline the urgency of our situation than to suggest that were God to attempt to take out an insurance policy on the world, he would not be able to afford the premium.

He continues:

> Of late, certain politicians have been attempting to play the green card in their grubby scramble for public support. Believe me, such tokenism is entirely cynical. The situation can never be reversed whilst market forces remain superior to political will. The politicians have always left us alone, and they will always leave us alone, because we pay the piper, and we call the tune. . . .
>
> We all hoped, of course, that market forces would produce a solution; that ecologically responsible activity would somehow become profitable. As we know it hasn't and that is just too bad. We had a duty to progress, to make money and create wealth, that was our bounden mission. If the earth had to die in the defence of a free market economy, then it is a noble death. . . . In modern times people worship money. Money is God in that it has been deified and can clearly be said to rule our lives.[21] Hence it is fitting that you, the super-rich, those who have worshipped money with a diligence and conviction far above the faith of lesser men, that you should board the Star Arks and carry our faith to a new civilization beyond the flood, on the moon.

The survival of the planet, the reduction of the obscene disparities of wealth both between and within nations which characterise today's world and its economic system, are issues demanding education in economics, politics and sociology not science and technology. Perhaps that is the point of the National Curriculum. After all if 20 per cent of curriculum time is devoted to topics which actually do not really matter at all, then that time cannot be used for other more subversive purposes, can it? This issue is considered later.

WHAT NO SCIENCE?

A number of challenges have been thrown down to those who promulgate an unquestioning 'institutional truth' view of the importance of science education. The weakness of this view has been demonstrated.

What contribution has science education to make to the general education of all young people? Arguably education designed to increase awareness of global environmental problems now facing Planet Earth should be a top priority. But such awareness is not dependent on understanding the science of acid rain, the greenhouse effect, desertification *et al*. Indeed, such education is trivial compared with education about the global economic and political changes a solution to these problems must entail. After all, no government has yet been elected that had, as part of its manifesto, a reduction in living standards.

We have reached a stage when politically neutral environmental education is a contradiction in terms. What, for example, does a 'green' science teacher do about the Prime Minister's view, expressed at the 1989 presentation of the Environmental Industry Award to ICI that:

> I find some people thinking of the environment in an airy-fairy way, as if we could go back to a village life. Some might quite like it, but it is quite impossible . . . we have created enough wealth to enable us to consider very carefully how to reduce pollution – how to design things for the better.
>
> We are not going to do away with the great car economy. . . . But we are going to have to find more economical ways of using fuel and more economical engines and more economical uses of cars.

This from the first Prime Minister [Margaret Thatcher] we have ever had who ought to have understood the limitations the Second Law of Thermodynamics imposes, even on politicians. But she was of course right. How many 16-year-olds, no matter how idealistic they are in the classroom, will forego the gift of a provisional driving licence on their seventeenth birthday? Or for that matter the car that, in the leafy lanes of Surrey, is increasingly likely to accompany it?

A 'green' teacher may well take the view that the world economic system rooted, as it is, in competition and consumption is inherently incapable of dealing with the problems facing the world today. But is a world economic system based on cooperation and conservation a realistic possibility? The United States with 2 per cent of the world's population consumes some 25 per cent of the world's oil supplies. Is it realistic to think it would ever tolerate only consuming 2 per cent? Which electorate in the world is going to help save the rain forests if it means going without hamburgers? What Dagenham family will tolerate education which might lead to reduced car production? And what will Europe do if the victims of African desertification do, as in a recent television play, take it into their heads to migrate across the Mediterranean in order to survive and claim their fair share of the world's goods? The problem for the 'green' science teacher is that her/his aims are, almost inevitably, subversive. The 'catch 22' such teachers face is that even the most liberal of governments only tolerate subversion as long as it is ineffective. Should there be any danger of 'green' science teachers being effective then the National Curriculum can quickly be amended to eliminate such subversion.

CONCLUSIONS

Education has always been a convenient whipping boy for society. Impatience with education for not delivering the economic goods is no new phenomenon and today's National Curriculum can be traced back at least as far as James Callaghan's 1976 Ruskin College speech blaming education for the economic difficulties the Labour government were then facing. If one believes this then it follows that one will want to have a curriculum designed to remove those difficulties. There are however, two problems with this. First, we do not actually have any evidence that education is as directly related to economic performance as this implies. In many countries it can be shown that investment in education is a consequence rather than a cause of prosperity. Second, even if it is related, we do not actually know what the right curriculum for economic prosperity in a post-industrial, information-technology-based society should be. All one can say with some confidence is that, in the absence of certainty, a monolithic curriculum is the last thing we need. Science educators really should be well aware that diversity and adaptation to the environment go hand in hand. How much anything we do to the curriculum will matter when the North Sea oil wells eventually run dry is another matter.

Unfortunately for the 'green' science teacher if education is impotent in the economic field it is probably even more impotent in the social field. Only if, and when, developed societies are prepared to make the necessary economic adjustments – sacrifices – will there be any hope of tackling the consequences of the environmental degradation now afflicting Planet Earth. Given that, as economic pressures in any country increase, minority ethnic groups are victimised, it is very difficult to be anything but profoundly pessimistic about a future in which each nation state continues to compete for a larger share of the world's resources than its neighbour. Does anyone really believe the government of a non-oil state would have got the same support as Kuwait did when it was invaded? Perhaps instead of worrying we should adapt Tom Lehrer's paean for a nuclear holocaust – We'll all go together when we go/Every Hottentot and every Eskimo/When the air becomes uraneus/We'll all go simultaneous/We'll all go together when we go – to one for an environmental Armageddon. A National Curriculum based on the principle of 'Eat, drink and be merry for tomorrow may not be' is really what today's young people need.

NOTES

1 *Review Guardian* 28–8–89. Commencement address to graduates of Smïth College, Massachusetts.
2 See, for example, Sir John Harvey-Jones, 1986 Dimbleby Lecture, 'Does Industry Matter?'
3 Quoted in *Daily Telegraph* British Association Science Extra: September 1989.
4 Letter to *Education Guardian* during the run up to the 1989 Education Reform Act. Reiterated in *Education 2000* article 14–8–90.
5 *Laboratory Equipment Digest* is almost totally concerned with equipment which automates out of existence traditional laboratory practical and measurement skills.
6 BBC 2 Documentary *9 to 5*, 6–3–90. In this programme the representative of a major Bristol-based manufacturing company acknowledged that his firm was unable to compete with the insurance and financial companies relocating in that city for the best-qualified school leavers.
7 Department of Education and Science, *A Survey of Balanced Science Courses in some Secondary Schools* (DES, 1990).
8 Biology A-level entries from 42,138 in 1989 to 44,362 in 1990 (+5.3 per cent); Chemistry 47,559 to 47,286 (-0.6 per cent); Physics 44,871 to 42,564 (−5.2 per cent).
9 'If you're a student or recent graduate you've probably contemplated working abroad. In fact, 84% of you have, according to a recent survey. . . . Our panel is waiting to hear what kind of recruitment plan is needed to attract top graduates to British Industry. . . . You've got until 20 April to help reshape the future of British Industry . . .'. Extracts from 1990 Royal Mail Enterprises Awards publicity.
10 'British Airways has a new breed of directors. They don't know much about planes; they know everything about marketing', *Airline*, BBC 2, 1990.
11 Anthony Sampson, *The Midas Touch* (BBC Books, 1989), pp. 87–9.
12 See, for example, Maynard Keynes, 1931 essay, *Economic Possibilities for our Grandchildren*.
13 Bryan Magee, 'Women's rights and wrongs', *Weekend Guardian*, 11–11–89.
14 *Physics Education*, 1989, **24**(3), 117–18.
15 *Wireless World*, Editorial, May 1982.
16 David Layton, *Science as General Education*. Paper presented to a University of Leeds Heads of Department INSET course, circa 1970.
17 'Britain has one of the lowest labour costs in the European Community – one half of the costs of Germany and one third of the costs in France or Italy. Only Greece, Spain and Portugal are cheaper. The workforce is also skilled and flexible, since it is not limited by rigid labour laws.' Eric Forth, the Industry Minister, opening a CBI conference on Japanese investment in Britain, March 1990.
18 Dr Jeremy Leggett, 'The coals of calamity', *Environment Guardian*, 20–1–90.
19 Ealing comedy in which shareholders, management and unions unite to ensure that the development of an indestructible totally dirt- and stain-resistant white

suit never sees the light of day. Even the inventor's laundry lady turns on him: 'What about my bit of washing when there's no washing to do?'

20 Ben Elton, *Stark* (Sphere Books, 1989).
21 Anthony Sampson, *The Midas Touch*, Chapter 1, 'The world's religion' (BBC Books, 1989).

Acknowledgements

Chapter 1 'The laboratory comes of age', from *Teaching Children in the Laboratory* (1980), by Joan Solomon, reproduced by permission of Routledge.

Chapter 2 'Why the science curriculum changes – evolution or social control?', by D. Hodson and R.B. Prophet, from *School Science Review*, September 1983, 65 (230), pp. 5–18, reproduced by permission of the authors.

Chapter 3 'The fallacy of induction in science teaching', from *The Pupil as Scientist?* (1983), by Rosalind Driver, reproduced by permission of Open University Press.

Chapter 4 'Teaching about electric circuits: a constructivist approach', by Michael Arnold and Robin Millar, from *School Science Review*, December 1988, 70 (251), pp. 149–51, reproduced by permission of the authors.

Chapter 5 'Pause for thought', by Philip Adey, from *TES*, 17 November 1989, p. 63, reproduced by permission of the author. Summary part of *Thinking Science* activity reproduced by permission of Thomas Nelson & Sons Limited.

Chapter 6 'Well, Mary, what are they saying here?', from *Words, Science and Learning* (1992), edited version of Chapter 9, by Clive Sutton, reproduced by permission of Open University Press.

Chapter 7 'Group discussions in the classroom', by Joan Solomon, from *School Science Review*, June 1991, 72 (261), pp. 29–34, reproduced by permission of the author.

Chapter 8 'Chemical compositions', by Andrew Burns and Mike Hamlin, from *TES*, 28 December 1990, p. 26, reproduced by permission of the authors.

Chapter 9 'A variety of methods', by Dorothy Dallas, from *Teaching Biology Today* (1980), pp. 72–8, reproduced by permission of Stanley Thornes (Publishers) Ltd.

Chapter 10 'Developing pupils' skills', by Terry Hudson, from *Open Chemistry* (1992), edited by M. Atlay *et al.*, reproduced by Hodder & Stoughton Limited.

Chapter 12 'Assessing and evaluating in science education', by John Skevington, from *Secondary Science Teachers' Handbook* (1993), edited by Richard Hull, reproduced by permission of the author.

Chapter 13 'Gender differences in pupils' reactions to practical work', by Patricia Murphy, from *Practical Science* (1991), edited by Brian Woolnough, reproduced by permission of Open University Press.

Chapter 14 'Teaching chemistry to pupils for whom English is a second language', by Maggie Farrar, from *Open Chemistry* (1992), edited by M. Atlay *et al.*, reproduced by permission of Hodder & Stoughton Limited.

Chapter 15 'Redefining and reorienting practical work in school science', by Derek Hodson, from *School Science Review*, March 1992, 73 (264), pp. 33–40, reproduced by permission of the author.

Chapter 16 'What is "scientific method" and can it be taught?', by Robin Millar, from *Skills and Processes in Science Education* (1989), edited by Jerry Wellington, reproduced by permission of Routledge.

Chapter 17 'Practical work in science – a task-based approach?', by Richard Gott and Judith Mashiter, from *Practical Science* (1991), edited by Brian Woolnough, reproduced by permission of Open University Press.

Chapter 18 'The overselling of science education in the 1980s', by Bryan Chapman, from *School Science Review*, March 1991, 72 (260), pp. 47–63, reproduced by permission of the author.

Notes on sources

Chapter 1   J. Solomon (1980) *Teaching Children in the Laboratory*, Croom Helm, pp. 13–29.

Chapter 2   D. Hodson and R. B. Prophet (1983) *School Science Review*, September, 65 (230), pp. 5–18.

Chapter 3   R. Driver (1983) *The Pupil as Scientist?*, Open University Press, pp. 1–10.

Chapter 4   M. Arnold and R. Millar (1988) *School Science Review*, December, 70 (251), pp. 149–51.

Chapter 5   P. Adey (1989) *TES*, 17 November, p. 63.

Chapter 6   C. Sutton (1992) *Words, Science and Learning*, edited Chapter 9, Open University Press.

Chapter 7   J. Solomon (1991) *School Science Review*, June, 72 (261), pp. 29–34.

Chapter 8   A. Burns and M. Hamlin (1990) *TES*, 28 December, p. 26.

Chapter 9   D. Dallas (1980) *Teaching Biology Today*, edited version of Chapter 4, Hutchinson, pp. 72–8.

Chapter 10   T. Hudson (1992) (extracts) from M. Atlay *et al.* (eds), *Open Chemistry*, Hodder & Stoughton.

Chapter 11   Commissioned for this volume.

Chapter 12   J. Skevington (1993) from R. Hull (ed.) *Secondary Science Teachers' Handbook*, Simon & Schuster.

Chapter 13   P. Murphy (1991) from B. Woolnough (ed.) *Practical Science*, Open University Press.

Chapter 14   M. Farrar (1992) from M. Atlay *et al.* (eds) *Open Chemistry*, Hodder & Stoughton.

Chapter 15   D. Hodson (1992) *School Science Review*, March, 73 (264), pp. 33–40.

Chapter 16   R. Millar (1989) from J. Wellington (ed.) *Skills and Processes in Science Education*, Routledge.

Chapter 17   R. Gott and J. Mashiter (1991) (extracts, pp. 55–65) from B. Woolnough (ed.) *Practical Science*, Open University Press.

Chapter 18   B. Chapman (1991) (extracts) *School Science Review*, March, 72 (260), pp. 47–63.

Index